MAKE YOUR MONEY GROW

Getting control of your finances instead of having them control you is one of the most difficult accomplishments. But it is the surest way to rest easier and build up your assets at the same time.

The trick is in knowing where to put your investment funds; what are the best deals on big ticket items, such as insurance; what kind of coverage you really need; how to take advantage of the tax breaks that are available to you; whether it pays to borrow; what you should watch for when buying a house; and how to get a handle on the dozens of other financial decisions you must make all the time.

It's knowing how to get the most mileage out of your income and your investments. It's the way successful people make *their* money grow.

A KIPLINGER *Changing Times* BOOK

MAKE YOUR MONEY GROW

Smart steps to success
in the exciting years ahead

EDITED BY
Theodore J. Miller

WITH AN INTRODUCTION BY
Austin H. Kiplinger

A DELL BOOK

Published by
The Kiplinger Washington Editors, Inc.
1729 H Street N.W.
Washington, D.C. 20006

Distributed by
Dell Publishing Co., Inc.
1 Dag Hammarskjold Plaza
New York, New York 10017

Dell ® TM 681510, Dell Publishing, Co., Inc.

ISBN: 0-440-06054-0

Printed in the United States of America
First printing—November 1981

CONTENTS

PART FIVE

PROVEN WAYS TO CUT TAXES

PART SIX

YOUR JOB, YOUR RETIREMENT, YOUR ESTATE

Acknowledgments

This book is the work of many people. Its content and style draw heavily from ideas developed for *Changing Times*, the Kiplinger magazine. Each month the writers and editors of *Changing Times* sift and sort their way through piles of facts and figures, separating the vital from the not-so-vital and honing what's left into the solid, readable, personal guidance that has become the magazine's hallmark. The volume you are holding in your hands grew out of the efforts of that talented staff.

These people will recognize their hand in the pages that follow: Robert A. Marshall, Jerome Oelbaum and Charles Schaeffer of the magazine's senior editorial staff; and Cherrill Anson, Janet Bodnar, Jack Kelso, Kevin McCormally, Morton Paulson, Paul Plawin and Ellen Roberts, all associate editors of *Changing Times*.

Thanks are due also to Priscilla Gichuru and Rona-leen Roha for their invaluable help with the research. Finally, the editor is indebted to Sidney Sulkin and Milton Christie for their expert guidance and generous encouragement along the way.

Introduction

The idea behind this book is a simple one. It is that you—if you are equipped with the necessary knowledge and a little bit of determination—can make a go of your own financial affairs in the years ahead. And despite what you may hear or read elsewhere, those years will be exciting ones, full of opportunities for people who know where to look.

What makes me think so? Just this: There are many forces in motion today—population, economic and business trends—that, taken together, will bring renewed growth and prosperity to our country as the years go by. Those who prophesize economic calamity ahead consider this view to be Pollyannish. In truth, it's just good sense, based on a realistic appraisal of the prospects.

Consider for a moment where prosperity comes from. It comes from people making things and doing things for other people, and from people with money to spend for those things. People get that money from their jobs and from their investments. The decade of the 1980s will be one of historic change in spending and working patterns and there will be plenty of new opportunities for everyone who has the vision and vigor to take advantage of them. For one thing, the number of 18- to 24-year-olds is getting smaller, and that takes pressure off business to create an abnormal number of new jobs for people just entering the work force. That, in turn, means more opportunities for those who do start working, and less unemployment.

What of those already in the job market? The single largest group will soon be the 25- to 34-year-olds. They will be experienced workers, approaching their peak earning years. They will also comprise the best market for homes, provided that the troubled housing market can cope with its present problems (which we think it can).

The larger proportion of experienced workers on the job should help boost productivity, for the simple reason that experienced workers tend to be more productive.

And there are other favorable signs. The federal government is adopting tax policies that will encourage investment by business and individuals. Government budgets are getting the ax in Washington. Regulations are being scaled back to more reasonable levels.

This doesn't mean there won't be problems. Business has some distance to go before it is humming along with solid growth. Inflation will continue for the forseeable future, though it will not be as high as it has been in recent years. Much of your time will be spent worrying about inflation, working to survive it, wondering what kind of damage it will do to your purchasing power and assets. You'll also be wondering how you should deploy your resources to give you the best chance of getting through the years ahead with your capital intact and perhaps making a little progress on your personal balance sheet.

That's where this book can help. It is based on material developed for *Changing Times* magazine, a monthly publication that shows readers how to protect what they have and make it grow. As you start reading this book, you will notice that it has a plan. The early chapters are designed to help you get your financial affairs in order—figure out where you stand, decide where you want to go and map a course for getting there. Then there's a section on insurance. It's one of life's necessities, because without it your financial resources could be wiped out in an instant. Without insurance, an unexpected death, a fire, an auto accident or an expensive illness could create a financial catastrophe.

Once you've taken care of necessities, you're ready to start looking for opportunities to make your money grow. Never before have there been so many different kinds of investments competing for your dollars. Equipped with the information and guidance in this book, you'll be able to find the investments that suit you now and you'll know when it's time to move along to something else. And of course, the more you make from your investments, the more you'll want to minimize your tax bill, so you'll find help with that problem, too. Finally, there's guidance for getting ahead on the job, planning a comfortable retirement no matter what your current age and developing a sensible estate plan that will provide for those you love.

Throughout these pages, the emphasis is on *you* and what *you* can do to get ahead and stay ahead in the years to come. You are the most important asset you have.

I commend this book to you. May you profit from it, and have good luck in all you undertake.

AUSTIN H. KIPLINGER

PART ONE

MAKING THE MOST OF WHAT YOU HAVE

1

How to take charge of your money

When you consider the importance most of us place on money—or at least on the sense of security money can provide—it is surprising how many people have only a vague idea of how much money they possess. If this book is to succeed at its main task, which is to show you how to use the money you have to build a more secure future, then it must begin by helping you perform some personal financial stocktaking.

Wealthy people ordinarily aren't guilty of inattention to their money. When Gerald Ford chose Nelson Rockefeller to be his vice president in 1974, Congress demanded a look at Rockefeller's great fortune. Among the details he provided was this fascinating statement of his overall worth:

ASSETS		
cash	$	394,898
cash advances		247,891
notes receivable		1,518,270
accounts receivable		713,326
New York State Retirement Fund (contributed cost)		21,803
securities		12,794,376
partnership interests		157,124
art (estimated market value)		33,561,325
real estate		11,252,261
furnishings		1,191,328
automobiles, other vehicles, boats and airplanes		1,767,900
jewelry		521,136
coins		12,600
total		$64,154,238

LIABILITIES	
notes payable	$1,567,500
miscellaneous accounts payable	5,513
total	$ 1,573,013
net worth	$62,581,225

Does a glance at those figures tell you more about Rockefeller's financial condition several years ago than you know about your own right now? If so, determining your current net worth will be a necessary first step in developing plans for enhancing it.

This isn't a complex or difficult chore. In fact it consists of only two basic steps: First you add up the value of everything you own, then you subtract from it the total of all your debts. The form on pages 6-7 is designed to help you accomplish that. But before you turn there, take a preliminary step, one that will pay off in valuable information about the state of your financial affairs and help you get them under control.

If you haven't been keeping close track of the dollars that flow through your hands on a regular basis, filling in the cash flow form on pages 3 and 4 should bring you up to date. It will give you a bird's-eye view of your getting and spending during the past year.

You can't remember every little detail, of course, but you should be able to locate exact figures for some expenses—mortgage or rent, for example, and insurance premiums—and you can estimate others by thinking of them in weekly or monthly terms and multiplying to get the year's total. Go over your checkbook, paid bills, credit card slips, receipts from stores, cleaners, garages, restaurants. The more actual expenditures you can pinpoint, the more you'll know about your spending habits when you're through.

YOUR CASH FLOW

INCOME	total for year	monthly average
take-home pay	————	————
dividends and capital gains received as cash	————	————
bonuses	————	————
other	————	————
total income	————	————
EXPENDITURES		
mortgage or rent	————	————
taxes not withheld	————	————
food	————	————

utilities and fuel   _____   _____

insurance premiums   _____   _____

household maintenance   _____   _____

auto (gas, oil, maintenance, repairs)   _____   _____

other transportation   _____   _____

loans   _____   _____

medical bills not covered by insurance   _____   _____

clothing purchases and care   _____   _____

savings and investments   _____   _____

charity   _____   _____

recreation and entertainment   _____   _____

miscellaneous   _____   _____

total expenditures   _____   _____

SUMMARY

total income   _____

minus total expenditures   _____

surplus (+) or deficit (−)   _____

No matter how this exercise comes out, you're confronted with the evidence of your spending and forced to make some judgments about it. The results will show one of three things.

• *Income and expenditures are roughly in balance.* Making it from one year to the next without getting into a hole may be something of a feat these days, but before you start patting yourself on the back, check your totals again. How much did you put into savings, compared with what you spent on recreation, gifts or clothing? Out-of-whack entries in those or other categories of discretionary spending could mean trouble is brewing. There's more to sensible spending than balancing the books. You have to balance your priorities, too.

• *You took in more than you spent.* This isn't necessarily a good sign either. Since your cash-flow statement includes savings and investments, you shouldn't have any money "left over." Any apparent surplus is probably created by a failure to remember and record all your spending.

• *You spent more than you took in.* This is the clearest signal of imminent danger. When current expenditures outrun income, the money has to come from somewhere it shouldn't. Either you've been dipping into savings, borrowing money or buying too much on credit. You can get away with it for a while, but it's bad money management that can cost you dearly in the long run.

Examine your cash-flow statement carefully, looking for places where your money might be dribbling away. As you proceed with this chapter, you should begin to spot some ways to plug the leaks.

HOW MUCH ARE YOU WORTH?

Now you have a picture of how you're handling the money that comes your way. But performing a cash-flow analysis for a single year doesn't give you much information about the cumulative impact on your financial worth of all the cash that's been flowing through your hands for all of your adult life. Compiling a net

YOUR NET WORTH

ASSETS

cash in checking accounts   _____

cash in savings accounts   _____

savings certificates   _____

U.S. savings bonds (current value)   _____

cash value of life insurance   _____

market value of house or apartment   _____

market value of other real estate   _____

surrender value of annuities   _____

equity in pension plan   _____

market value of securities   _____

    stocks   _____

    bonds   _____

    mutual fund shares   _____

    other   _____

current value of durable possessions   _____

    automobiles   _____

    household furnishings   _____

    household appliances and equipment   _____

    furs and jewelry   _____

    precious metals   _____

collectibles _____

recreation and hobby equipment _____

loans receivable _____

interest in a business _____

other assets _____

total assets _____

LIABILITIES

current bills outstanding _____

installment debts _____

auto loan _____

taxes due _____

balance due on mortgages _____

other liabilities _____

total liabilities _____

SUMMARY

assets _____

minus liabilities _____

net worth _____

worth statement will show you this, and a form for doing so is located on pages 6 and 7. Here's how to use it.

Assets. In compiling this part of the statement, begin with cash: what you've got on hand, what's in your checking account and what you may have squirreled away elsewhere. Next come funds in savings accounts and certificates of deposit. If you own U.S. savings bonds, check with an institution that sells them to get the current (not face) value. Premium payments on a whole life insurance policy contribute to your assets by increasing the policy's cash value—the amount you'd get if you cashed it in. A table in the policy or your agent can tell you the current cash value. Ditto for finding the surrender value of any annuities you own.

Settling on figures to enter as the current value of your pension and profit-sharing plans is probably the toughest part. A program that will provide you with retirement income is surely an important asset, but it's hard to put a present-day dollar value on what you're supposed to receive in the future. Include in your net worth only the amount you could withdraw in cash if you quit your job. Your personnel office should be able to provide that figure. If you have an Individual Retirement Account or a Keogh plan, list its current balance, but remember that you'll be charged a penalty if you withdraw funds prematurely (see chapter 24).

Your home is likely to be your biggest asset, so it's especially important that the value you assign it be accurate. Don't list what it cost you or take a wild guess at its present value. Find out what similar homes in your area have sold for recently (a list of such sale prices should be available in the local land records office) or ask a real estate agent for an estimate of current market value. Try to get reliable estimates of the value of any other real estate or business interests you own, too.

The current dollar value of securities—stocks, bonds, mutual funds—can be found by checking the financial pages of a newspaper. If you run into problems finding information, ask a stockbroker.

You can get a good idea of what your car is worth by consulting a car price guide, such as the *Kelley Blue Book*. Banks that make auto loans usually have copies of these guides. Be realistic in valuing your auto and remember that any sentimental value you attach to an old clunker can't be counted among your financial assets. For help in putting a value on a boat, motorcycle, or other vehicle, contact a dealer.

You'll probably have to rely on ball-park figures when valuing household furnishings, appliances and other personal belongings. It's best to be conservative in your estimates. One conservative approach is to "guesstimate" that what's inside your home is worth about 5% of the value of the home itself. Or make your own item-by-item estimate and then slash the total by 50%. Include the estimated value of any antiques, furs, jewelry, or stamp or coin collections.

Liabilities. If you're like most Americans, there's a string of debits tied to your list of assets. Filling out this portion of the form may be painful, but it shouldn't be difficult. Most liabilities are obvious, and whoever you owe probably takes the time to remind you of the debt.

Start with current bills—what you owe the doctor and plumber, for example, and this month's utility bill, college tuition payment, etc. Next, list all charge accounts and installment debts, with the balance due in each case. There's a separate category on the form for your car loan and another one for taxes coming due. Your home mortgage is probably your largest single liability, and an amortization schedule should indicate exactly how much you still owe on it. Do you have any other loans outstanding, or stock bought on margin? Whatever you owe is a liability that diminishes your net worth.

Now it's time to fill in the bottom line. If you liquidated all your assets and paid all your debts, what would be left over? That's your net worth.

The bottom line. With all the figures at hand, it's easy to compute your asset-to-debt ratio and compare your position with that of the average American. Just divide the total of your assets by the sum of your liabilities. If you have $100,000 in assets, for example, and liabilities totaling $20,000, your asset-to-debt ratio is 5 to 1. Recently the overall asset-to-debt ratio for U.S. households was about 5.3 to 1, meaning that for every $1 of debt, consumers had $5.30 in assets. That's based on 7.16 trillion dollars in assets and 1.36 trillion dollars in liabilities. (The ratio of Rockefeller's assets and liabilities listed earlier is 41 to 1.)

But the importance of figuring your net worth goes beyond satisfying any curiosity about how you stack up against Rockefeller or the mythical average American. Pulling all the figures together can be a first step toward starting or revising a budget that can show you ways to beef up your assets and trim your liabilities. To do that, you need to set some goals.

HOW TO SET FINANCIAL GOALS

You probably don't expect to attain great wealth in your lifetime. Plain old "financial security" would do fine, if only you knew what it meant. It's a slippery notion, all right, but it does have a few characteristics you can grab onto.

• *It means having a steady source of income.* This means your job, of course, or your business if you're self-employed, or income from investments. Future income is the bedrock on which financial security is built.

• *It means anticipating long- and short-term needs.* Cars break down, household appliances wear out, roofs spring leaks. Kids grow to college age, and someday you'll want to retire. These are expenses you should provide for with savings and investments.

• *It means being protected against financial catastrophes.* In a word, insurance. You need it in sufficient amounts to cover your life, health, family and possessions. Without insurance, the best-laid financial plans can be wiped out in an instant.

• *It means getting further ahead each year.* If you stand pat, inflation will loot your financial reserves just as surely as if you were throwing the money away. You have to be alert for opportunities to make your money grow.

First, you've got to translate financial security into your own terms. What, exactly, are your personal financial goals? If you have trouble sorting them out, try classifying them as either "wants" or "needs." Go a step further and add long-term or short-term to the description. Now you have a double-barreled label for figuring out your priorities.

Here's how you might use it. Say you're going to need a new car soon. Gathering together the money for a down payment without dipping into savings would be a short-term need, priority number one. Same for your youngster's braces, perhaps, or a badly needed new winter coat.

Long-term needs, such as contributions to a retirement fund, can get priority number two. Yearning for a vacation in Bermuda this spring? That's a short-term *want*, priority number three. The outboard motorboat you'd like to own before too many years go by is a long-term want, so it gets a four.

You could shift priorities around, of course, and use lots more numbers. Actual goals and their priorities will vary with your circumstances. The important thing is to give serious thought to your goals and try to anticipate the expenses coming up, be they close at hand or several years away.

A good way to ride herd on goals is to assign target dates to each of them. If you think October would be the best time to buy a car, for instance, and you want at least $2,000 on hand for a down payment, solidify that objective by putting it in writing: "Need $2,000 for new car by October." That gives you a basis for action: You have to find some way of allocating expenditures that will allow you to accumulate $2,000 by October. The progress you make toward this and other specific goals becomes the gauge of your progress toward the ultimate goal, which is financial security.

Trouble is, the cash often runs out before the priorities do. That's where budgeting can help. It's your best bet for distributing limited resources intelligently among competing priorities.

WHAT A BUDGET CAN DO

You'll find a suggested budget format on pages 14 and 15. Think of it as a planning device, a means of setting and reaching goals. You project future expenditures now, record them when they're made and see whether your projections were any good. If not, you adjust either your planning or your spending, whichever is out of line.

Some of the projections you make will be easy. You know probably what your mortgage payments will be in the months ahead. Same for the premiums coming due on insurance policies you currently have in force. So why "budget" for them? Because by recording these and other fixed expenditures as monthly outgo, you can see at a glance how much of your income is committed to current or future expenses. That should stop you from spending it on something else.

Under variable expenditures go the items over which you have some degree of control. This is the place to test your cost-cutting skills. Watch for patterns developing that may signal trouble. If the electric bill is climbing faster than the rates are going up, family members may be leaving lights on or running appliances unnecessarily. If the long distance telephone bill goes up, somebody's talking too long. If the miscellaneous line keeps growing bigger, your record keeping may be careless.

Use the record of last year's spending that you compiled on pages 3 and 4 as the basis for the coming year's budget projections. Work only a couple of months ahead at first, until you get the hang of it. Then you can budget further ahead. After a while you'll want to apply the same principles to long-term goal-setting by forecasting the growth of your net worth and all the little pieces that compose it. Then you can keep track of the progress you're making by comparing each year's projected growth with the actual results.

MAKING THE BUDGET WORK

The beauty of a budget is that it alerts you to trouble while you still have time to do something about it.

A BUDGET FORMAT FOR THE 1980s

	MONTH			MONTH		
INCOME						
take-home pay	$			$		
other						
total	$			$		

FIXED EXPENDITURES	projected	actual	(+) or (−)	projected	actual	(+) or (−)
mortgage or rent	$	$	$	$	$	$
taxes not withheld from pay						
installment and credit card payments						
insurance premiums life						
auto						
home						
health and other						
savings and investments						
emergency fund						
investment fund						
vacation fund						
other						
subtotal	$	$	$	$	$	$

VARIABLE EXPENDITURES								
food and beverages		$____	$____	$____	$____	$____	$____	$____
fuel and utilities	gas or oil							
	electricity							
	telephone							
	water and sewer							
household operation and								
maintenance								
automobile	gas and oil							
	repairs							
public transportation								
clothing	mom							
	dad							
	kids							
pocket money	mom							
	dad							
	kids							
personal care (haircuts, cosmetics, etc.)								
recreation, entertainment								
medical and dental								
charity								
special expenses (tuition, alimony, etc.)								
miscellaneous								
subtotal		$____	$____	$____	$____	$____	$____	$____
fixed expenditures								
total		$____	$____	$____	$____	$____	$____	$____

You're forced to find out why expenditures are climbing and take action. If the electric bill is higher because the rates were raised, you'll have to revise your monthly forecasts for that budget item and figure out which other items can be cut to pay for it.

Sometimes, though, your budget may be flashing danger signs that are more difficult to pinpoint. If you start picking up distress signals, run your budget through these checks:

• *Have you been inattentive?* Perhaps you got in this fix because you didn't watch what was going on. Examine the budget categories where your spending overshot allocations. Pay particular attention to items that involve charge account buying and credit card spending. The finance charges generated by revolving credit alone may be enough to force you out of bounds.

• *Are you behind the times?* If the record reveals that carefree spending and charging is what blew the fuse, you're in luck. Presumably, you should be able to get back on the right track simply by staying alert and spending less.

But matters may not be that simple. You may be in trouble not because you've been doing unnecessary spending but because your necessary spending now costs more. This is everyone's inflation experience, whether you budget or not. In fact, those who budget sometimes have more trouble coping with inflation than other people because budgets usually tie spending objectives to pre-existing price levels.

When prices change as rapidly as they do these days, it is risky to assume that a working budget will continue to work for any length of time. It can't. So what do you do? The only answer is to revise your budget from time to time to keep it in touch with reality. These days an annual review probably won't be frequent enough. You're going to have to watch it constantly.

• *Do you need more flexibility?* Consider the young couple who thought they were doing fine without a budget of any kind—until their checks suddenly began bouncing all over town. It was humiliating. With their two-salary income, they told each other, there was simply no excuse for such embarrassment. So they vowed to budget and for the first time ever sat down to list their normal expenses and match them against their normal income.

To their delight, they found not only that there was enough money to go around but also that it would be perfectly realistic to fund a savings program, which they had talked about but never started. They promptly drew up a budget that included a heroic chunk of savings each month and happily set forth on their road to affluence.

Well, it didn't work. In their enthusiasm they had been both too ambitious and too rigid. They had tried to shovel too much into savings. They budgeted every penny of the remainder but neglected to allow for the little unforeseen expenses that are too petty to budget for but add up nevertheless.

Moral: Don't torture yourself. Don't aim for Spartan goals. Allow yourself leeway. It is better to budget a bit too much in a few headings (certainly including "miscellaneous" or "contingencies") than to end each month robbing Peter to pay Paul. After all, the purpose of a budget is not to make impossible dreams come true but to make attainable goals come easier.

• *Are you doing somebody else's thing?* The Bureau of Labor Statistics invented a hypothetical urban family of four, and periodically it computes itemized budgets for this family, just to see how much it would cost them to live.

This is a useful exercise and often revealing. But if by wild chance yours happens to be an urban family of four with precisely the income the BLS concludes you need, it is unlikely that you could live by the BLS budget.

Next to a will, a budget is probably the most intimate financial document known to man. It embodies decisions you make about how you will allocate your resources. And so many intangibles help shape those decisions—your goals, aspirations, values, hopes, anxieties, life-style, commitments, and, to an important degree, even the expectations of other people whose expectations you regard as worthy of honoring.

Thus, you may be John Doe Average and pull off-the-rack pants over one-size-fits-all socks every morning of the year, but you can't live by somebody else's budget. Yours has to be tailored to your measure, by you.

Most people approach this task by listing first the expenditures about which they feel they have no choice whatever. If anything is left over, only then do they consider expenditures they might make from free choice. Budgeting doesn't have to proceed this grimly, however. A few people begin at the other end. First they put down their desired goals, such as "enough money to buy a 30-foot boat by 1985." Then they budget to attain those goals of choice before distributing the remainder among items most people would rank as first-order necessities—shelter, food, clothing and the like.

It takes a strong-minded person to budget wishes first, needs later. But it can work, which only goes to show how highly personal the whole budgeting process can be.

2

Managing the day-to-day flow

If you operate like most people, you probably deposit a good part of your salary in a checking account on payday and then write checks as needed—20 a month if you match the average. Add up all the checks you write in the course of a year and you will come up with quite a large sum. That money can be managed to produce additional income.

You have to start with a good checking account. NOW accounts, which many financial institutions started offering at the beginning of 1981, offer opportunities to earn interest on checking-account funds, but NOW accounts don't always pay off (see chapter 4). Sometimes you're better off with a free checking account or one that offers a sizable number of free checks and requires only a small minimum monthly balance.

The gaps between the time you receive income and the time you have to pay it out represent interest-earning opportunities. For example, if you receive your salary on the first of the month but don't have to make your mortgage or rent payment until the 15th, you could deposit the money in a day-of-deposit to day-of-withdrawal savings account on payday and transfer it to the checking account 15 days later. This maneuver yields a modest amount over the course of the year, but you could generate considerably more interest by bunching several bill payments into a couple of days of the month so you have larger amounts working for you. And if you're writing checks for $500 or more, you could increase your yield by using a money-market fund (see chapter 17). Some savings and loan associations will pay bills directly from your savings account.

Take the time to shop for a good account, because the cost differences can be surprisingly large. A survey in Texas found one bank's checking account charges were ten times that of a nearby competitor. (There's guidance on choosing a good bank in chapter 4.)

Follow these additional pointers for getting the most out of your dollars:

• *Don't prepay bills.* Paying bills before they are due won't improve your credit standing; it's the persistently late payers who worry the stores and other creditors. Prepaying only reduces the time your money can be earning interest.

• *Don't overwithhold taxes.* Many people deliberately have too much taken out of their salaries to avoid a large tax bill in April or to accumulate a refund. Those excess withholdings could be put where they will earn interest to help pay taxes.

• *Don't accumulate idle cash.* Do you often delay

depositing checks? Do you neglect to cash traveler's checks after a trip? Do you keep large amounts of cash around? All those practices deprive you of the opportunity to increase your interest income.

• *Maximize your savings.* Never before have ordinary people had such abundant opportunities for maximizing the return on their savings as they do today—certificates of deposit with a wide range of maturities and rates, money-market mutual funds, interest-paying checking accounts. With those facilities you can use many of the cash management techniques developed by large corporations, even though you deal in far smaller sums.

To succeed, however, you must begin with an accurate, up-to-date record of the funds you have. Use the form on page 22 to list all your savings funds, the institutions where they are held, the names in which the accounts are registered, the rate the money is earning and when the money can be withdrawn.

Standard passbook account money can be considered immediately available. So, too, can money-market funds and U.S. savings bonds, although you won't receive the full interest on the bonds if they are cashed in before their initial maturity. For certificates of deposit, enter the maturity dates. Certificates may be redeemed beforehand, but normally you must pay an interest penalty for premature redemption. The registered owner's name is important because his signature is required for withdrawal.

Once you have mapped out your present savings position, you can see how your return can be improved by applying basic cash management principles:

• *Rotate your funds.* One formerly reliable principle of saving held that the longer the term, the higher the rate. A 30-year bond, for example, should offer a higher rate

SAVINGS RECORD

account, institution	registered owner	amount	when available
standard savings accounts			
	total		
certificates of deposit			
	total		
U.S. savings bonds			
	total		
other (e.g., money market funds)			
	total		
	grand total		

than a 10-year bond. A 6-year certificate of deposit normally provides a better return than a 1-year certificate, and a 1-year certificate pays more than a savings account.

Unfortunately, periods of rapid inflation can knock these relationships cockeyed. Frequently in the past few years, short-term rates have been much higher than long-term rates, making it unwise to commit your money for too long if you can help it.

With certificates you can reduce the risks of long-term commitment by staggering the maturities so that some certificates are always coming due in the near future. Then, if you don't need the cash, you can rotate the maturing certificates back into long or short maturities, depending on the rates at the time.

If you want further protection against getting locked into a low rate or caught short for ready money, arrange to have the interest from some of the certificates paid out on a quarterly or semiannual basis. That gives you a constant stream of cash for use or reinvestment. You may lose part of the extra return from leaving interest in the account for compounding, but it's a relatively small cost to pay for retaining your liquidity. Also, remember that in an emergency you can pledge a certificate as collateral for a loan.

• *Use the money-market funds.* The money-market mutual funds provide an excellent cash management tool, particularly when you want to park savings temporarily between investments or hitch a ride with climbing interest rates.

The money-market funds invest in very short-term debt instruments, such as corporate IOUs (known as commercial paper), which typically don't fluctuate much in price. During the past several years the funds have usually yielded much higher returns than savings accounts and short-maturity certificates.

You can open an account in some of the funds with $1,000 or less. Shares are generally redeemable at any time by telephone, and you can arrange to have the proceeds wired or mailed directly to your bank.

Most of the funds offer a checking service for large payments, usually with a $500 minimum. There are technical differences between fund and bank checks, but for ordinary purposes they can be used the same way. Actually, the fund-check system gives you a financial premium because your money continues earning until the check clears. (For more information on these funds, see chapter 17.)

MONEY MANAGEMENT
IN THE TWO-INCOME FAMILY

The typical American family of statistical fame, in which the husband goes off to work and the wife stays home to tend to the house and the two kids, really isn't very typical at all. In fact, the vast majority don't fit that mold. More than 24,000,000 wives are now bringing home paychecks, and that means nearly half the nation's families face the challenge of managing two incomes. Some of the second paycheck may have to go to sop up the effects of inflation on the first, but what are you going to do with the rest?

If the second income is a temporary condition, you can't afford to dress up your life-style and extend your debt obligations to levels that devour both paychecks. Doing so could transform the financial flexibility that should come with the second income into a straitjacket that locks both spouses into the job market. Even when you expect both jobs to be permanent, take care not to let the added income be blithely absorbed by routine family spending.

One approach for dual-income families is to try to cover day-to-day living expenses with one salary while using as much as possible of the other for savings, investments, longer vacations and other goals. Some two-income families pool all their income, paying all the bills and setting aside funds for savings and investments from a single account. Others keep their paychecks and each spouse contributes to joint expenses. Another alternative is to put part of each paycheck into a family pool and retain the rest for individual use.

It's important for you and your spouse to agree on a workable method and cooperate to make your financial partnership run smoothly. That means deciding how financially independent each of you is going to be. You may want to set aside a certain amount each month for each of you to spend as you please but agree that both of you must approve any other expenditures.

KEEPING THE RIGHT RECORDS

Good record-keeping is an essential part of sound money management. The following is a guide to the kinds of records to keep, and why.

Tax records. Cancelled checks, receipts and a myriad of other documents may be required for federal and state income tax purposes, both to calculate how much you owe and to justify deductions, exemptions and other tax items. You should be prepared to present concrete evidence to the government in case of an audit. However, you can lighten your files by eliminating superfluous items and discarding records after they have served their purpose.

You can dispose of weekly or monthly salary statements once you have checked them against the annual W-2 wage form.

Often, a cancelled check that directly relates to an entry on your return is sufficient without supplementary documents. The cancelled check for a medical expense doesn't have to be supported by the original bill unless the nature of the expense is ambiguous. A check to a physician leaves little doubt as to the service involved, but you would want to back up a check to a drugstore with a detailed receipt because the check could cover either deductible drugs or nondeductible cosmetics.

Sometimes you can—and should—create a record to protect yourself. If a charity fails to give you a receipt for donated goods, draw up a list with the used-market value of each item, the name of the organization and the date of the contribution.

Precise records are particularly important for business travel and entertainment expense deductions. If you expect to claim business expenses, write to your Internal Revenue Service district office for a copy of Publication 463, which explains the regulations and record requirements.

How long should you keep tax records? The law allows the IRS three years to challenge a return under ordinary circumstances and six years when you understate income by more than 25%. (In cases of fraud, there is no limit.) Even if you're certain the six-year rule will not be used against you, it's best to keep five years' returns—four back ones plus the latest one filed. The extra returns will make it easier to use certain income-averaging provisions of the law if your income increases substantially.

You may be able to obtain substitutes for lost tax

records from the person who made the payment to you or to whom you made the payment. The IRS generally stores returns for six years and can furnish copies for one dollar for the first page and ten cents for each additional page. Write to the IRS center to which the return was originally sent. Include your social security number and notarized signature.

For detailed suggestions on tax record-keeping, see chapter 21.

Stock and bond certificates. These should be kept in your safe-deposit box or, if you prefer, in the brokerage firm's vault. Mutual funds retain custody of shares unless the owner requests the certificates.

Should you lose a certificate, immediately notify the issuing company or its transfer agent (your broker can find the name for you). You will probably be sent a set of replacement forms, including an application for an indemnity bond. The bond insures the company against loss if the missing shares are cashed in illegally. You can expect to be charged a fee for the bond based on the value of the shares. Once the bond is obtained, the company can issue a new certificate.

Stock purchase and sale confirmations. The broker's purchase statement showing the number of shares, the price, and commission and taxes, if any, should be filed with the certificates. You will eventually need that information to figure your gain or loss for tax purposes when you sell the shares. The broker's sales statement goes with your current year's tax material.

Investment dividends. It's helpful to log dividend payments each year in a separate record to guard against company errors or lost checks. You can discard your tally after matching it against the annual dividend summary the company sends you (and the IRS). However, you should maintain an ongoing record of capital-distribution dividends because they have to be figured into the gain or loss reported for taxes when the shares are sold.

Savings passbooks and certificates. They're not as difficult or costly to replace as stock certificates, but their loss could cause some inconvenience. Bank procedures for handling lost passbooks and certificates vary. You may be given new ones with no fuss and bother. In some cases, though, withdrawals from the account might be temporarily restricted.

Homeownership and rental records. When you buy or sell a house, keep all the records you receive. They are not all necessarily essential from a legal viewpoint, but they may have other important uses. The deed, for example, doesn't fully protect your ownership of the property until it is recorded at the county or municipal land office. However, it may give a precise description of the property. Similarly, the survey map provided is a convenient reference for location boundaries when you put up a fence, a tool shed or other structures.

The payment records of the transaction will probably be needed for tax purposes either that year or at some future time. Your share of the regular real estate tax is deductible the same year you pay it. Special land transfer taxes are ordinarily not deductible, but they can be added to the cost of the house in calculating the capital gain when you sell it.

Any permanent improvements you make to property—central air-conditioning, a porch, a patio, etc.—can be added to the cost of the property. The cancelled checks to contractors or the receipted bills should be put away for long-term safekeeping.

Maintenance costs for painting, papering and the like do not qualify under that rule, but they can be deducted from the sales proceeds of a property as a fixing-up expense if the work is done within 90 days before the sale. If there's any possibility that you might sell in the near future, hang onto those records.

When you rent a house or apartment, your legal and financial relationship with the landlord rests on the lease. You may need it to verify particular provisions from time to time. Keep it handy.

Warranties, service agreements. Try to assemble all your warranties, appliance instruction booklets and agreements covering such services as lawn care and termite inspection in one place and periodically remove the out-of-date ones. If you buy an appliance without a printed guarantee, retain the cancelled check or paid bill in case you have to make a claim against the retailer or manufacturer. They could be obligated to correct defects, even without an explicit warranty, under the legal principle that any product should adequately perform its designated function.

Automobile records. If your state issues automobile titles, keep the certificate in a safe-deposit box. You can probably obtain a replacement, should you need it, from the state motor vehicles department, but that could be difficult, particularly if the dealer who sold the car has gone out of business and you haven't kept the original bill of sale.

Keeping receipts or a running log of work you have done on the car can help you maintain it properly and, presumably, lengthen its life. At the very least, put those little stickers that show when the oil was changed in a protected location like the back of the glove compartment door.

Passports. Don't throw out an expired passport. You can use it to satisfy some of the application requirements for a new one. If you lose your passport while traveling abroad, notify the nearest American consular office immediately. If you're at home, report the loss to the Passport Office, Department of State, 1425 K St., N.W., Washington, D.C. 20524.

Insurance policies. Life policies are best kept in a safe place, quickly and easily accessible to your heirs. A safe-deposit box might not always be the best location because there may be a delay before your heirs can get permission to open the box. Ask your bank how long it usually takes to gain access. The company can replace lost policies.

Auto, house and other property policies should be readily accessible at home so you can verify the provisions when making claims.

Birth, death, marriage records. These are vital for many legal and financial purposes, so protect them in your safe-deposit box. If you've lost any, apply for a replacement now, before it's needed, because you could run into a long wait.

For the names and addresses of the state agencies to get in touch with for copies, write to the National Center for Health Statistics, Rm. 1-57, 3700 East-West Highway, Hyattsville, Md. 20782. Specify the type of record involved.

Many people leave the original copy of their will in the custody of their attorney and keep one duplicate in their own safe-deposit box and another at home. If you don't have a regular lawyer, put the original in your safe-deposit box.

Pension and profit-sharing records. Before retirement your prospective pension benefits are likely to change in line with your salary and length of service, so you need keep only the last annual statement issued by your employer or union. If you leave the company before retirement with rights to a pension that starts at some future date, make absolutely sure to preserve a record of how much you will receive and when payments will begin. In some plans the employee is given the annuity policy that will provide the pension payments. In others your rights may be recorded only in the plan's files and it is up to you to apply for that pension when you retire.

Loan contracts. Even though you may be keeping the cancelled checks for the payments on a loan, the contract spelling out the credit terms might be required to settle differences with the lender and for tax purposes. Similarly, when you make a loan to someone, the note constitutes the best evidence of the terms.

Unfortunately, the one loan document borrowers rarely receive before the debt is paid off is their home mortgage and the attached note covering the payments. You should be able to obtain a copy of the note and the mortgage from the lending institution or a copy of the mortgage and deed from the land office where it was recorded.

Military service records. The two key documents for most veterans are the discharge certificate and the service record. If you qualify for disability benefits, retain the original letter from the Veterans Administration specifying the amount to which you are entitled. You might need it if you should have to enter a VA hospital.

Put the discharge, service record and disability letter in your safe-deposit box, and make copies for home reference if you like.

To replace lost VA records, contact the nearest VA office.

3

Using Credit Wisely

**HOW TO TELL
IF YOU OWE TOO MUCH**

Are you approaching your debt limit or have you already surpassed it? Should you be borrowing more and counting on inflation to help you pay it back with cheaper dollars?

There are no easy, definitive answers to these questions. Just as people's incomes and expenses differ, so do their debt limits. A long-standing rule of thumb holds that monthly payments on debts—not including the home mortgage, which is considered more of an investment—should not exceed 20% of take-home pay. The closer you get to that 20% ceiling, the greater your risk of overindebtedness. And as mortgage payments consume more and more of pay, that 20% may even be a little bit generous. But there are so many variables involved that a general guideline isn't much help. Debt is a personal thing, and the answer to that riddle of how much you can afford must be based on your own situation.

It's relatively easy to know whether you're heading toward or already are in trouble. Too much debt gives off these warning signals:

- You find it more and more difficult each month to make ends meet.
- You rely heavily on overtime pay and income from moonlighting.
- You pay only the minimum due on your charge account bills and sometimes juggle payments, stalling one creditor to pay another.
- You have to struggle to save even small amounts and don't have enough set aside to get you through such upsets as a pay cut or the need to replace a major appliance.

Even if you're getting along fine now, you should take a hard look at your debt situation and set a debt limit.

Setting your debt limit. Begin by filling out the form on pages 36-37. Use your checkbook for help with the section on expenses. Where you have to estimate, be realistic, not hopeful. (If you filled out the cash flow form in chapter 1, this form will be easy.)

Add the total of current monthly expenses to the amount that equals one-twelfth of your annual, non-monthly expenses. Subtract that sum from your monthly income and you'll have the maximum amount you can commit to monthly payments. The current total of monthly payments on installment debt tells you how much you've already committed. What's left over is available to use for new debt. But first determine how prudent it would be for you to incur a new debt.

Your total outstanding debt must also be considered when you set your debt limit. You're interested not only in how much you have to pay each month but also in how many months into the future you'll be stuck with those payments. If you quit using credit today, for example, how long would it take to pay off all your installment debts? Six months? A year? Longer?

Using the form shows you the maximum amount you can afford to pay on debts each month. How close you want to come to that limit is a personal decision.

How much future flexibility have you forfeited to your debts? How secure is your household income? Can you count on raises every year? Are you locked into your present job because your monthly payments won't let you take the pay cut that might go along with a change in careers? How far down the road have payments on today's debts pushed the starting date for your retirement investment program?

There's no hard-and-fast rule on how much outstanding debt is prudent or makes sense. What's important is to set a debt limit that considers what you can afford today and, just as important, what it means to your future.

THE SMART WAY TO MANAGE YOUR CREDIT

You won't get the full benefit of your credit capacity unless you manage it like the asset it is. That means shopping for the best terms and making credit work for you, not against you. In the face of persistent inflation, many people are taking on more debt than they otherwise would in anticipation of repaying it in depreciated dollars. They also figure that paying finance charges now could turn out to be cheaper than waiting to buy an item that might have increased significantly in price by the time they've saved enough cash.

This is perfectly rational economic behavior. But remember that even though you'll be paying a loan back in "cheaper" dollars, they'll be dollars nonetheless.

SIZING UP YOUR DEBTS

Use this form for help in setting a personal debt limit.

MONTHLY INCOME

your take-home pay $ _____

spouse's take-home pay   _____

other regular income   _____

total $ _____

MONTHLY EXPENSES

rent or mortgage $ _____

food   _____

utilities (oil, gas, water, sewage,
telephone, electricity)   _____

savings and investments   _____

insurance   _____

charitable contributions   _____

transportation and auto expenses   _____

entertainment   _____

all other   _____

total $ _____

ANNUAL EXPENSES

taxes not deducted from pay or
included in mortgage payment $ _____

insurance (not paid monthly)   _____

medical and dental bills   _____

school costs   _____

major purchases and repairs   _____

vacation   _____

clothing   _____

all other   _____

total $ _____

Divide the total by 12 to find the amount that should
be set aside each month to cover these
expenses: $ _____

See page 34 for directions on how to use these numbers in setting a personal debt limit.

PAYMENTS ON CURRENT DEBTS

personal loans
(lender and purpose)

	monthly payment	balance	months left
	$	$	

charge accounts and other installment payments

	monthly payment	balance	months left
	$	$	
total	$	$	

Borrowing to beat inflation assumes not only that inflation will continue but also that your income will increase at the same rate or even faster. Otherwise, you could find yourself in a cash-flow squeeze—and even a cheap loan is no bargain if you don't have the money to keep up the payments.

There are different kinds of credit, sources of credit and prices for credit, and it pays you—literally—to know what the differences are. For instance, here are some credit truisms worth bearing in mind:

- Finance companies generally charge higher interest rates than banks, which charge higher rates than credit unions.
- Secured loans cost less than unsecured loans, but some kinds of collateral provide better security than others. For example, you'll get a lower rate on a new-car loan than on a used-car loan.
- Monthly payments will be lower on a three-year loan than on a two-year loan for the same amount at the same rate, but you'll end up paying more in interest.

How interest is stated. When you're shopping for the best deal, the basis of comparison to use is the annual percentage rate (APR), which is the relative cost of credit on a yearly basis. The federal Truth-in-Lending Act requires that lenders always use the APR when referring to interest rates, so you can be sure you're comparing apples with apples. However, lenders also use other methods of computing interest—notably add-on and discount rates—which make the interest sound lower but can actually be double the equivalent APR. For example, a 12% add-on rate on a 12-month loan is equivalent to an APR of 21.46%, and a 12% discount rate for the same term is equivalent to an APR of 24.28%.

The basic difference between add-on and discount rates and the APR is that in the first two cases the interest is expressed as a percentage of the original amount, whereas the APR is figured on the unpaid balance, which shrinks as you pay off the loan. This difference can result in significant variations in the amount of interest you pay. On a $1,000 loan at 12% add-on for 12 months you'd pay $120 in interest; on the same loan at 12% discount you'd end up paying $136.36. But at 12% APR the total cost to you would be only $66.19.

If the interest rate you're quoted sounds suspiciously low, or if the lender quotes you only a monthly dollar payment, make sure to get the APR. The mathematical computations involved are complicated, but all lenders have tables that do the work. Check the quoted rates and payment with another lender or with a library reference, such as *The Cost of Personal Borrowing in the United States*.

CREDIT CARDS

Used wisely, credit cards can be the closest you'll ever come to "free" money. The wisest way to use bank cards, such as Visa and MasterCard, and other cards that charge interest on the unpaid balance, is to pay your bill in full each month. These cards may allow a grace period of 25 to 30 days from the date you're billed before you're assessed interest, but such grace periods are getting harder to find. If you do have one and you pay the bill in full before it runs out, you get, in effect, a free loan. And if you make your purchases right after your billing date, you can stretch the term of this free-money period to nearly two months.

But change has come to the credit card industry during the past couple of years. The short-lived credit controls program of early 1980 is long gone now, but the differences it made in your credit card options appear to be quite permanent. You may now confront higher fees and less favorable terms. But you can still keep the cost of your multipurpose cards—Visa and MasterCard—under control if you keep an eye on the charges you're paying.

• *Annual fees*. Among banks that have levied them, the charges range from $10 to $20, with $12 and $15 most common.

• *Transaction fees*. The rationale here is that each cardholder should pay his own way. Crocker National Bank in California, which began charging its Visa and MasterCard customers 12 cents per transaction in 1980, pointed out that its fee would cost its average customer, who uses the card four to seven times a month, between $7 and $8 a year—less than most annual fees.

Some banks take a different tack, charging customers even if they pay their bills in full each month. Cardholders who extend their payments and run up interest charges aren't charged the fee.

Transaction fees take dead aim at those people at the top of bank hit lists—the so-called free riders who use credit cards as a convenience but pay off their balances before incurring any interest charges. Visa says about a third of its cardholders fall into that category.

• *Higher interest rates*. Interest rates are set by the bank that issues your credit card, not by the card company. Banks have to keep under the interest limits set by the state in which their headquarters are chartered. Some states have raised these limits from their traditional 18% level to 20% or more. And there is a possibility that state ceilings eventually could be eliminated entirely by federal law.

• *Elimination of the grace period.* It used to be that you could avoid interest charges by paying for a purchase the first time it showed up on your bill, but that practice is going by the boards. More and more banks are shifting to a system under which new purchases start accumulating interest on the date of the purchase if you carry over a balance from the previous month. This system is also popular among department stores that issue their own credit cards. Sears and J.C. Penney both use it.

• *Other fees and charges.* These include minimum monthly payment requirements, transaction fees and interest rates on cash advances, charges for paying late and charges for exceeding your credit limit.

FINDING THE BEST DEAL

Though all of this may sound confusing, the variety of credit card charges can work to your advantage. If you aren't satisfied with the terms your bank is offering, you may be able to find a plan that's less expensive somewhere else. The way you use your credit card will determine which pricing deal works out best deal for you.

• Do you pay your bill in full every month? If so, a 24% APR won't affect you, but being charged interest from the date of purchase will.
• Do you use your card frequently? If you do, paying a flat annual fee may be a better deal than paying each time you use the card.
• Do you rely on your card mostly as a form of identification? In that case, a transaction fee could end up costing you very little.
• Do you carry over balances from month to month?

Then look for the lowest interest rate and fee combination.

Here's how much an account would cost annually under three pricing schemes, assuming an unpaid balance of $200 a month:

	BANK A	BANK B	BANK C
percentage rate	18%	21%	24%
interest charges	$36	$42	$48
fee	$12	12 cents per transaction, or $8.64 a year based on six transactions per month	none
total annual cost	$48	$50.64	$48

BANK CARD OR T&E?

If you have two bank cards and you're being charged a $15 annual fee for each of them, you can save yourself an easy $15 by dropping one of the cards. Since both Visa and MasterCard are accepted just about equally in this country, it doesn't much matter which one you choose.

Paring the plastic in your wallet can save you money in another way, especially if you make lots of charges and extend your balances from month to month. In many states interest ceilings fall as balances go higher, so you could manage to get yourself a lower rate of interest by putting all your charges on one card instead of splitting them up.

As more bank cards levy annual fees, they'll lose some of the edge they've enjoyed over travel and entertainment (T&E) cards—American Express, Diners Club, Carte Blanche—which have always charged fees. If you're going to pay a fee anyway, would you be better off putting your money into a T&E card?

Not if you've gotten along perfectly well without one until now. Charges for T&E cards have gone up too, so you'd still probably end up paying more than you would for a bank card. Besides, your decision on which kind of card to carry should depend as much on what you need it for as on what it costs.

T&E cards are still most useful for frequent travelers and business people who value the travel services these cards offer and aren't deterred by having to pay each bill in full. If they don't pay, they're charged a late fee, which has been rising along with the basic cost of the card.

T&E cards impose no preset spending limit, compared with an average credit limit of $900 to $1,000 for bank cards. But if you want to make an unusually large purchase with your T&E card, the merchant may have to phone the card company for an okay based on your payment history, income or assets.

Though you may be able to get more credit with T&E cards than you can with bank cards, bank cards are accepted by more merchants. T&E cards are accepted at many retail stores—especially pricier department stores and specialty shops in cities frequented by tourists—but travel-related services and restaurants are still their mainstays.

The bottom line: If a single multipurpose credit card is what you're looking for, Visa or MasterCard is probably the best deal, despite their increased costs.

OTHER LINES OF CREDIT

Credit cards are convenient, but they also can be expensive. You have additional sources of "instant" credit, a few of which are available at bargain rates.

Overdraft checking accounts. This special setup, which allows you to write checks for more money than you have in your account, is one of the easiest sources of credit to use—and one of the easiest to misuse.

As with credit cards, interest rates vary among banks. Because checks cost much less to process than loan applications, banks may offer lower rates on overdraft accounts than on personal loans, especially small loans.

You can lose the interest rate advantage if the bank imposes a transaction fee each time you write a check. Even if the fee sounds small, it can have a significant effect. Suppose your overdraft account carries a 12% APR (1% per month) and a 50-cent fee for each check. And suppose you write a $100 overdraft check and pay it back one month later. You will have paid a total charge of $1.50 for the month—the same as an APR of 18%. Whatever interest is charged, it will be charged from the date of the transaction; overdraft accounts don't have grace days.

Be sure to find out whether your bank will advance you money in the exact amounts you request or only in multiples of $50 or $100. If it uses the $100-multiple system, don't write an overdraft for $210 because you'll have to pay interest on $300. Far better—and cheaper—to write a check for $200 and dig into your pocket for the extra $10.

Since the interest on overdraft accounts is usually less than the interest on credit card balances, these accounts can come in handy if you want to pay credit card bills in full but don't have the cash; you'll incur interest but at the rate of perhaps 12% to 15% instead of 18%.

One potential drawback to overdraft credit lines is that there's often no compulsion to repay them in full right away. Some banks automatically deduct a minimum monthly payment from your checking account, but as with all minimum payments, you don't make much headway. You may find that your supposedly revolving line of credit has turned into a permanent debt.

Cash advances. Credit card cash-advance privileges have much the same advantages and disadvantages as overdraft accounts. Interest rates are usually lower than on charges, but as a rule, they're assessed from the date of the transaction with no grace period. And a low interest rate can be hiked considerably if there's a transaction fee.

Retail installment credit. When you buy a big-ticket item—furniture, a major appliance, an expensive stereo—you often have the option of paying the retailer in equal installments over a set number of months. This kind of "closed-end" credit may sound convenient, but it can also be expensive.

Before you sign on the dotted line, see how the retailer's APR stacks up against what you would pay if you got a loan from a credit union, wrote a check on your overdraft account or used your revolving charge account or bank credit card.

BORROWING ON YOUR ASSETS

Your assets can give you leverage on a loan. Pledging security might help you get a bigger loan than you could on an unsecured basis. And maybe you'll get a break on the interest rate in exchange for giving the lender an extra hedge against the risk that you won't pay.

Most lenders want only highly liquid assets as collateral, things that can easily be converted to cash if they must be used to pay off the loan.

Savings account. Cash in the bank is the epitome of liquid assets, and borrowing against savings will get you the most favorable rates. By law the rate must be at least 1% over the interest rate being earned by your passbook account. In effect, you're borrowing from yourself, with the bank or savings association serving as a middleman to make sure you pay yourself back. During the term of the loan your savings account continues to earn interest but you can't withdraw the funds pledged as security. As the loan balance decreases, more of your savings is freed for your use.

Certificates of deposit (CD), in which your money is already tied up for a certain period of time, can also be used as collateral. Here, too, the interest rate can be as little as 1% above what your CD is earning. If a money pinch has you tempted to cash in a CD early, consider whether it might be cheaper to use the certificate as collateral for a loan rather than suffer the penalty for premature withdrawal.

Stocks and bonds. You can use them as security, but you can't borrow their full value. If you want a loan to buy more stocks, a bank can't legally lend you more than 50% of your stocks' value. On loans for other purposes bank policies may depend on what kind of stock you use as collateral. One New York City bank, for example, recently would lend up to 70% of the value of stocks traded on the New York Stock Exchange, up to 60% of those on the American and up to 50% on over-the-counter stocks. The same bank would lend up to 90% of the value of Treasury bills. Federal regulation prohibits the use of U.S. savings bonds as collateral.

If you pledge securities, the bank will hold them for the life of the loan and keep an eye on the market. If the value of your stock tumbles, the bank can require additional collateral and might call in the loan if you can't provide it. That could force the sale of your stock at a depressed value.

Household goods. Your refrigerator, color television set and similar items are acceptable collateral for certain loans. Some banks accept such security, but this sort of loan is really the province of consumer-finance and small-loan companies. The majority of the personal loans made by such lenders are secured by household goods. Even though the resale value may not cover the loan in case of default, lenders view security interests in household goods as evidence of the borrower's good faith and commitment to repay. Note, too, that when you buy something on the installment plan, you are in effect using it as collateral for a loan because the seller who is financing the deal can repossess the item if you default.

Home equity loans. Tapping home equity for money can be done either with a second mortgage or by refinancing the existing first mortgage. With refinancing you negotiate a new first mortgage, use part of the proceeds to pay what's due on the existing loan and pocket the difference. If the interest rate on your existing loan is low—say in the 7% to 9% range—a lender might let you refinance for less than the current rate just to get that old low-rate loan off the books.

You may, however, recoil at the thought of surrendering a low-interest loan. If so, you can keep it and still borrow against your equity via a second mortgage, also called a junior mortgage. Transaction costs are often lower than for refinancing, but interest rates are higher.

Other arrangements are possible. You could reduce the interest cost of refinancing by borrowing for a shorter term, or you could lower the monthly payment by taking a longer mortgage.

Life insurance loans. Borrowing against accumulated cash values in your permanent life insurance is quick, easy and cheap. You can usually borrow up to 95% of the cash value at as little as 5% or 6% interest; on more recently issued policies the rate may be as much as 8%, and there is talk of raising it further. There is no set date for repayment, but any balance due at your death will be deducted from the proceeds your beneficiary receives.

OTHER KINDS OF LOANS

Unsecured personal loans. This is the most common type of loan made by banks, credit unions and finance companies. It's based on your signature, and perhaps your spouse's, and your promise to repay. Usually the top amount you can get fairly easily and quickly at a bank is a couple of thousand dollars or so, perhaps more from some specialized finance companies. Interest rates can run to 36%; the length of time you'll have to repay the loan normally ranges from 12 to 36 months.

You can arrange to pay back a personal loan either in fixed monthly installments or in one flat payment at the end of a set term. There are advantages either way. Lenders usually prefer monthly installments, which enable you to climb slowly and steadily out of debt. On the other hand, if you can count on some future sizable lump-sum income, such as a bonus, you might prefer a single payment. The repayment plan selected may have a bearing on the interest rate you'll be charged.

Debt consolidation loans. There is nothing basically wrong with the idea of borrowing money to pay your debts—as long as you realize that consolidating bills doesn't eliminate them. Used wisely, a consolidation loan can get you through a period of income reduction or an emergency that puts a sudden drain on funds that are normally available for debt payments. It can be a way to get back on course if you find yourself temporarily over-extended. In fact, it might be a more convenient, even cheaper, way to pay off some debts.

But you should know that many specialists in personal credit say that taking a consolidation loan is a sign of money mismanagement, is habit-forming (many consolidation loans end up being refinanced) or, even worse, is a prelude to bankruptcy or financial suicide.

If consolidate you must, figure out precisely what you need to do the job and borrow that amount—no more, no less. Aim for the lowest possible interest rate on an installment schedule that fits your situation. Don't take on bigger payments just to reduce the term of the loan or you may end up as harried as before. Don't secure the loan with your car, furniture or equity in your home, and avoid interest-only loans with a final balloon payment calling for all of the principal in one lump sum. If you don't have a monthly obligation to pay, you may be lulled deeper into debt.

HOW LENDERS SIZE YOU UP

Imagine that you have just applied for a loan or a credit card. What's more important to your potential creditor: your income or whether you have a telephone? The age of your auto or an unblemished credit record?

The answers may surprise you. If you are being sized

up by a computer rather than a loan officer, your income and credit history might not even be considered, but having a telephone in the house and a two-year-old car in the garage might weigh heavily in your favor. Because scoring by computer systems is being used increasingly to decide who will get credit and who won't, you need to know how it works.

In essence your application becomes a test, and how you score depends on how many points you get for your answers to such questions as: time on job? own home or rent? number of credit cards? Owning a home might be worth 15 points, for example, compared with 5 for renting. If you score enough points on a dozen or so questions, you get the credit; too few and your application is rejected.

The questions that make up the test and the score needed to pass often depend on where you live, as well as on what kind of credit you want and the creditor's experience with previous customers. A computer identifies the characteristics that most clearly distinguish between customers who paid as agreed and those who did not and assigns point values to specific attributes. It then predicts the creditworthiness of applicants whose answers add up to certain scores. A score of 115, for example, might translate into a prediction that 95 of 100 customers will repay as agreed. As the score increases, so does the probability of repayment. The creditor chooses a cutoff score that is expected to limit losses to an acceptable level.

One reason behind the use of computer analysis as a basis for credit decisions is that the growth of credit markets to include nationwide retailers and credit card issuers makes it comparatively rare for a lender to know applicants or their references personally. With the loss of such firsthand information the methods to winnow out bad credit risks have grown impersonal.

Moreover, federal law limits the criteria that can be used to decide who will get credit. The Equal Credit Opportunity Act (ECOA) prohibits discrimination on a number of grounds. A lender can program a computer to consider only legally permissible information. The lender then applies the same standards to all applicants.

This does not mean that all credit-scoring systems use the same criteria. A trait that is valuable in one system may carry little weight in another. A doctor, for example, might win high points for his profession from a bank but very few from a finance company. Commercial Credit Corporation, a nationwide consumer finance company, uses different scoring standards for different types of loans and for applicants under and over age 30. (Lenders are permitted to score age provided that applicants 62 and older receive no fewer points for this factor than anyone under 62.)

Geography may also play a role because the characteristics of a good credit risk in one part of the country don't necessarily apply in another. Homeownership is generally a plus, for example, but Sears has discovered some communities where this is not the case.

A typical credit-scoring system. Creditors keep their scoring criteria close to their chests. This secrecy, and the fact that scoring systems differ according to area and lender, make it impossible to know precisely how you'll be scored when you apply for credit.

Fair, Isaac & Company, Inc., a major developer of scoring systems, prepared the following illustration for the Federal Reserve Board as a "reasonably typical" example of what a credit-scoring system looks like. Because neither occupation nor income is scored, a house painter making $15,000 a year could score higher

	PAINTER	DOCTOR
age	50 yrs. old (31)	32 yrs. old (0)
time at address	12 yrs. (21)	1½ yrs. (0)
age of auto	4 yrs. (13)	2 mos. (12)
monthly auto payment	$0 (18)	$125 (4)
housing cost	$200 (10)	$400 (12)
checking and savings accounts	both (15)	both (15)
finance company reference	no (15)	no (15)
major credit cards	2 (15)	4 (15)
ratio of debt to income	5% (16)	12% (20)

The painter scores 154 points, the doctor 93 (the highest possible score is 196).

than a doctor with a $45,000 annual income. Points assigned to each answer are in parentheses.

Many credit screening systems don't score income because their computer analyses have found that it has little value in predicting repayment performance. Other factors not included on the above list that may be scored in other systems are occupation, time on the job, whether you have a telephone, even your zip code.

Although the way you've handled credit in the past is considered by most lenders the best predictor of your future performances, it might not be scored. Many creditors check with the local credit bureau only if a score falls in a gray area between automatic approval and automatic rejection. When it is considered, a bad credit record—several late payments, for instance—can knock down an otherwise passing grade; a good record might boost your score to the approval level.

YOUR CREDIT RIGHTS

When you apply for and use credit, you should expect a fair deal from the lender. Your credit rights are protected chiefly by three federal laws: the *Truth in Lending Act*, which requires the lender to disclose the terms of the deal in a way you can understand; the *Equal Credit Opportunity Act*, which prohibits unfair discrimination in the granting of credit; and the *Fair Credit Billing Act*, which is aimed at preventing foul-ups on your bills and helping to straighten them out when they do occur. You could benefit from detailed knowledge of the latter two laws.

The Equal Credit Opportunity Act. It says that you cannot be denied credit because of sex, marital status, age, race, color, religion, national origin, your receipt of public assistance income or exercise of your rights under truth-in-lending and other credit laws. Understand that neither this law nor any other guarantees anyone credit. There are many valid reasons for a creditor to deny you credit. What the law does is to guarantee that your creditworthiness will be evaluated on the same basis as that of all other customers. The law contains a number of special provisions designed to protect women.

- When evaluating a joint application for credit of a husband and wife, creditors must consider the wife's income—even if it is from a part-time job—in the same way they consider the husband's in determining the couple's creditworthiness and allowable credit limit.
- If you want them to, creditors must count as income any alimony and child support payments to the extent that they are likely to continue. If these payments are included as part of income on a credit application, then the creditor can ask for proof that this income is reliable (copies of court judgments, checks and the like), and he is also entitled to check on the credit

record of the ex-spouse if it is available under other applicable credit laws.

- Creditors must permit a woman to open and maintain credit accounts in her birth-given first name and married surname or combined surname, whichever she prefers, regardless of marital status. For example, Jane Doe married to Robert Smith has a right to obtain credit as Jane Doe Smith.

- When checking on the history of any kind of account—joint or separate—used by a woman or her husband, late husband or ex-husband, the creditor must consider any additional information she presents to show that the credit history being considered does not accurately reflect her willingness and ability to repay debts. This protects her from getting poor marks as a result of an unpaid bill that was solely her husband's responsibility or from such things as a creditor's failure to clear the record on an account mix-up.

- When creditors pass along information about your account to credit bureaus or other agencies, they must report all information on joint accounts in the names of both spouses if both use the account or are liable for it. This is to insure that both husband and wife get equal acknowledgment for the credit history of the account.

- If a creditor denies you credit or closes your account, you have the right to know his specific reasons so you can compare them against anything you might have been told that leads you to believe sex or marital status discrimination was the reason.

- Creditors must not discourage you from applying for credit because of your sex or marital status or consider your sex or martial status in any credit-scoring systems they have for evaluating creditworthiness.

- They cannot refuse to grant husband and wife separate credit accounts if each is creditworthy without relying on the other's income or credit history.
- Whether a woman is applying individually or jointly with her husband, creditors cannot ask about child-bearing intentions or capability, or birth control practices.
- They cannot require a co-signature on your loan or credit account unless the same requirement is imposed on all similarly qualified applicants—that is, others whose income, existing debt obligations and credit history are comparable.
- They must not change the conditions of a credit account or close it solely because of a change in your marital status while you are contractually liable for it. However, they can require you to reapply for the credit when your marital status changes if the credit was initially granted in part because of a spouse's income.
- They must not ask for information about a woman's husband unless he will be liable for or will use the credit account or loan, or they live in a state with community property laws, or she is relying on alimony provided by him as part of the income listed in the credit application, or she is applying for a student loan.
- They cannot require a woman to use a courtesy title, such as Mrs., Ms. or Miss even though these may be printed on application forms. They are not part of anyone's legal name.

The Fair Credit Billing Act. The heart of the Fair Credit Billing Act obligates credit card issuers and firms that extend revolving-type credit to do the following:

- Credit payments to your account the day the payments are received at the address the company has specified so that you don't run up finance charges after you've paid the bill.

- Mail your bill at least 14 days before payment is due if your account is the type that gives you a period of time to pay before finance charges are assessed.
- Send you a detailed explanation of your rights and remedies under this law twice a year, or, if the company prefers, enclose a brief explanation with every bill and send the longer explanation when you ask for it, or when you complain about a billing error.
- Follow certain procedures in resolving complaints you may make about billing errors. Six types of possible complaints are:

1. An unauthorized charge on your bill from which you received no benefit, or a charge that is for a wrong amount or a wrong date or is not correctly identified.
2. A charge or debt for which you want an explanation or clarification. (Example: You need to see the creditor's documentation before paying an item.)
3. A charge for goods or services that were not delivered to you or were not accepted by you in accordance with your agreement with the seller. (Example: A charge for something that was delivered in the wrong quantity or wrong size.)
4. A failure to properly reflect a payment or a credit to your account.
5. A computation or accounting mistake. (Example: Computing finance or late-payment charges incorrectly.)
6. An additional finance charge or minimum payment due that resulted from the creditor's failure

to deliver a bill to your current address. However, if you moved, you must have notified the creditor of your address change at least ten days before the closing date of the billing cycle involved.

If you run into any of those problems, here's what the law says you should do:

Write to the creditor at the address that must now be noted on every bill after a phrase like "send inquiries to." Telephoning may not preserve your rights under the law. Include in the letter your name and any account number, a description of the error, including why you believe it to be an error, the dollar amount involved and any other information, such as your address, including zip code, that will help identify you or the reason for your complaint or inquiry. You have 60 days from the postmark on the questioned bill to get your letter to the creditor. The creditor must acknowledge your letter within 30 days of receiving it and resolve the matter within 90 days.

While an amount on a bill is in dispute, you needn't pay the disputed item. If you have a checking or savings account and a credit card account at the same bank and your payments are made automatically, you can stop payment on the disputed amount or have it restored if you mail your complaint notice within 16 days.

During the dispute settlement period the creditor must not dun you, sue you, report you to a credit bureau as delinquent, close your account, deduct money from your other accounts to pay the amount or otherwise hassle you about the disputed amount. It can, however, continue to include the disputed amount in your bills and levy finance charges against it as long as it notes on the bill that disputed amounts don't have to be paid, at least until the argument is over.

The law says your complaint has to be resolved in one of two ways: If your contention proves right, the creditor must correct the error and subtract any finance charges added as a result of it, then notify you of the correction, either in a revised statement or on your next bill.

If the company turns out to be right, it must show you why the bill is correct. Then you'll have to pay the amount you disputed plus the finance charges added during the dispute. If you don't, the credit card company can start normal collection procedures against you.

4

Choosing and using a bank

It pays to shop around for a bank. Finding one that really wants your business and getting to know your banker can return unexpected dividends: help with your income taxes, a loan when no one else you know is able to get one, assistance in preparing for an overseas vacation, advice on settlement procedures when you buy a new home, quick credit when you are out of town. Some banks even offer special counseling services to assist survivors in settling an estate. A few provide, usually for a fee, courses in financial planning with special programs on the fundamentals of investing, employment benefits and retirement planning. You may even be offered computer analysis of your financial resources and a plan for using them for best results.

HOW TO PICK A GOOD BANK

For most people the biggest single factor in deciding where to bank is convenience. Before you choose strictly on that basis, though, see how well the bank nearest you handles its customer traffic at the peak lunch-hour rush, particularly on Fridays. Is there an express line for customers with simple deposit or withdrawal transactions or a single line that allows customers to go to the first available teller? Are there enough tellers? Or would going an extra block or two to another bank that moves its customers more efficiently reduce the time you spend in line?

Test the bank on the quality of its service, too. See how accessible the branch officers are, how familiar they are with the services their bank sells. In larger banks offering a myriad of services, don't expect the tellers to know answers to detailed questions; their chief job is to clear customer transactions accurately and as quickly as possible. The teller can introduce you to a "platform" officer, usually located in the area behind the teller counter, who should be able to describe the principal services and quote their costs. For those he is not readily familiar with, he should know where to get the information or direct you to someone who does.

Finding yourself shunted from one person to the next or getting incomplete answers to your questions could be a taste of what lies ahead.

Introduce yourself to the branch manager. Explain the services you are considering: perhaps you are planning to open a checking and savings account at the branch, or to rent a safe-deposit box. He'll probably welcome you as a customer and offer his personal service should the need arise. If it does, take him up on it.

THINGS A GOOD BANKER CAN DO

In most banks the growth of new customer accounts is a key factor in the job performance ratings for branch managers. They do not want to lose customers, particularly those doing more than one kind of business there. So it is not uncommon, for instance, for managers to waive penalty charges against an overdrawn checking account when they might lose a good customer if they don't.

Being known by your banker can come in handy under other circumstances—for instance, when you need a loan and money is tight. A banker who says there is a temporary shortage of lendable funds usually means that what money is available is being saved for his better customers. If you are one of the customers he hates to lose, you have a better chance of getting your loan, tight money or no.

Or say you are buying a new home but cannot settle because the down payment you need is tied up in the sale of your old house and the closing on it has been delayed. Banks normally prefer to make large, short-term loans to their corporate customers. However, on request many will arrange "swing" or "bridge" loans of up to 90 days to enable valued customers to complete such a purchase.

Many larger banks that do business on an international level have representatives to help customers plan foreign travel. Some operate their own travel bureaus. Some have foreign exchange specialists who can advise you on foreign currency exchange rates.

A bank that does business abroad should be willing to arrange advance credit for you at foreign banks with which it has regular dealings. This can be helpful if you plan to make more overseas purchases than can be accommodated by credit cards and traveler's checks.

FINDING A BANK IN A NEW TOWN

Almost all banks maintain what are called correspondent relationships with other banks. They process one another's checks, participate in large loans, sell data processing and other services back and forth, lend each other money and extend mutual courtesies. If you're moving to another city, ask your branch manager whether his bank has correspondent relationships there. Request an introduction by phone or letter testifying to your good customer status and creditworthiness, and ask your banker to make a personal introduction on your behalf to an officer at the bank he is recommending—the more senior the officer, the better.

On the basis of this introduction, your new bank should be willing to accept your out-of-town checks, tide you over in case of a cash emergency, help you with short-term financial problems in the purchase of a new home, and provide you with other financial assistance you might not get if you walked in cold.

If you find yourself without banking contacts in your new location, consult Polk's *World Bank Directory*, found in major public libraries. It gives brief financial histories of the more than 14,000 commerical banks in the United States, locations of branch offices, and, in many cases, the major divisions and departments, with the names of the officers who head them.

Write to the banks before you move. Tell them you are moving into their area and ask for information on their services. Many banks offer "welcome-wagon" programs for newcomers. Which bank responds most quickly? How good is the information you receive? Which bank strikes you as most interested in having you as a customer? From that starting point, check out the bank branches most convenient to you.

When you are comparing services, be aware that

claims of "no-charge" or "free" checking accounts can be misleading. There are often strings attached. In many areas of the country banks that tried free checking to lure new customers or keep up with competition have found it to be an expensive giveaway and have reverted to some form of direct or indirect charge. Some that advertise free checking require that you maintain a monthly minimum balance in your checking account if you want to avoid service charges. (The bank makes its money by lending out your funds without paying you interest. Your "free" checking account actually costs you whatever the excess balance in the checking account would earn in an interest-bearing account.)

Some banks charge a flat monthly fee plus a smaller charge for each check written during the month. Based on your check usage, compare what these service charges would amount to in a year before selecting a bank.

"NOW" ACCOUNTS

Since December 31, 1980, federally regulated banks and savings and loan associations throughout the country have been able to offer NOW (Negotiable Order of Withdrawal) accounts to their customers. These are, in effect, interest-earning checking accounts. But there are strings attached, often enough to keep some depositors from sharing in the potential benefits.

Picking your way through those strings may be difficult. The profusion of service charges, minimum balances, fees for checks and other fine print can form what seems to be an impenetrable jungle.

The key to choosing the right NOW account lies in the minimum balance requirement. If you don't meet it, you'll have to pay a service charge, and what you pay could actually exceed what you earn in interest. Suppose, for example, you kept an average balance of about $900 in a NOW account, on which you got 5% interest but which had a $1,000 minimum balance requirement. You'd earn $3.75 a month but you'd also pay a service charge because your balance was under the minimum. If the charge were, say $5, you'd lose $1.25.

Savings and loan associations generally require smaller minimum balances than banks, and many credit unions offer even better terms on share draft accounts, their equivalent of NOW accounts. Only about 5% to 6% of credit unions that offer share drafts have set any conditions at all, even minimum balances. But you could end up losing out on interest because of the way many credit unions compute dividends on share draft accounts. (See below under *How is interest calculated?*)

Questions to ask about NOW accounts. Minimum-balance requirements and service charges are the most obvious strings attached to NOW accounts, and they can trip you up in many subtle ways. Here are some questions to consider when trying to decide whether a NOW account will pay off for you.

• *How is the minimum balance determined?* Standard procedure is to tote up your balance at the end of each day; if it falls below the minimum for even one day in a monthly cycle, you're charged the full service fee.

• *How are charges assessed?* If your balance dips below the minimum, you may be charged for every check written during the month, or only for those written while your balance was too low. Sometimes check fees aren't charged at all, no matter how little you have in your account, unless you write more than a specified number of checks, usually around 15 to 20.

In addition to monthly service and check fees, you may run into another kind of NOW account charge— loss of interest for all or part of the period when your account dips below a certain amount.

Of course, you can avoid all service charges simply by keeping the required minimum balance. But even this tactic could cost you money: If you had to increase your NOW balance by shifting money from a higher-paying account, you'd lose interest on the transferred funds.

There's still a good chance you'd come out ahead, though, especially if your alternative is a 5½% passbook account. If your money is earning considerably more, you could be better off leaving it where it is.

• *Which are better—NOW account service charges based on an average balance or charges based on a minimum balance?* An average balance gives you more leeway. Your account can drop to zero for days at a time, but as long as you deposit enough to bring the average up to snuff, you won't have to pay a service charge.

On the other hand, it's more difficult to keep track of an average balance. Although the minimum balance required at one bank may sound like a better deal than the higher average balance required at another, it may not be. Industry studies show that the average balance in a checking account usually runs anywhere from less than two to more than three and a half times the minimum balance. At that rate, a $500 average balance requirement could be considered comparable to a minimum-balance requirement of about $250.

• *How is interest calculated?* You'll get the best deal if

interest is figured from day of deposit to day of withdrawal or on your average daily balance. In either case you get credit for all the money you have in your account, and compounding sweetens the deal even more.

NOW accounts generally pay interest daily, but there are some exceptions. At credit unions, for instance, dividends paid on share draft accounts are commonly based on the lowest balance during a dividend period, which is often a month or a quarter. This quirk can dull the interest edge credit unions have over bank and savings and loans (S&L) NOW accounts. Although federal credit unions have been permitted to pay as much as 7%, the effective rate usually turns out to be under 4% when dividends are paid on the lowest quarterly balance. (In such an account the effective yield is normally a little more than half the stated rate.)

But since credit unions by and large haven't set minimum-balance requirements or service charges, share draft accounts can still be a good deal, especially if fees would eat into your earnings at a bank or s&l.

• *Would you be better off with a traditional checking account that pays no interest?* You might be if you're accustomed to keeping a very low balance. Regular checking account fees are generally set below the fees for NOW accounts, so even though you're not earning any interest, you could end up better off with the traditional account.

SAVINGS ACCOUNTS

Most banks and savings institutions pay the maximum rates on savings deposits. But enough don't to make it unwise to assume you will automatically get the best deal. Moreover, your real yield, usually referred to as the effective yield, depends on how often interest is compounded, when interest is credited to the account and other factors.

For example, a 5½% nominal interest rate increases to a 5.66% effective yield if interest is compounded daily, as is shown in the table below. What you gain on compounding, however, can easily be lost to infrequent crediting. If the interest isn't credited to your daily compounded account until the end of the quarter and you withdraw, say, $1,000 five days before the quarter ends, you usually lose all the interest earned on that amount up to that point.

The ideal account is one that pays the maximum rate, compounds interest daily (or "continuously," a formula that yields fractionally more) and credits interest daily to the day of withdrawal. Many institutions offer such day-of-deposit to day-of-withdrawal accounts.

Compounding practices also affect the yield of certificates of deposit. Certificates are commonly advertised with their nominal and effective yields, so you can spot the differences fairly easily. The more frequent the compounding, the higher the effective yield, as this table shows.

| | ANNUAL EFFECTIVE RATE | |
stated annual percentage rate	if compounded quarterly	if compounded daily
5.25%	5.3543%	5.3899%
5.50	5.6145	5.6536
6.00	6.1364	6.1831
6.50	6.6602	6.7153
7.00	7.1859	7.2501
7.50	7.7136	7.7876
7.75	7.9782	8.0573
8.00	8.2432	8.3278

BANK PACKAGES

Within the past few years more and more banks have begun to package financial services to induce you to bring them all of your profitable financial business.

A set monthly fee entitles you to a variety of services—perhaps checking; protection against charges for overdrafts; traveler's and cashier's checks; money orders; and a safe-deposit box. As an example, for a small monthly charge, a bank may provide a free checking account, specially designed checks, discounts on group travel plans and purchases from local merchants, individual accidental death insurance, traveler's and cashier's checks, and discounts on tickets to local movie houses. It may also offer special bank seminars on such subjects as income taxes, the economic aspects of homeownership, trust services and budgeting.

To figure out whether a package would be worth its price to you, list the services you currently use, then consider which of the other services in the package you would like to have. Compare what they would cost on an individual basis against the cost of the package. If you regularly use several of the services offered, chances are you will save money by taking the package plan. If you use only one or two basic services or if you deal regularly with two or three different banks, it may not pay.

TRUST DEPARTMENTS

Perhaps the most obscure of all bank services are the trust departments, not because what they do is that difficult to understand, but because banks have not aggressively promoted them. Trust departments have traditionally been viewed, often by banks themselves, as preserves of the wealthy. In these times, however, many families who don't rate themselves as wealthy need trust services as part of their overall personal money management plan.

For a fee a trust department will help you manage your personal property. You can arrange to have the bank simply act as a custodian of your assets and follow your instructions in carrying out your investment decisions, or you can assign it complete management of your financial affairs. A trust department will also execute the terms of your will and manage your estate for your children.

Most larger banks will consider you as a trust customer if your estate is valued at more than $100,000. This includes the current value of your home and any other real estate, savings, stocks, bonds, business interests, life insurance and personal property, including stamp or coin collections or antiques.

If you are thinking about the possibility of using trust services, ask your branch manager to introduce you to a trust officer of the bank. If nothing else, you will probably come away with good free advice on managing your finances. If you are seriously considering trust services, you should also consult your lawyer and an accountant.

QUESTIONS PEOPLE ASK ABOUT BANKS

Who's responsible if something is missing from a safe-deposit box?

That depends on the circumstances and on state law. Generally, a bank is obligated only to employ ordinarily adequate safeguards to prevent the opening of a safe-deposit box by unauthorized persons. The lease agreement you sign when you rent a box spells out the details. The bank carries insurance that might in some cases cover losses from your box, and homeowners policies provide limited coverage. You can also purchase additional protection as a rider to your homeowners policy or with separate policies.

I got a car loan from my bank for a lower interest rate than the prime rate reported in the newspapers the same day. Isn't the prime the best rate you can get?

The prime rates set by big-city banks don't automatically apply elsewhere or to every bank. And a consumer may get a better break than a big company. The prime rate is subject to frequent change, and corporations often borrow for short periods. The bank may get a better return by lending you money at a lower rate for a longer period. Also, consumer loans are sometimes subject to state limits that don't apply to business borrowing, and banks might use a low car-loan rate to attract customers for other services.

Is it true the government will actually insure more than $100,000 of my bank deposits even though the limit is $100,000?

The limit applies, in the word of the law, to all accounts owned by an individual "in the same capacity and the same right." In effect, you can obtain more than $100,000 of insurance by opening accounts in different capacities and rights at the same bank, and you can duplicate that coverage with accounts in other banks. For example, a couple could stretch its coverage to $500,000 in one bank with the following series of accounts:

husband, in his own name	$100,000
wife, in her own name	$100,000
husband–wife, joint account	$100,000
husband, in trust for wife	$100,000
wife, in trust for husband	$100,000

They could be insured, too, for accounts opened in trust for their children or grandchildren. They can't extend the limits, though, by opening more joint accounts at the same bank. All of your interests in joint accounts at one bank are considered as one. If you have $100,000 in a joint accounts with your spouse, another $100,000 with one child and still another $100,000 with a second child, you are insured as an individual for only $100,000.

Although banks, savings and loan associations and credit unions are insured by different agencies, their rules don't differ materially.

What's the best way to transfer a large sum of money from one bank to another when you move to a new city?

Probably the best procedure is to open an account at your new location and have the funds wired directly to the account. You will be charged for the service, but you will have immediate use of the money.

Many people use bank or certified checks, but they can be difficult to cash at places where you are not known. Like other merchants, bankers want to avoid being victimized by phony checks and identification papers. In a government survey, about 30% of the banks queried would not immediately cash checks issued by other banks.

A bank check, also known as a cashier's check, is issued by a bank against its own funds. You buy the check from the bank. A certified check is essentially a personal check backed by funds that the bank has segregated from your account.

What are mutual savings banks?

They function largely as thrift institutions, taking in savings deposits and investing in residential mortgages.

But many offer such commercial bank services as safe-deposit boxes, credit cards and checking accounts. The Connecticut, New York and Massachusetts mutuals also sell low-cost life insurance (you have to be a resident or work in the state to buy it).

Savings deposited in member mutual savings banks are insured by the Federal Deposit Insurance Corporation, which covers commercial banks, rather than the Federal Savings and Loan Insurance Corporation, which covers savings and loan associations.

About 465 mutuals operate in 17 states. The first two savings banks in this country opened in 1816 and are still operating. The Philadelphia Saving Fund Society has grown to be the largest in the country, with over five billion dollars in deposits.

What are mortgage bankers?

Mortgage bankers make construction and mortgage loans on their own for later sale to investors, or they act as agents for banks, insurance companies and other major investors.

Mortgage bankers usually service the loans they make, collecting the borrower's payments and taking care of delinquencies. They are not commercial banks.

It often takes several days for my bank to credit my account for a check I deposited. Yet I understand that the bank somehow has use of that money while I'm waiting. If that's so, why should I be forced to wait?

Ordinarily, a depositor doesn't receive credit until his check is accepted for payment by the bank at which the person making the payment has his account. Until then, there's always a possibility the check might be rejected: You might have been given a check that was drawn on insufficient funds or even forged.

Banks will sometimes make exceptions, so if you want the money quickly, talk it over with a bank officer.

It is true that banks have use of the money while checks are awaiting acceptance. Say you live in New York and deposit a check sent to you by someone in California. It might take six to eight days for that check to be transmitted and accepted by the California bank. However, the Federal Reserve Bank through which the New York bank clears the checks for transmission to California will usually credit the New York bank's reserve account within two days. In effect, the New York bank enjoys an interest-free loan for the few days' difference.

I've read that banks "create" money. How is that done?

They don't print currency, but they do create spendable funds. Stripped of a multitude of complexities, it happens this way:

Assume you pay a contractor $1,000 for home repairs. He deposits that money in his bank. The bank is required to hold part of the deposit as a reserve; the rest can be used for loans. If the mandatory reserve is 10%, the bank sets aside $100 and makes the remaining $900 available for loans. Someone borrows the $900 and pays it to another person, who deposits the money in his bank. That bank sets aside $90 as reserve and uses the remaining $810 for loans.

In theory, with a 10% reserve the process can continue until the original $1,000 produces approximately $10,000 in deposits. Looked at from another angle, every $1,000 addition to the banking system's reserves makes it possible to expand loans by $10,000. However, it's estimated that $1,000 would be more likely to produce $6,000 than $10,000 in new loan money because banks are subject to differing reserve requirements.

The Federal Reserve Board controls the money-creating process through various measures, including transactions in government securities and changes in reserve requirements.

Do I have to set up a trust in order to have a bank manage my investments?

That depends on what kind of management you want. Bank trust departments operate through two basic arrangements: agency accounts and trusts.

With an agency account the bank can serve as a custodian of your securities, collect dividends and interest, notify you when bonds are maturing and so on. The bank acts as your agent, subject to specific terms. The conditions may be covered in a letter of instructions similar to a power of attorney.

With a trust account you appoint the bank a trustee and it takes over full management of your investments, including making new investments at its own discretion. The bank's powers and duties are spelled out in a formal trust agreement.

Many banks offer standby trust arrangements designed for people who want to maintain overall control now but would like the bank to take over completely if they become disabled or otherwise unable to handle their affairs. At that point the bank would assume responsibility for paying housekeeping expenses as well as managing assets.

5

Your kids and your money

TEACHING KIDS ABOUT MONEY

Today's money worries certainly should make it easier for parents to teach their children that money doesn't grow on trees. That was a hard point to make when children hadn't experienced anything but seemingly unending prosperity. Now, though, it's important to pay close attention to the dollars and cents that pass through family hands. And if family belt-tightening is going to work, it must include the kids.

That's easier said than done, of course. You can train a four-year-old to close the front door, but you can't expect him to understand the reason why—namely that you don't want to pay for air-conditioning the whole neighborhood. A teen-ager should understand that and more. While lessons in financial responsibility must be geared to a child's age and level of maturity, there are some general guidelines you can follow.

• *Give your child an allowance.* Although child specialists aren't unanimous on this point, most agree that the best way for kids to learn about handling money is by having some to handle. An allowance is a teaching tool from which a child begins to learn about living within his means.

How big an allowance is reasonable? When should it be started and how often should it be given? The answers depend largely on the child and will be discussed later. For now, note this rule: Every allowance should include some money the child can spend however he wants. If every cent is earmarked for lunches, bus fares and the like, the child gets no experience in choosing among spending alternatives. Another rule: Don't come to the rescue every time your youngster runs out of money. The allowance should be realistic and determined by mutual agreement. If the child consistently spends fast and needs more, either the allowance is too small or spending habits are sloppy. Find out the cause and act accordingly.

• *Don't use money to reward or punish a child.* Giving bonuses for good grades or withholding part of an allowance for misbehavior may be an effective way to teach a youngster about an economic system based on monetary rewards, but many child specialists fear it puts family relationships on the wrong footing. Such actions mix love with money, and in the minds of the young the two concepts can become confused. A better approach is to reward good behavior by showing pride and affection and to punish wrongdoing with some penalty that fits the crime. Don't give kids the idea that money can be used to buy love or to buy your way out of a jam. Paying older kids for doing extra jobs around the house is fine, as long as they realize they also have regular family responsibilities that they are not paid for performing.

• *Remember that your own example is the best teacher.* Your attitudes toward money, the way you handle it and discuss it make an impression on your children just as surely as your attitudes toward religion and other personal matters. If you speak longingly of the neighbor's new car or television set, if you spend impulsively, if you often quarrel about money with your spouse, the children will take note. Your behavior reveals the place of money in your life. It's unrealistic to expect your children to develop an attitude toward money more mature than your own.

Those are general guidelines. The problems parents face are usually more specific. What can you do to encourage financial responsibility in children of various ages and how much can you expect of the child?

Preschoolers. Three- and four-year-olds aren't too young to start learning about money. At least they can be shown that money is something you exchange for something else. You might want to give your child a few pennies when he accompanies you to the store to spend on a piece of candy or fruit. This will demonstrate the use of money, even though the relative merits of different purchases are still beyond the child's comprehension.

Does an allowance make sense at this age? Probably not, since children's concept of time isn't developed enough to grasp the idea of receiving a regular income. Besides, what would they spend it on?

Nevertheless, there are a few specific money-related exercises for the preschooler. As your child learns to count, you can demonstrate the relationship between pennies and nickels, then dimes and quarters. Also, children like to play store with play money, acting as salespersons or customers. It's a good way for them to learn the role of money in buying things.

Actually, situations that don't appear to be connected

with money at all may be the most important influences. If preschoolers are encouraged to share things, to take care of their toys and pick up after themselves, this sense of responsibility will be reflected in the attitude they develop about money. Psychologists generally agree that a person's attitude toward money is really an extension of attitudes toward other things. Thus, if children feel secure at home, are given freedom to explore their environment within reasonable limits—in short, given a healthy, happy start in life—then they are off on the right foot where money is concerned, too.

Elementary school youngsters. Most youngsters are ready for a regular allowance when they start school. A weekly interval is probably best. The amount depends on what you expect the child to buy. If he has to pay for lunch and bus fares, then the allowance must be bigger than if you paid those expenses yourself. Either way, remember the rule that kids need free money, money to spend or save as they see fit. Handing out exact change for lunch each day doesn't teach the child much if he merely conveys the money from your hands to the hands of a cafeteria cashier. With an extra dollar to spend each week, deciding what to do with it is a more valuable experience than just carting lunch money to school each day.

You must judge how much of an allowance your child can manage. Start small, then increase the child's responsibility for lunches and other expenses gradually as he matures.

With a little extra money at their disposal, kids in the elementary grades become serious shoppers. Help them learn to compare items and their prices. Allow them to make small choices on their own, such as gifts for friends or toys for themselves. As they mature, give them more say in buying clothes for school and play, pointing out along the way why one purchase may be a better buy than another because of quality, appropriateness or price. This will equip them for making intelligent choices on their own.

Of course, allowing kids to do their own shopping means you have to expect some mistakes. There will be a cheap toy that breaks the first day or too much candy or a garment that doesn't fit. Allow your child to make mistakes. Then do your best to make it a learning experience, not simply an occasion for you to say, "I told you so."

Including older elementary school youngsters in some family financial discussions is a good way to demonstrate the kinds of choices adults face. They needn't be in on every detail, but some financial decisions present natural opportunities for including the kids. For example, the cost of a family vacation depends largely on where you go. Would the kids rather spend one week at the beach or two weeks at grandma's house? Or say you're thinking of buying a dog. Even though a pedigreed animal may not be under consideration, you can point out how much more it costs than a dog from the pound. Including the kids in discussions of this type shows them how the relative costs of things affect family decisions.

Teen-agers. One thing known for sure about American teen-agers is that they have a lot of money to spend. If you wait until the teen years to give your youngster money-management experience, you're waiting too long. Your influence is waning.

The allowance is very important at this stage of life because it is the teen-ager's ticket to independence. It can now be on a monthly basis to encourage long-range planning, and it should cover most daily expenses as well as discretionary income. Discuss your teen-agers' expenses with them and arrive at a mutually agreeable figure. Then stick to the amount, giving it periodic reviews. Make the payments on time, without having to be reminded.

If a teen-ager takes a job to earn extra money, fine. This adds to the all-important feeling of independence. Don't penalize initiative by reducing the allowance, unless financial circumstances leave you no choice.

Teen-agers' savings should be kept in banks, credit unions or savings and loan associations, not piggy banks. Introduce your youngsters to the services of financial institutions and let them see their advantages. You can't force them to save, but they should be familiar enough with the family's financial circumstances to know whether they'll have to pay for all or part of college themselves, or whether you can help with a car plus the expenses of gasoline, repairs and insurance.

Teen-agers should be participating regularly in family financial discussions. They still needn't know every detail, such as total family income or the size of the mortgage, but they should know what the pressures on the budget are. Seeing how dramatically the electric bills have increased over the past year might encourage them to turn off lights and appliances when they're not being used. Participating in the decision to fix up the old car instead of buying a new one can be a valuable lesson in the importance of taking care of things. And purchases that involve them directly—a lawn mower a boy will use, for instance—provide opportunities for comparison shopping.

A couple of cautions about including kids in family financial affairs: First, don't expect them to shoulder the weight of a financial crisis. Second, don't make them feel guilty about costing you money. Show them how mom and dad cost money, too. Dad's golf clubs, mom's new typewriter—everybody incurs expenses and nobody should get the idea he or she is a burden. If financial setbacks occur that make cutting some expenditures necessary, deciding where to trim the family budget can be an educational exercise.

Before you know it, your kids will be on their own, worrying about how to teach their kids the fiscal facts of life. Between now and then, you can't teach them everything they need to know. But with your guidance, they'll learn how to use money properly. Your job is to see that they get easy lessons when they're young and don't have to learn the hard way later.

SAVINGS PLANS FOR THE CHILDREN

Setting up a savings plan for your child's future can provide not only a nest egg for your child but also a tax break for you.

In the first place the federal government allows you to give as much as $3,000 a year ($10,000 starting in 1982) to each of as many individuals as you like without having to pay a gift tax; for you and your spouse, that makes an annual exclusion of $6,000 ($20,000 in 1982 and after). You can also save money on your income tax by using the Uniform Gifts to Minors Act to shift to a child income produced by such assets as savings and securities. The child's tax bill, if any, is likely to be considerably smaller than yours. Finally, if done properly, gifts can result in reduced estate taxes and a saving in probate costs.

The government's generosity is not without a catch: In return for your tax savings you have to give up control of the asset involved and the way it is used.

Before setting up any savings plan, have a clear idea of your objective. Do you want to give an outright gift to your children? Do you want to encourage them to save their own money? Or perhaps you're looking for a plan that will force you to save for some long-term goal—a college education, for example.

Suppose you're interested in making a gift. To realize the tax savings to which you're entitled and still maintain adult management of the gift, you have two options: Setting up a custodial account under the Uniform Gifts to Minors Act or setting up a trust.

The Uniform Gifts to Minors Act. Every state and the District of Columbia has adopted some form of this law, under which you can give money and securities (and usually life insurance and annuity contracts) to a minor. Custodial accounts are promoted under various names: an example is the Savings and Loan Foundation's "College Savings Plan." Whatever the name, the principle is the same: You choose a custodian to manage the account until the minor comes of age, but the asset is held in the name of the child, so he is liable for taxes on income the asset earns.

The benefits of this arrangement are readily apparent. Let's say you wish to start a savings plan for your infant daughter with the annual dividends you earn from a group of securities. You are in the 35% tax bracket and the dividends total $500 a year (after the $200 exclusion for federal taxes), so you'd be able to set aside $325 after paying $175 in taxes. But if you gave securities yielding $500 to your daughter, she'd get to keep it all, as long as her total unearned income was less than $1,200 ($1,000 personal exemption plus $200 dividend exclusion). Even if it did exceed that figure, her tax bracket is almost certain to be lower than yours.

It's relatively easy to use the gifts-to-minors law. All you have to do is go to a financial institution or broker and arrange to open your gift account, which will be set up in a form similar to this: "[name of custodian] as custodian for [name of minor] under the [name of state]

Uniform Gifts to Minors Act.'' Besides the tax advantage, you'll get the benefit of knowing that the custodian you name will control the account until the child reaches the age of majority.

All the income distributions from the account must be used for the child's benefit but not for any purposes that are part of your legal obligations to support the child. If you use income for support purposes, it will be taxed to you, not to the child. To avoid any future wrangling, make sure to keep records of all transactions and consider appointing someone other than yourself as custodian to keep the value of the assets out of your estate (you can't appoint yourself custodian when giving bearer securities).

A gifts-to-minors account is particularly useful when you're giving securities. Although stocks and bonds can be registered directly in the name of a minor, trading in such an account can present problems. Brokers, bankers and others are understandably reluctant to deal with minors, who usually can't be held to contracts, and who can revoke transactions when they reach majority.

Just because the gifts-to-minors act is easy to use doesn't mean you should use it lightly. It has its limitations, notably:

- Your gift is irrevocable (you can't take it back), and the minor is legally entitled to receive the principal and any undistributed income when he reaches the age of majority. Then the minor is also entitled to use the money as he wishes, even if those wishes don't coincide with yours. (Some states have lowered the age of majority but retained age 21 in their gifts-to-minors laws.)

- If you are both donor and custodian and die before the child reaches majority, your gift would be considered part of your estate for federal tax purposes. This is an argument for appointing someone other than yourself as custodian. The amount of a gift that exceeds the annual exclusion would be considered part of your estate even if you weren't the custodian.

Trusts. A gifts-to-minors account is probably all you'll need to provide for small gifts. But if your gift is large enough or complex enough to warrant professional management, or if it involves an asset that isn't covered by the gifts-to-minors law, such as real estate, you might consider setting up a trust.

A trust is a way of shifting income-producing assets to a trustee for the benefit of someone else—in this case a child. In a properly created trust, the income can be taxed either to the trust itself or to the trust beneficiary if the income is distributed to the child. The trust is managed and the income controlled by a trustee until the child reaches an age you specify.

Among the advantages of setting up a trust are:

• You can instruct the trustee to use the income for a specific purpose. (If that purpose is college tuition, check first to see whether tuition is considered a support item in your state—if so, you might lose your income tax advantage.) Though you don't have to turn control of the trust over to the child as soon as he reaches majority and can pick any age you wish, you could lose your gift-tax exclusion if you choose to extend the term of the trust past age 21.

• You don't necessarily have to give your property away forever, as you do under the gifts-to-minors act. Instead, you can set up a Clifford trust—also called a reversionary trust or a short-term trust—under which the asset will revert to you after a certain period (the minimum is ten years and a day from the date the

property is transferred to the trust). The child does have a right to the income from the trust.
• Unlike a gifts-to-minors account, a trust can have more than one beneficiary.

Setting up a trust is a more complex and more expensive arrangement than setting up a gifts-to-minors account. You shouldn't proceed without getting professional guidance. Attorneys' fees vary with the type of trust and the amount of property involved. To avoid legal and tax hassles over who is reaping the benefits of trust income, it's recommended that you appoint someone other than yourself as trustee, and that too can cost you money in service fees. In contrast, gifts-to-minors accounts cost nothing to set up.

Though both trusts and gifts-to-minors accounts can save you money on income taxes, the situation with estate taxes is a bit trickier. As far as the federal government is concerned, value of gifts falling within the annual gift tax exclusion will not be included in your estate, but annual gifts in excess of the excluded amount will be. Of course, your estate will be given credit for any gift taxes you've already paid. Each state has its own inheritance and gift tax rules; be sure you know the law that applies to you.

CULTIVATING THE SAVINGS HABIT IN CHILDREN

Suppose you're not so much interested in giving your child money as you are in teaching him how to save it on his own. The simplest way to begin is to open a savings account for him. In fact, your child can open an account himself and have full control over deposits and withdrawals as long as he has reached the age of "competence." This is a rather subjective standard that depends on state law and the policy of each financial institution. It's almost always required that the child be able to write his name.

If you would prefer to have some supervision over your child's account, work out an arrangement with the financial institution whereby you'll have to countersign any of your child's withdrawal slips. For an account in the name of a very young child, you, as parent or guardian, can make deposits and withdrawals on the child's behalf until he's able to act on his own.

But don't be tempted to use such an account as a tax shelter for yourself. If you're in control of an account and you use it for your own benefit, then in the eyes of the IRS you are responsible for paying taxes on the interest income.

Other kinds of savings options are available to you if you want to accumulate money for a specific purpose or if you need prodding to save. Remember, though, that what you gain in compulsion you frequently give up in yield and flexibility. Here are some of your choices.

Payroll savings plans. If your employer has an employee investment program, check to see whether your contribution can be put into a gifts-to-minors account on behalf of your child.

If you buy Series EE U.S. savings bond through a payroll plan, they can be registered directly in your child's name. If they are, they can also be cashed in by the child when he is old enough to write his name and understand what he's doing. If you want to maintain some control over use of the bonds, you'll have to place them in a gifts-to-minors account.

However, you don't need such an account to get the benefit of tax savings on Series EE bonds. If your child owns the bonds directly, he can defer paying taxes on the interest earned until the bonds are cashed in. Better still, he may be able to avoid taxes altogether by reporting the interest each year as it accrues. He'll only have to file a tax return for the first year, stating that interest is being counted as income annually, to establish intent with the IRS; after that he won't have to file until his income warrants it—that is, until he receives $1,000 or more in a year in unearned income or $3,300 or more of total income.

"Systematic savings," or "bonus," accounts. The complexity of these plans and the proliferation of higher-yield savings instruments have made these programs unpopular, but they are still available through many federal savings associations. They usually work like this: You agree to make fixed monthly deposits for a period of up to eight years; in return the savings institution promises to pay you a higher-than-passbook rate of interest. If you fail to keep up your payments or if you make a premature withdrawal, the interest drops back to the regular passbook rate.

The Insured Tuition Payment Plan, offered by the Richard C. Knight Insurance Agency of Boston. In this variation of the systematic savings idea, you make fixed monthly payments, which the Knight agency, a specialist in college tuition loans, deposits in a 90-day, notice-of-withdrawal account earning about 5½%. You can drop out of the program after giving written notice. As an additional feature, Knight will sell you insurance that will complete the payments for you if you die or become permanently disabled. Though college tuition is the usual goal of this savings plan, you're not legally bound to use the money for that purpose.

PASS accounts. Available only to New York residents, these accounts (officially known as Parent's and Student's Savings Plan) were authorized in 1978 by the New York State legislature. You can deposit up to $750 per year per child and get a state income tax deduction. In addition, state income tax on the interest earned will be deferred until your child graduates from college, after which he'll have to pay the taxes due over a five-year period. If your child doesn't use the money for higher education, the interest and principal become taxable to you. Generally, you can make deposits only on behalf of your own children or dependent relatives who are under age 21.

FINDING THE MONEY
FOR COLLEGE

Read the numbers and weep: The average cost of four years away at college is running as high as $40,000 these days. A few years from now it will cost even more. If you didn't start planning for bills like that years ago, you're probably going to need help.

Fortunately for many parents and students, help is available—more than 14 billion dollars of it each year, by recent count. It comes from the federal and state governments, private agencies and the colleges themselves. But the money has a way of running out before everyone who wants some can get it. The best way to increase your chances of finding aid is to start looking early. Even if college is a couple of years or more away, it's not too soon to familarize yourself with the possibilities and begin mapping your search.

The key forms. Most financial aid is awarded on the basis of need, and most aid programs rely on one or more of the standard need-analysis systems to sort out their applicants. At a minimum you'll have to complete either the Financial Aid Form (FAF), which is published by the College Scholarship Service of the College Board, or the Family Financial Statement (FFS), which comes from the American College Testing Program. The colleges to which your youngster applies will tell you which they accept. Along the way you may also have to fill out additional forms for specialized kinds of aid programs. Both the FAF and the FFS are multipaged documents that demand detailed information about family income, expenses, assets and debts. The forms don't look alike, but they ask essentially the same questions and result in identical assessments of need. The high school guidance office or the financial aid department of any college can tell you where to get the forms.

How you come out in the need analysis will depend on how your finances stack up against others in the applicant pool. Computers process the information you supply and calculate a precise estimate of how much you'll be expected to contribute. Using that figure, financial aid officers at individual schools decide how much aid, if any, they can give you. Their decision will be based on the cost of the school, the amount of money on hand for financial aid and the competition for funds. Applicants showing the greatest need generally get first crack at the money.

Although the money comes from a variety of sources, the great majority of it is funneled through the colleges themselves, so the assessment forms and college financial aid offices should be the early targets of your efforts. If your need is judged great enough, you may not have to look any further.

Successful aid applicants are commonly offered a package of aid, part of which is an outright grant, part a loan and part the opportunity for a part-time campus job. If you don't survive the need test, or if you aren't offered enough money to make ends meet, your search for help gets considerably more difficult. That doesn't mean the situation is hopeless: Scholarships, loans and jobs aren't always tied to need. But since most of them are, let's examine need-based programs first.

Help that's based on need. The federal government is by far the single largest source of financial aid to college students. Aid from state governments, once paltry, has grown increasingly important in recent years. A look at the details of the major programs will give you an idea of whether you might qualify.

• *Basic Educational Opportunity Grants (BEOG).* Also called Pell Grants, these constitute the largest of the government's programs. Grants can be up to $1,800 a year or half the cost of attending school, whichever is less. Actual grants are rarely that large, however.

The program was expanded and liberalized in the late 1970s to make students from higher-income families eligible for help. Students still have to show need to get a grant, but the gap has been narrowed between the government's definition of need and the way a family faced with the bills probably sees it. This was accomplished by using a less restrictive formula to decide whether a student needs help. Students from families with incomes up to about $26,000 have received BEOG grants, compared with the old income cutoff of around $15,000. The size of the grant depends on the family's financial situation. A student from a typical family of four whose income is $20,000, for example, might qualify for a grant of about $700. If the family income were $14,000 the grant might be about $1,100.

The $26,000 income cutoff was under fire in Congress

as this book was being printed, and some sort of lower figure seemed certain to be written into the law. Even so, applicants should remember that the cutoffs aren't rigid. Special circumstances—several children in college at the same time, for instance—can make higher-income families eligible for aid. That's why it is important to follow through on the application process, no matter what your expectations may be.

• *Supplemental Educational Opportunity Grants (SEOG).* For students who have greater financial need than can be met by a BEOG, the SEOG program offers grants ranging from $200 to $1,500 a year. The average grant in recent years has been about $550. Financial aid officers at each school decide which of their students get the money.

• *College Work–Study (CWS).* Higher-income students have a better chance of getting a part-time job under the CWS program than of getting most kinds of grants. Jobs can be on- or off-campus and commonly take about ten hours a week of the student's time. The school's financial aid office picks the workers.

• *National Direct Student Loans (NDSL).* Under this program eligible students can borrow up to $3,000 during their first two years of undergraduate work and up to $6,000 for four years of study. Interest is below market rates. Repayment needn't begin until six months after the student graduates or leaves school and can be stretched out over ten years.

Lenders may be individual schools or the federal government, and applications should be submitted through the college's financial aid office. An important thing to remember about the NDSL program is that students, not parents, are the borrowers, and students must pay back the money.

• *State aid programs*. Some 250,000 students normally receive grants averaging $500 each from joint federal–state programs. Thousands of more students are helped each year by programs sponsored by the states alone. Some grants can be used only at state-supported schools; with others the student can attend any school within the state's boundaries. Only a few states let students use their grant money in another state. Information about such programs is available at the higher-education department of your state government. Ask your state legislators to help you apply.

• *Private agencies*. Labor unions, fraternal organizations, corporations and other private agencies often sponsor scholarship and loan programs for the sons and daughters of people affiliated with them. Some programs, like the National Merit Scholarships, are open to everyone, with awards being determined on the basis of competitive examinations and financial need. A few programs rely on the results of competitive exams, projects or school records without considering need.

The amount of money available through private agencies is nothing to sneeze at, but the sources are so diffuse that it is perhaps the hardest to find. Check with employers and local, state and national organizations with which you or any member of your family may be affiliated, and watch high school bulletin boards.

• *Colleges and universities*. Schools themselves support many different aid programs for students who need the money. If you start your search at the colleges' financial aid offices, you'll find out about such programs.

Aid if you can't show need. Parents living on what they thought were modest incomes, especially compared with the size of college bills, are often surprised to learn that the standard need-analysis systems judge them too affluent to qualify for the bulk of financial aid. The fact is that the aid money peters out pretty quickly for families earning more than $25,000 a year. But it isn't gone completely, as an examination of the possibilities will show.

• *Guaranteed Student Loans*. Under the Guaranteed Student Loan program, undergraduates from families with under $30,000 annual income can borrow up to $2,500 a year to a maximum of $12,500. (Students independent of their parents' support can borrow $3,000 a year, up to a maximum of $15,000.) For graduate students the maximum is $25,000.

Loans carry a competitive 14% interest rate, and the government pays the interest during the four years of school and, usually, for six months after graduation. At that time you pick up the interest payments and begin repaying the principal; some lenders give you up to ten years to repay. There is a 5% loan origination fee.

Many banks, savings and loan associations, credit unions and colleges are lenders under the guaranteed loan program. Check with your school or ask local financial institutions for information on how to apply, and for information on recent changes in the program.

• *Parents' loans*. A change in the law enacted in 1980 created a new class of government-backed college loan. Parents may borrow up to $3,000 a year, up to a total of $15,000, to help pay the bills for any one student. Unlike student borrowers, parents must begin repaying their loans, with interest, within 60 days after the loan is made. Financial need is not a criterion. Check with local lenders; these loans may not be available everywhere.

• *No-need scholarships*. A growing number of financial awards are going to students for their academic achievements. At many colleges and universities good high school grades and high test scores are being converted to cash to help pay the bills. Check with colleges your child is considering.

• *Commercial loans*. Sometimes institutions unwilling or unable to make guaranteed loans will lend money for college at regular commercial rates or under special programs they have set up for education loans. Interest rates will be higher than under the guaranteed loan program, and repayment periods are likely to be shorter. Shop for these loans the same way you would for an auto loan or a mortgage—by checking with several lenders and comparing rates and terms. And remember, loans of this type are generally available only to parents, not students.

• *Part-time jobs*. Although many jobs are offered to students only if they need money, many others are available to whoever asks for them first. Pay for part-time campus work is generally at the minimum wage or above, and earnings of $1,000 or more during the school year are not unusual. Check with the college's financial aid and employment offices to get a reading on opportunities.

PART TWO

THE ROOF OVER YOUR HEAD

6

Buying, selling and renting a home

SHOULD YOU BUY OR RENT?

The turmoil in the housing market over the past few years has taken its toll on the psyches and pocketbooks of many Americans. A lot of people who figured that they had solved the old rent-or-buy riddle once and for all now find themselves back at square one, reconsidering.

House prices are sky high. Likewise mortgage interest rates. And often a would-be buyer can't get a loan at any price. Result: If you would like to buy but can't, you have to reconsider renting.

But rentals can be scarce, too. This is not exactly a new problem, of course, but things have been especially tough lately. The people who frequently prefer to rent—young marrieds, singles, the elderly, empty nesters—have been getting more numerous. Building for their needs not only hasn't kept up, it's occasionally been a disaster scene. Furthermore, the epidemic of conversions to condominiums has forced tenants to buy or be evicted and reduced the supply of existing rentals.

So there are reluctant home buyers and reluctant renters. There also are reluctant landlords and sometimes tangled webs of people doing things reluctantly.

An example: A homeowner gets a new job in another city. He can't sell his old house, though, and so he rents it involuntarily to somebody who really would rather buy but can't. Then the reluctant landlord moves to his new location and there's another twist of the screw. Much as he would like to buy a new home there, he can't do it because he can't unload that old house. So he rents, becoming simultaneously a reluctant landlord in one city, a reluctant tenant in another. And it may be that he is the tenant of a landlord who is every bit as reluctant as he is.

The case for ownership. Reflect on the advantages of homeowning for a moment. To begin with, it is a respected life-style. It stands for such well-regarded virtues as independence, prudence, thrift, stability and, with any luck at all, a nice profit. It also is widely popular. Homeowners are a national majority, and they have been for more than 30 years.

For the average person, furthermore, this much admired institution has very solid, practical foundations.

- Homeownership offers the best chance, perhaps the only chance, to amass a lump of capital big enough to be visible to the unaided eye.
- Homeownership also offers the best chance, perhaps the only chance, to shield a little of your worldly worth from the flames of inflation.
- And, finally, homeownership is subsidized. The subsidy is indirect, of course. The homeowner collects his subsidy on his tax return, where he can deduct the property taxes levied against his home and the interest

charges on his mortgage payments, two items that usually amount to enough to make itemizing deductions worthwhile, which in turn opens the way to itemizing other expenses.

Of course, taxes and interest are charged against the renter's premises, too. The tenant pays them in his rent, but it is the landlord who gets to take the deductions.

While it is true that there has been a long-term trend for homes in general to appreciate in value, nobody can promise how much any particular home will appreciate or even that it will appreciate at all. Some houses don't. A well-designed, well-built house that has been well-maintained and is in an attractive neighborhood that is not declining probably will grow in value. But it is neither impossible nor unknown for houses to depreciate, particularly in a severe recession. Between 1925 and 1933, prices of one-family houses in 22 sample cities declined almost 29%.

The case for renting. Plenty of thoughtful people find merit in tenancy.

• *You're freer to move.* You have no long-term financial investment to consider. You may not even be bound by a lease. When you need to leave, perhaps to grasp an unanticipated opportunity elsewhere or perhaps simply to get away from whatever grates on you, you can go. No waiting to sell out first. And you are freer psychologically, not just economically. A renter simply feels unbound.

• *You can adjust to change more easily.* If your fortunes improve, you can step up to better living readily. If they decline, belt-tightening comes more readily, too. When your family expands, moving to a bigger apartment is simpler than adding onto the home. Moving is simpler when the family contracts, too.

• *You don't worry about property values*. If property values slump, the worst that happens to a renter is that you pay too much rent for a time, until the lease expires. Then you try for a rent cut or move where rents are reasonable. The same slump could be a disaster to an owner.

• *You can resist spending*. Home improvement is a big business not just because homeowners must spend to maintain their homes. It's also because they often have an almost irresistible itch to make their homes even better, to fix up and upgrade. The renter, on the other hand, spends on furnishings, but usually that's about it. His lease may even forbid other kinds of fix-up. And if the place looks tacky, he complains and lets his landlord do the worrying.

Those are positive advantages. And a common thread runs through all of them: freedom from the commitments that a homeowner makes the moment he decides to buy a home.

Can you afford to buy? Suppose you want to buy a house or apartment. Can you possibly afford it these days? Once upon a time conventional wisdom held that a home buyer shouldn't pay more than two and a half times the household's gross income and shouldn't spend more than 25% of income for carrying costs—mortgage payments, taxes, insurance, utilities and maintenance.

These days those guidelines are out the window. For one thing, people are willing to spend more for housing because it has been such a good hedge against inflation. For another, chances of many people finding some place they'd want to buy that falls within those limits are pretty slim. As a result, the ratios have been creeping steadily upward.

In this environment the prudent home seeker should consider carefully the traditional advantages of home-ownership. Is housing still a good investment, even at today's costs? How much can you afford? Would it be smart to overextend in anticipation of future increases in income and in the value of the property?

The answer to the first question appears to be yes. Those forces that have driven up prices—rising costs of land and materials (and, to a lesser extent, labor), and strong demand—show few if any signs of abatement. Indeed, demand is almost certain to increase in future years.

As for ability to pay, those old benchmarks still make some sense, but your housing budget is an intensely personal matter. You should figure out your capabilities for yourself and not be influenced by the fact that others flout the old rules.

The work sheet on pages 100-101 will help you assess your home-buying potential. If you anticipate sizable financial obligations, your employment outlook is uncertain, your down payment fund is low, your family is likely to grow or you'll be needing money for improvements or furnishings, it would probably be wise to spend less per month than the calculations indicate you can afford. On the other hand, you might consider spending more if you expect increased income, if the price is low compared with similar properties or if you have resources not shown on the work sheet that could be tapped in an emergency. Depending on your expectations about your future income, you might consider getting a graduated payment mortgage (GPM), payments for which are lower in the early years and rise gradually to a given level. GPMs are described later on.

HOW MUCH CAN YOU SPEND FOR HOUSING?

I. Before you can know how much house you can afford, you need to calculate your other expenses. Do that in the blanks below, then subtract line B from line A to see how much you have available for housing (line C).

MONTHLY INCOME

    net pay (after taxes) $_____

    other income   =========

                        total $_____ **A**

MONTHLY NONHOUSING OUTLAYS

    food and household supplies $_____

    transportation   _____

    insurance   _____

    health care   _____

    clothing and cleaning   _____

    education   _____

    debt and installment payments   _____

    recreation and vacation   _____

    telephone   _____

    personal (haircuts, lunches)   _____

    taxes (not deducted from pay)   _____

    savings   _____

    charity   _____

    other   =========

                        total $_____ **B**

AMOUNT AVAILABLE FOR HOUSING

    monthly income (A) minus
    nonhousing expenses (B) $_____ **C**

II. With the figure on line C in mind, plus a firm idea of the size of the down payment you plan to make, you're ready to begin assessing individual homes. Real estate agents or current owners can give you reasonably precise estimates for the categories of expenses listed below. Under "other" you might include any additional cost of commuting to work from that location or new expenses, such as community association fees. If you would reduce any of your current nonhousing expenses by buying a particular home, estimate your saving and subtract it from anticipated expenses. Then add up the housing costs and compare the total on line D with line C. If C is larger than D, you've probably found a place you can afford.

ANTICIPATED MONTHLY HOUSING EXPENSES

mortgage payment	$_____
insurance	_____
property taxes	_____
utilities	_____
maintenance and repairs (figure at least $1/12$ of 1% of the price)	_____
other	_____
total	$_____ **D**

In figuring how much you have for a down payment, remember that you'll have to pay settlement costs, which could run 3% or more of the house price. You should hold back some cash as a reserve for emergencies, too.

Is it really smart, as many home buyers think, to pay as little down as possible? Not always. True, the bigger the mortgage, the bigger your tax deduction for interest, and any spare cash you may have left over could be invested. But those advantages could be offset by the greater amount you'd pay out in interest over the life of the loan and the cost of private mortgage insurance, which is usually necessary to obtain a low down-payment mortgage.

A MORTGAGE YOU CAN AFFORD

Prior to the squeeze in the mortgage-lending market that began in earnest in the 1970s and continues today, the loan options for most home buyers remained virtually unchanged for decades. The traditional long-term, fixed-rate, fixed-payment mortgage was the only game in town.

Today, however, shopping for a mortgage is a lot like shopping for an automobile. You can pick and choose among different models, even adding options on some if you wish. And, though all of the new kinds of mortgages available aren't necessarily competitors in the sense that different models of cars are, they do offer an array of possibilities for getting you where you want to go. Any discussion of the mortgage market in the 1980s must begin with a rundown of its inventory.

Standard fixed-rate mortgages. These loans once accounted for most residential mortgage lending, but their role in the marketplace is growing increasingly smaller. They carry fixed monthly payments and a fixed interest rate, usually run for 25 to 30 years, and are made by banks, savings and loan associations and other lenders. Some lenders, however, have stopped making them.

FHA mortgages. Insured up to a maximum amount by the Federal Housing Administration, FHA loans often carry an interest rate that is a little bit below the going market. Unfortunately, that usually doesn't mean very much. Lenders can refuse to make loans under the program unless they receive lump-sum amounts called points to make up for the difference. (One point is 1% of the amount of the loan.) The buyer must also pay the cost of the FHA insurance, and processing of the application can take longer than for a conventional loan. FHA mortgages made at interest rates fixed for the life of the loan are growing less popular with lenders.

VA mortgages. The main advantage of mortgages guaranteed by the Veterans Administration is that they usually require little or no down payment on the part of the buyer, who must be a qualified veteran. Here, too, points and red tape may cause headaches. But VA loans are available in most places, and you can find out whether you qualify by calling or writing the nearest VA office. It will ask for your military service number, social security number, birth date, date of entry into the service, date and place of separation, name of the unit you were with when discharged and the type of discharge.

Graduated payment mortgages. They're designed primarily for young people who expect their incomes to increase. GPMs insured by the Federal Housing Administration have been available for a few years now. A significant portion of all FHA-insured mortgage loans are GPMs. The Federal Home Loan Bank Board authorized federally chartered savings and loan associations to write non-FHA GPMs in 1979.

Buyers who obtain FHA-insured GPM loans can choose among five payment schedules. Payments are relatively low at first—lower than they would be with a fixed-payment mortgage—then increase at regular intervals, usually yearly, until they reach a fixed amount after six to ten years. By then, payments are higher than they would have been under a level-payment mortgage.

What are the drawbacks of GPMs? For one thing, you pay more interest. That's because reducing the principal takes longer with the smaller payments. The outstanding balance can even increase for a period when payments do not completely cover the interest actually due.

Few mortgages run their course. Houses change hands every eight years, on the average. But because the principal of the loan has been reduced so little in those first years, and may even have increased, your payments will not have increased your equity as much as payments under a standard loan would have. That means you will get less cash when you sell, perhaps not enough for a down payment on the next house you want to buy.

GPMs also entail more risk of default. If your income fails to increase as you anticipated, or if it declines because you or your spouse stop working, you might be unable to keep up with the rising payments and could lose the house.

HOW MUCH WILL THE MORTGAGE COST?

This table shows the monthly payment required per $1,000 of mortgage amount at various interest rates for three common mortgage terms. The numbers shown include principal and interest only; insurance and property taxes would be additional. To determine the monthly payment for a mortgage you're considering, multiply the appropriate amount in the table by the number of thousands of dollars involved. Example: For a 30-year loan of $50,000 at 13% interest, multiply 50 × $11.07 = $553.50 monthly payment.

Interest rate	20 years	25 years	30 years
10 %	$ 9.96	$ 9.09	$ 8.78
10¼%	9.82	9.27	8.97
10½%	9.99	9.45	9.15
10¾%	10.16	9.63	9.34
11 %	10.33	9.81	9.53
11¼%	10.50	9.99	9.72
11½%	10.67	10.17	9.91
11¾%	10.84	10.35	10.10
12 %	11.02	10.54	10.29
13 %	11.72	11.28	11.07
14 %	12.44	12.04	11.85
15 %	13.17	12.81	12.65
16 %	13.92	13.59	13.45
17 %	14.67	14.38	14.26
18 %	15.44	15.18	15.08
19 %	16.21	15.98	15.89
20 %	16.99	16.79	16.72

Pledged-account mortgages (PAM). These are GPMs with a major difference: All or part of the down payment is kept in an interest-bearing escrow account. During the early years of the mortgage, money is withdrawn from that account each month and added to the payment made by the borrower. This enables the borrower to pay less during those years than he would with a regular mortgage. The most widely-known PAM arrangements are called FLIPs, for flexible loan insurance program.

There is another variation of the GPM—a mortgage on which only the interest is paid during the early years. This is more likely to be available from an individual selling a home than from a financial institution.

Floating-rate mortgages. What makes these relatively new types of mortgages different from the rest is the fact that the interest rate, instead of being fixed, can move up or down with changing economic conditions. Lenders like these loans because they protect them from getting stuck with mortgages agreed upon at rates than turn out to be woefully low as time goes by. After a slow start, floating-rate loans seem to have found a permanent place in the market, partly because some big lenders now refuse to make any other kind. They come in two varieties.

• *The variable-rate mortgage*, also called an adjustable-rate mortgage, permits the interest rate to be adjusted up or down by the lender after the loan is made. At federally insured savings and loan associations and credit unions rates may change as often as once a month, but few lenders can cope with that, so adjustments generally are scheduled less often.

Rate changes can be hooked to any number of interest-based indexes published by the federal government and readily verifiable by a borrower. There is no limit on adjustments, either up or down. In some cases, increases in the rate can be accommodated without actually raising the borrower's monthly payment. Instead, the lender either extends the life of the loan—meaning the borrower will be making payments longer than originally contracted for—or tacks on the additional amount in the form of "negative amortization." With negative amortization, the loan amount is increased and the monthly payment stays the same, an arrangement that eats into the borrower's equity.

National banks can make variable-rate loans on which the interest can be raised as much as 1% every six months, with no upper limit.

When you accept a variable-rate mortgage, in effect you are gambling on interest-rate trends. If you think they are going to fall as time goes by, you'll want the variable-rate loan. If you expect rates to rise, you'll try to stay away from it. Variable-rate mortgages represent a shift of historical proportions in the mortgage market because they put the risk of rising rates on the borrower where they once resided with the lender.

• *The renegotiable-rate mortgage* is the other floating-rate form. On most loans of this type, interest rates can be adjusted up or down every three, four or five years. The allowable change per year is ½ of 1%, with a total limit of 5%. If the contract calls for adjustment every three years, the maximum adjustment each time would be 1½%. There is also a 5% limit to decreases. However, limitation on the frequency or size of adjustments have been lifted for loans made since mid 1981.

This loan resembles the Canadian "rollover" mortgage in concept but differs from it in many details. The main difference is that the Canadian version involves a series of short-term loans amortized over 25 years. The entire loan comes due at the end of each adjustment period and is replaced by another, new short-term loan, whereas in the U.S. version the entire series of short-term loans is secured by a single long-term mortgage or deed of trust of up to 30 years.

To call this a "renegotiable" loan actually sugarcoats the facts. That term suggests that when rate-adjustment time comes, some bargaining will take place, which is hardly the case. The lender tells you what the new rate will be; you tell him whether you accept it. End of negotiation. If you do not accept, the loan then becomes payable in full, with no penalty for prepayment.

As with variable-rate loans, lenders are required to explain to borrowers how renegotiable-rate mortgages differ from standard, fixed-rate ones. But they are not obliged to offer a fixed-rate alternative.

The renegotiable-rate loans may use a different index to signal rate adjustments. Older loans use the "monthly national average mortgage rate index for all major lenders," computed and published by the Federal Home Loan Bank Board. Because this index is a mortgage-rate index, it is normally sensitive to mortgage market conditions.

CREATIVE FINANCING FOR TIGHT MARKETS

When interest rates are so high that few people can afford a mortgage, how can buyes and sellers of homes still manage to strike deals? They have been doing it increasingly in recent years with "creative financing," a phrase used to describe a number of unorthodox, even exotic loan arrangements ordinary homeowners would doubtless shun in less stringent times. Creative financing makes possible purchases and sales that might not otherwise take place, but it sometimes entails risks not present in traditional mortgages. If you're in the market as buyer or seller, don't attempt any of the following arrangements without competent legal and tax advice.

• *Take-back mortgage.* This is a form of seller financing in which the seller takes a mortgage from the buyer for part of the purchase price. Take-backs can be attractive to sellers who don't need the entire proceeds from the sale right away and to buyers trying to work out a contract with terms they can handle. Though payments on such mortgages may be figured as though the loan would be paid back over a 25- or 30-year period, the loans are often due in full—in a balloon payment—three to ten years after the sale. This means the buyer will have to sell or refinance by that time.

• *Purchase-money second mortgage.* Here the seller agrees to finance part of the buyer's down payment through a second mortgage, usually of three to five years. The primary mortgage lender should be told of such an arrangement, since the payments on the second mortgage may affect the buyer's ability to meet payments on the first. The seller's interest is protected by a lien on the property that is subordinate to the primary lender's.

• *Subsidized interest rate.* Sometimes a developer or individual seller can enhance the marketabilty of a home by offering to subsidize the buyer's mortgage interest rates for a limited period of time. Here's how it might work: The seller guarantees a mortgage interest rate of, say, 11% for the first two years. Along comes a qualified buyer who gets a mortgage at 14%. To complete the deal, the seller agrees to pay the difference in the monthly payments between a 14% mortgage and an 11% mortgage for the two years. In the case of a $50,000, 30-year mortgage, the difference would be about $116 a month, or a total of nearly $2,800 for the two-year contract. Such an arrangement pays off for the individual seller only if he can keep the price of his house high enough to make up for the payments. For the buyer the subsidy provides a deferral of high interest rates and a chance to refinance if rates fall.

• *Wraparound mortgage.* This sort of deal involves an existing mortgage plus additional financing to complete the purchase. Say a house is selling for $100,000. The seller has a mortgage on the place with an outstanding balance of $40,000. A buyer makes a down payment of $20,000. He finds a lender, often the seller, who gives him a new mortgage that covers the old loan balance plus an additional $40,000. The buyer makes payments on the wraparound mortgage to the lender, who uses part of the money to make payments on the old mortgage. The rate on the wraparound loan is higher than the rate on the old mortgage, and the lender profits from the differential. Thus he can afford to offer a rate on the wraparound that is lower than prevailing rates. However, it may be difficult to find a lender for such an arrangement, since the existing mortgage contract usually forbids it.

• *Land contract.* Also known as a contract of sale or contract for deed, this is actually an installment sale. The buyer doesn't get title to the property right away but must wait until some point agreed upon in the contract—usually years down the road. The main advantage in such deals belongs to the seller. If anything goes wrong during the course of the contract, he still owns the property. And much can go wrong. As part of the deal, the buyer may agree to take over payments on the seller's existing mortgage—an arrangement that many mortgage lenders contend violates the "due on sale" provision of their standard mortgage contracts. Lenders who find out about it may be able to foreclose on such mortgages, leaving the buyer with nothing to show for his payments except a worthless contract. Neither buyer nor seller should draw up a land contract without expert legal help.

• *Shared appreciation*. The idea is simple enough: In return for a lower interest rate, the home buyer cuts the lender in on any profit the home may bring when it is sold. In early versions of these loans, the size of the discount generally corresponded to the portion of future profit the buyer agreed to share with the lender. For example, a one-third discount off the going interest rate would entitle the lender to one-third of the eventual profit from the future sale of the home. Thus, if a lender's usual rate is 12%, he might offer a shared-appreciation mortgage at 8%. Naturally, a lender would be inclined to make such loans only on property thought likely to appreciate in value. And in order to insure that the lender won't have to wait indefinitely for his profit, agreements may include a requirement that the home be sold or refinanced within a specified period, say ten years.

• *Land leasing*. Some real estate developers are attempting to make their projects more affordable by separating the house from the land. Investors buy up the land, then lease it to homebuyers for 99 years or some other period, often with an option to buy. Since the buyer then needs to purchase only the house, his down payment is lower and he is more likely to qualify for a mortgage. Land rent is often paid on an escalating basis—lower in the early years than it is later on. If a land lease can get you into a home you wouldn't otherwise be able to afford, it may make sense. But buyers should inspect the documents carefully so there are no surprises later on. And the arrangment may limit the market at resale time.

USING A REAL ESTATE AGENT

- In California, a rancher hired a real estate agent to sell his property but later changed his mind and took it off the market. Although no sale took place, he was forced to pay a $15,000 commission.
- In McLean, Virginia, a couple whose home was sold in ten days for their asking price of $159,500 paid a brokerage fee of only $1,000—$8,570 less than the prevailing rate.
- In Daytona Beach, Florida, a couple bought a choice home at a bargain price, thanks to a tip from an agent.

The lesson from all this? It's important to know the ropes when dealing with a real estate professional. If you ever buy, sell or rent a home, apartment or any kind of real property, you'll be confronted with such questions as these: What can I expect an agent to do for me? Do I really need one? How much should I pay? What recourse do I have if something goes wrong?

Before looking at the answers, it's helpful to review the nomenclature. *Agent* is the popular term for a salesperson who is licensed to work for a real estate broker. A *broker* is licensed to conduct a real estate business and to negotiate transactions for a fee. Both may properly be called agents because they act as agents for clients. *Realtors* are brokers who belong to the National Association of Realtors (NAR), a trade and lobby group. *Realists* are members of the National Association of Real Estate Brokers, a smaller group.

Usually it is the seller of real estate who engages professional assistance. But an agent can also assist a buyer in several ways: by telling about and showing properties that are listed for sale and by providing information about market conditions, cities, neighborhoods, schools, public facilities, tax rates, zoning laws, proposed roads and construction, and other essentials for evaluating a real estate purchase. And he can tell you about properties that are about to come on the market, giving you an opportunity to submit a purchase offer before a property is advertised.

Occasionally an agent is hired by a prospective buyer as a consultant for a negotiated fee, but in most cases agents work for sellers and are paid by sellers if they make a sale. Most work strictly on commission. The higher the price you pay, the bigger the agent's commission.

An agent can't possibly know everything about a particular property, nor is he likely to be a construction or engineering expert. An honest one will, however, tell you about the problems he's aware of, and an agent could be held accountable for providing wrong information on something he ought to know about. (A buyer could also sue an owner who conceals known defects.)

To get a broad perspective of what properties are on the market, values, trends, neighborhood characteristics and such, talk with several agents before you select one to work with. They'll be only too happy to help you; the real estate business is fiercely competitive, and prospects are avidly courted.

If you find out about a home for sale from sources other than an agent, you may be able to get a lower price by dealing directly with the owner, provided no brokerage agreement is in force. By avoiding a commission, an owner can lower the price.

Should you opt for assistance in selling, there are several possibilities. The vast majority of brokers charge commissions of 5% to 7% of the selling price of residential property and 10% for vacant land and farms. The amount is negotiable, however. Some will accept less, especially if business is slack or the property is particularly valuable or appears to be easily salable.

Also, as we shall see, discounters are emerging in growing numbers.

What agents should do. An agent who stands to receive a regular commission from you, the seller, should:

- Obtain a full description of the property, plus information about tax and utility rates, mortgage balance, the neighborhood and nearby facilities, such as parks and public transportation.
- Brief you on things you can do to make the place as appealing as possible, such as painting, making repairs, tidying up the yard, seeing that appliances are working.
- Help you set the price. You should be provided with "comparables" (recent selling prices and current asking prices of similar properties).
- Prepare forms for prospective buyers giving detailed information about the property and terms of sale.
- "Sit" on the property; that is, be there or have another agent there to receive prospects, at least one afternoon a week.
- Be available to show the property during regular business hours and some evenings and weekends.
- Know where mortgage money can be obtained and provide prospects with information about rates and other terms.

- Screen prospects to find out whether they're financially able to make the purchase.
- Promptly present you with all offers to purchase and advise you of any problems with them.
- Assist in the settlement of the transaction as your representative. You should also have an attorney because real estate agents aren't supposed to give legal advice.

If this sounds like a lot, remember that the salesperson and broker stand to collect a good sum if the property is sold—$5,950 or more for an $85,000 home, for example.

Commissions. The uniformity of commission rates throughout the country is a subject of curiosity and criticism. Commissions do not necessarily reflect the amount of work and expense required to sell a particular property; some sell instantaneously, whereas others take months or years. Critics say the rate structure results from tacit understandings among brokers and is enforced by boycotts and other reprisals against those who refuse to go along. The industry denies this, insisting that price fixing would be impossible in a competitive industry with hundreds of thousands of independent operators.

Actually, the rate structure has been cracking for some time. A number of discount brokers have set up shop in the past few years. Some will perform specified services for a flat fee, regardless of the home's selling price. There are also companies that will help you sell your home by providing signs, contract forms, information sheets and some advice for a small fee.

Whether you seek a low-fee or a full-fee agent, make your choice with care. Ask friends, neighbors or business contacts which agents are the most active in your area. If time permits, talk with several. Ask how extensively your property will be advertised, and when and how it will be shown to prospective buyers. The agent should be familiar with your area and willing to put forth the effort necessary to sell your home quickly and at a good price.

Listing the property. When you've made your choice, you'll be faced with another decision: how the property should be listed. These are the principal ways:

• *Exclusive right to sell.* This arrangement, the most widely used, provides that a commission will be owed to the listing broker whether he or someone else sells the property. Since the broker is sure to benefit from his efforts, he is likely to try harder to make a sale.

• *Exclusive agency.* This is similar except that no commission will be owed if the owner sells the property himself. There may be less incentive for the broker because he's not assured of a fee.

• *Open listing.* With this, an owner can list his property with several brokers at the same time. Only the selling agent gets a commission, so this type offers the least incentive to brokers. No commission is owed if the owner makes the sale himself.

Through the widely used multiple listing services, information on listings is made available to participating brokers in a community so they can gain the greatest possible sales exposure for their properties.

You will be asked to sign a listing agreement, a type of employment contract that sets forth the kind of listing and other specifics, including a description of the property, the price, the terms of sale and the fee or commission. Such agreements usually provide that the commission will be payable when a purchaser is produced who is ready, willing and able to buy on the terms provided or on any modification approved by the seller, whether or not settlement occurs.

That means you could be obligated to pay a commission if you should change your mind about selling or be unable to sell for whatever reason during the listing period. The provision has been enforced and upheld by courts in nearly every state.

Real estate people say that in practice the provision is seldom invoked. Nevertheless, for your protection, ask that it be stricken. Your agreement with the broker, like the commission itself, is negotiable.

Listing agreements often run for 60 days but can be longer or shorter. They commonly provide that a commission will be owed if within 30 days after expiration you sell the property to someone who inspected it as a result of the listing.

What if you have a grievance? If the broker doesn't resolve it to your satisfaction, take it up with the state real estate commission and, if the company is a member, the local real estate board.

TAX ANGLES OF BUYING AND SELLING

For many people, the act of buying or selling a home serves as a startling introduction to the often-baffling kinds of considerations that go with sound tax planning. With tens and sometimes hundreds of thousands of dollars involved in the typical home sale, a misstep can have expensive tax consequences. Here are answers to questions that often occur when deals are struck.

What's the "adjusted basis" I'm supposed to use to figure my profit or loss when I sell my home?
The basis generally starts out as the price of the

house plus certain settlement charges. Over the years the basis can be adjusted—up to reflect the cost of permanent improvements that increase the value of the property, for example, or down because of casualty losses or depreciation deductions you take if you use your home for business or rental purposes.

It is vital to keep records to substantiate the basis and any adjustments to it. You need the purchase contract and settlement papers, of course, and also receipts, cancelled checks and other evidence of improvements that add to the basis.

When you sell your home, the profit for tax purposes is the difference between the adjusted basis and the amount realized on the sale. The amount realized is the selling price minus certain expenses, such as commission and advertising and legal fees.

Which settlement charges can be added to the basis of the home?

State and county transfer taxes, appraisal fee, assumption fee, attorney's fees, credit report fee, mortgage origination fee, notary fees, property inspection fee, recording fee, title examination fee, title insurance premium, utility connection charges, and amounts owed by the seller that you pay, such as part of the selling commission or back taxes and interest. (You can't deduct taxes and interest owed by others even if you agree to pay those bills yourself.) If you qualify, you may be able to deduct settlement costs as moving expenses.

Why worry about profit on the sale? Don't you escape taxes as long as you buy another home?

Not quite. Basically, what the law allows is deferring taxes on the gain if within 24 months before or after the sale (for sales completed after July 20, 1981) you buy and occupy a home that costs as much as or more than the adjusted sales price of the old home. The 24-month rule also applies to earlier sales for which the old 18-month rule had not expired before July 20, 1981.

You can do this any number of times, delaying taxes on each transaction. But you don't escape the tax completely. The liability for it remains.

Here is how deferral works. Say that after expenses you realize $42,000 on the sale of your home, $15,000 more than its adjusted basis. Within the replacement period you buy a new home for $60,000. You defer paying taxes on the $15,000 gain, but that amount is subtracted from the basis of the new home, dollar for dollar. When you sell the second house, the $15,000 profit from the first one will be included in your gain.

Once you or your spouse reaches age 55, however, you may be eligible for the once-in-a-lifetime opportunity to escape taxes on up to $125,000 profit on the sale of your home (this is discussed later in this chapter).

Is it true that I cannot take advantage of those tax-deferral provisions if I sell my house before I've lived in it for 24 months?

Generally, you can't postpone tax on the profit from more than one home sale within a 24-month period. Assume, for example, that you sold a house in March 1980 and deferred the tax by buying another principal residence the same month. Then, in April 1981, you sold your home and bought another one. The 24-month rule would prohibit you from postponing tax on the gain from the sale of the intermediate house. However, if the third home is purchased within 24 months of the time you sold the first one, profit from the first house is considered reinvested in the third, and therefore the tax is deferred. You'd have to report only the profit that accrued during the months you owned the second home. The rule doesn't apply if the sale of your home is connected with a qualified job-related move.

We sold our home for $110,000. That's $84,000 more than the balance on the mortgage. We put only $25,000 down on our new $125,000 home and used the rest of the cash to buy into a business. Can we postpone paying tax on our gain even though we didn't reinvest it in the new house?

Yes. What matters is that the new home cost more than the adjusted sales price of the old one.

I just sold a house in a depressed market and took a $3,000 loss. Since Uncle Sam would demand a share of my profit if I had made one, will he share my loss by letting me deduct it?

No. Losses on the sale of a personal residence are not deductible, nor do they affect the cost basis of the next home you buy.

When we bought our home, there was a dilapidated wooden fence around the backyard. Last summer we replaced it at a cost of nearly $1,000. Can we add that amount to the basis of the house?

Yes, because the fence is a capital improvement. The tax law draws a line between repairs, which are considered nondeductible personal expenses, and improvements, which, though nondeductible, are added to the cost basis. It's an important difference because expenditures that qualify as improvements cut the taxable gain when you sell the house. In other words, Uncle Sam helps pay for improvements but not repairs.

To qualify as an improvement, the expense must add

value to your home, prolong its life or adapt it to new uses. Adding a bathroom, putting in new plumbing or wiring and paving a driveway are examples of improvements that increase the basis.

Repairs, on the other hand, merely maintain your home's condition. Replacing a broken window pane or painting a room would count as repairs. However, the cost of some work that would ordinarily be a repair—such as painting a room—can be added to the basis if it is done in connection with an extensive remodeling project. Also, some major repairs, such as extensive patching of a roof, may qualify as improvements.

The IRS doesn't have a list of what qualifies as an improvement and what doesn't. It's often a judgment call, and two IRS agents could disagree over any specific expenditure. So it's important to keep detailed records of any expenses that might affect your home's basis. When you think a bill might qualify as an improvement, keep the receipt.

Our refrigerator gave up the ghost last winter, and we replaced it with the latest deluxe model. When we sold the house during the summer, the new refrigerator went with it. Do we count the $895 it cost as an addition to basis?

It depends on whether local law considers the appliance a fixture that must be sold with the house (your real estate agent should know). If so, its cost is added to the basis. But if the refrigerator is considered personal property, its cost is not included. However, the refrigerator's value when you sell (distinguished from its cost when new) does cut the profit on the house sale.

Here's an example of how to handle buying and selling a home when the price covers personal property as well as real estate: You bought your home five years ago for $63,000, a price that included a stove, refrigerator, washer and dryer—all of which are considered personal property rather than fixtures where you live. You estimate that at the time of purchase the appliances had a fair market value of $1,800. Subtracting $1,800 from the purchase price gives the home a basis of $61,200.

Shortly before selling you replace the stove and refrigerator; the estimated value of the appliances sold with the house is now $2,400. You realize $90,000 on the sale, but for purposes of determining your profit, use the figure $87,600 ($90,000 minus the $2,400 attributable to personal property).

Your taxable gain is the difference between $61,200 and $87,600, or $26,400.

After arduous negotiations we agreed to pay half of the real estate commission owed by the couple who was selling us a home. It cost us $2,200. Can we deduct it?

No, but add that amount to the basis of the new home.

My sons and I spent the last two summers building a garage. It cost $4,600, but if we'd hired all the work out, I'm sure the price would have been twice as much. When calculating the addition to the basis of the property, how do I figure the value of our labor?

You don't. The addition to the basis is the actual cost of the improvement to you. If you hire workers, you include their wages, but you get no credit for your own time and skills.

A job switch this year meant moving my family from Kansas to Texas. We sold our home and bought a new one in Austin. Which of the buying and selling costs are deductible as moving expenses?

You must meet several tests before you can deduct moving expenses. For example, the move has to be related to a full-time job—which you must hold for at least 39 weeks during the 12 months after the move—and your new place of work must be at least 35 miles farther from your old home than your former workplace was. (People who move to take their first job can also qualify.) Since you are apparently eligible, you can write off many buying and selling expenses that would ordinarily only affect the gain on the sale of the old house or the basis of the new one. It's worth doing. If you use $100 of selling expenses to cut the gain on the sale of the old house, for example, it would trim just $40 from your taxable income (because 40% of long-term capital gains is taxable)—and if you're rolling over your profit into the new house, this year's tax bill wouldn't be affected anyway. Claiming that same $100 as a moving-expense deduction would cut taxable income by $100 for the year in which the expenses are paid.

Selling costs that can be written off as moving expenses include real estate commissions, attorney's fees, title fees, escrow fees, points or loan placement charges, state transfer taxes and similar expenses. Purchasing expenses that can qualify include the settlement charges listed in the answer to an earlier question (see page 117). There is a $3,000 limit on such deductions.

We recently inherited some money, enough to pay off the mortgage on our home. If we do, we'll be stuck with a prepayment penalty. Would it be deductible?

Yes. It is treated as interest and may be deducted in the year paid.

We sold our home for $87,500 and the real estate commission took $5,250 of it. Can we deduct that charge?

No, but the commission does reduce the amount realized on the sale and therefore cuts the profit by $5,250.

After several years in Washington, D.C., we moved to Indianapolis. We discovered that we'd have to buy a mansion here in order to reinvest the $138,000 we received for our modest three-bedroom home on Capitol Hill. The house we bought cost $96,000, leaving us with $42,000 we didn't reinvest. Here's our question: The house has a garage we're considering converting into a guesthouse. If we spend $20,000 remodeling it, can we count that as part of our investment for purposes of figuring how much of the gain from the old house we can postpone paying taxes on?

Yes, as long as you complete the work within 18 months of the time you sold the Washington home. The purchase price of a replacement residence includes costs for reconstruction, extensive rebuilding, capital improvements and additions to the new house.

I sold my house for a $22,000 gain and moved to Denver, where I'm living in an apartment. I don't intend to buy another house for a while, so I guess I'll have to pay taxes on the profit this year. Any way to trim what looks like a whopping tax bill?

You might try income averaging. If you qualify, part of this year's bulge in income would be treated as though you earned it in equal chunks over a five-year period. Spreading it out this way could substantially reduce your tax bill. A key test for determining whether you can use income averaging is to compare this year's taxable income with your income during the four previous years. Generally, to qualify, this year's income must be over $3,000 more than 30% of that four-year total.

We sold our home last month and aren't sure whether we're going to buy another one. If we do, we want to defer paying taxes on the gain from the old house. But how do we handle the sale on this year's tax return?

Simply attach a statement (or Form 2119, "Sale or Exchange of Personal Residence") to your tax return, notifying the IRS of the amount of profit and stating that you have not yet purchased a replacement residence. You also have to file Schedule D (for reporting capital gains), but don't report or pay tax on any part of the gain at this time.

If you buy a new home within the replacement period and it costs enough that you can roll over the entire profit from the old house, notify the IRS in writing of the dates of purchase and occupancy of the new home and its cost. If you don't buy another home within the specified period or if the one you buy costs less than the adjusted sales price of the old one, you'll have to file an amended return for the year of the sale and report the gain on Schedule D. The IRS will charge you interest on your late taxes, but there will be no penalty.

We sold our house and deferred the tax on our profit by reinvesting all of it in a new home. Even though there's no tax payable, do we have to report the sale to the IRS?

Yes. You should attach a completed Form 2119 to your tax return. Or you may file a statement with your return showing the purchase price of the new home, the dates of purchase and occupancy, how you computed the gain on which tax is postponed and the basis of the new home.

HOME SWEET TAX SHELTER

When you turn 55, the tax law gives you a valuable birthday present: The chance to escape taxes on up to $125,000 of profit from the sale of your home. This break can be worth thousands of dollars, money to make your retirement years more financially secure. It also adds new flexibility to your retirement planning.

- To be eligible, you must be 55 or older when you sell your principal residence.
- The exclusion applies only to a principal residence that you have owned and lived in for at least three of the five years preceeding the sale.
- If you're married, only one spouse needs to meet the age, ownership and residency tests.
- You can take the exclusion only once in your lifetime. For purposes of this limitation married couples are treated as one; if one spouse used the exclusion before marriage, the other spouse forfeits his or her right to use it later on.
- The $125,000 limit is not cumulative. If you exclude $45,000 of the profit on the sale of one home, for example, the other $80,000 is forfeited. You can't carry an unused portion forward to be applied against the gain on the sale of another home.
- You can use the exclusion in conjunction with the part of the law that lets you defer taxes on profits that are reinvested in another home. If you realize a $150,000 gain, for example, the exclusion will let you escape the tax on the first $125,000 of profit. And you can postpone tax on the rest if you buy a new home that

costs at least $25,000—what you sold your house for minus that amount of excluded gain. The gain you roll over into the new home will not be taxed until you sell it and fail to replace it with a more costly house.

To illustrate the savings offered by the exclusion, consider the case of a married couple, ages 57 and 54, who've been living in their present home for 14 years. The kids are grown, and the couple have decided the house is too big and too expensive to maintain. They want to sell and rent a smaller house or an apartment. Still in their high-earning years, the couple's taxable income is $40,000.

They figure that if they sell their house and make a $100,000 profit, taxes will be $20,212. However, if they use their once-in-a-lifetime exclusion, the couple can sell the house and not have to pay taxes on any of the profit.

This new tax break confronts many taxpayers with questions about how to make the best use of it.

What if you meet the age and residency tests and want to sell your home but your profit is only $40,000?
Using any part of the exclusion uses it all up. If you don't intend to buy another house, you don't really lose anything. If you do plan to buy another, more expensive home, you should roll over your gain rather than exclude it. As the new house appreciates and your profit grows toward $125,000, so will the value of your exclusion.

But say you want to buy a less expensive home and therefore can't roll over all your profit. Should you use the exclusion now to shelter the $40,000 of gain, even though doing so means forfeiting the unused $85,000 worth? If you don't take the exclusion, you'll have to pay tax on the gain you don't roll over. On the other hand, using the exclusion now means any profit on your new home will be taxed when you sell it. Since you can't be certain what your tax bracket and the amount of taxable gain you'll realize will be at that time, it's difficult to compare the benefits of using the exclusion now with the advantages of saving it for later.

What if you put off taking the exclusion and defer the gain by buying a more expensive home but then decide to sell the new house and move into an apartment before you meet the residency test to qualify anew for the exclusion?

As long as the tax return for the year in which you sold the old home is open to amendment—which it is for at least three years after its due date—you can retroactively elect the exclusion. That would eliminate up to $125,000 in taxable profit on the first house. The cost basis of the second home, which had to be reduced when you deferred the gain, will be increased by the amount of the newly excluded gain.

What if you're 54 and want to sell your home and move into an apartment or small home?

You can still take advantage of the exclusion by renting out your house until you're 55. Make sure that ultimately when the house is sold, you still qualify for the exclusion by having lived in the house as your principal residence for three of the five years preceeding the sale. If you need the proceeds from the sale of your home to buy a retirement place, consider taking out a second mortgage against the equity in your house to make a down payment.

7

Condominiums and cooperatives

When you first start to look into it, buying a condominium or a cooperative apartment can seem a lot like taking a legal exam. It is a complicated process, and a miscalculation could have wrenching financial and emotional consequences. Since condos are far more common than co-ops, most of this chapter is devoted to them. But aside from differences in the legal forms of ownership, life in condos and co-ops is quite similar, and much of the advice given here can be applied to both.

What is a condominium? Though different from any other kind of real estate, a condo is not a special type of structure. It is a legal plan of ownership. Under such a plan, the owners of individual dwelling units in a housing development also own proportional interests in common facilities, such as grounds, hallways, elevators and recreation areas.

In a new condominium the common property is usually conveyed by the developer to an owners' association after a period of time or after a specified percentage of units have been sold. (This is stated in the documents and may also be in state statutes.) Thereafter the development is controlled and operated by directors of the group, often through a hired manager.

Garden apartments, high rises and connected town-houses are the most common types of condominiums. The genre also includes small buildings with two, three or four living units, and even detached houses, although these are rare.

What is a cooperative? In a cooperative, residents own shares in a corporation that owns the development; they do not hold titles to their individual units. Thus, cooperative ownership cannot normally be financed with a mortgage. Instead, you must take out a personal loan, usually at an interest rate higher than the going rate for mortgages. You pay back the loan and make separate monthly maintenance payments to the cooperative corporation, which pays for the mortgage on the building, the real estate taxes and general upkeep. As a partial owner of the corporation, you deduct on your tax return your proportional share of the mortgage interest (plus the interest on your own loan, of course) and your share of the corporation's taxes.

Advantages. The better condos and co-ops have amenities that few residents could afford as individuals— swimming pools, saunas, game rooms, squash courts, even golf courses. In most projects there is no lawn mowing or leaf raking to do.

Condos often cost less than detached houses in comparable locations. You can deduct mortgage interest and property taxes from taxable income, something renters cannot do. You have a say in how the project is run. The value of your unit may rise.

Disadvantages. Operating costs of condos and co-ops—which you help pay through your monthly assessment—can and often do exceed projections. Your neighbors could be noisy or otherwise objectionable. You'd probably have less space than in a conventionally owned, detached house. You couldn't enlarge your unit. You would be subject to strict rules adopted by the majority of owners. Certain activities and hobbies, such as gun collecting or amateur radio, may be banned or restricted. The same may be true of pets.

Abuses. Among the most prevalent abuses in condos are unfair leases on recreation facilities, poor construction, incomprehensible legal papers, misuse of purchasers' deposits and underestimation of maintenance costs (called low-balling). There have been instances in which monthly charges, set unrealistically low to promote sales, later doubled or tripled.

Leases on recreation facilities have provoked many complaints and many a lawsuit. In some projects the developer retains ownership of one or more of the amenities, such as the pool, leases them to the owners' association for up to 99 years, and can raise the monthly charges as he sees fit. Thousands of people have complained bitterly that they had no idea when they bought that the recreation facilities belonged to the developer and not to the condo owners.

Then there are "sweetheart contracts"—long-term agreements that obligate the owners' association to obtain management services or do other business with firms designated by the developer.

Before you shop. Generally, the best locations are residential areas where you see a good mixture of quality apartment buildings and homes in the middle-to upper-price range—and where property values are rising.

Convenience to stores, hospitals and parks is a big plus, of course.

Try to visualize the neighborhood in ten or twenty years. Could your view be obstructed by a future high rise? Could a factory or highway be built nearby?

Check the vacancy rate, too. The condo explosion in the mid-1970s resulted in vast overbuilding in some sections of the country, particularly resorts. More than 50,000 units stood empty on Florida's lower east coast. There and elsewhere builders resorted to distress sales and auctions, sometimes getting less than half of their original asking prices. The glut eventually disappeared but prospective buyers should carefully check the local supply-and-demand situation. In 1981 the Florida condo glut was showing small signs of a reappearance.

• *Buying into a new development.* It's obviously less risky to buy into an unfinished project when it is at a late stage of construction and organization. Never buy into an uncompleted project unless you are provided with site drawings, floor plans, maintenance-cost projections and other descriptive material. Model apartments are sometimes built larger than those to be sold. What's more, some developers have used scaled-down furniture to make rooms look larger. Pace them off yourself if you have doubts. Another thing to think about: Will you have any recourse if the project isn't finished when you're ready to move?

• *Buying into an older project.* This may be the safer route, since you can judge the construction, talk with residents, see how things are working out. What you won't get are the uncertain joys of pioneering that go with participating in a new development.

If your apartment goes condo. Thousands of people are

faced with this problem every year as more and more rental buildings convert to condominium ownership. Your choice is stark—you can buy or get out.

You could rent another place, but it might go condo, too. Besides, there's the cost and inconvenience of moving. Yet if you buy, you'll assume some risk, and your monthly costs could jump.

Those are the negatives. The brighter side is that here's your chance to stop collecting rent receipts and start building equity. If you like the place and the price is right, you may have a golden opportunity.

The rules for sizing up a converted rental unit for possible purchase are the same as for other kinds of condos. Learn all you can about the structure and equipment. Some states require owners to supply such information in writing. But if this is not done, you and the other prospective purchasers should get a statement of condition from an independent engineer or other expert. Warranties should be provided; be sure to ask whether you'll get them on common property as well as your own unit.

The owner may have renovated the building before putting it on the market, but the improvements may be purely cosmetic. Getting an appraisal of the entire development would be too costly for individuals, but if a lender has agreed to finance purchases of units, you may be able to obtain a copy of its appraisal.

Make a special effort to estimate the expenses you'd incur as an owner. They could be considerably higher than the rent you're paying. When the property is reclassified on the tax rolls as a condominium, real estate taxes could be raised sharply because of new assessments. Of course, this could be partly offset by the federal income tax deduction for mortgage interest and property taxes.

Naturally, you'll be asking your fellow tenants whether they plan to buy. If many of them say no, it could be a bad sign. Find out why.

If you don't want to buy *or* move check out your legal rights. The owner probably can't throw you out until your lease expires. In some areas condo conversions are permitted only if certain conditions are met. It may be necessary for a certain number of tenants to give their assent before a conversion can take place.

And find out whether the owner will continue to rent some unsold units. You may be able to stay put—at least for a while.

What to ask when you buy. Whether you're considering a new development, an existing one or a conversion, there are literally hundreds of facts you should have, so keep your list of questions ready. "Don't hesitate to ask anything—even questions that may seem silly to you," advises the Department of Housing and Urban Development. "It's better to feel silly now than sorry later." Some questions:

How good is the developer's reputation? Is there a cooling-off period during which you can cancel the purchase contract? Are the recreation facilities adequate for the number of residents? Could the development be enlarged? Would that put a strain on facilities? What provisions have been made for parking, storage, refuse disposal? Are the units equipped with individual heating and cooling controls? How are utility costs apportioned? Are equipment warranties provided?

How much would you pay in settlement costs? Could you rent your unit? Find out whether the place will be occupied mainly by unit owners or whether many occupants will be renters, tenants or people who have bought units as investments rather than as homes. Owner occupancy usually results in better control and management in the interests of the people who live there.

Ask an officer of the owners' association whether lawsuits are pending or planned against the developer. Was an engineer's report obtained when the association took possession of the project? Were defects found?

Visit the property several times and at different times of day. Is litter lying around? Do the residents seem congenial? Is the place well maintained? Are the facilities crowded?

The documents. Answers to many questions will be in the documents you should be given if you start getting serious about buying. These include:

• *Sales contract, or purchase agreement.* It's basically similar to other real estate contracts, but there are differences. In signing you may acknowledge receipt of the other documents. Check for conditions under which you could back out of the deal, such as your inability to get mortgage money. If the contract doesn't give you the right to withdraw within a specified period, don't sign until you have studied it and the other papers, with professional legal assistance. There should be assurances, if appropriate, that the project will be completed as promised, and you should have a right to make an inspection prior to settlement. It would definitely be advantageous to you to have your deposit placed in an escrow account, preferably one that pays interest. But not all states require escrow accounts.

• *An enabling declaration.* Also called the master deed, plan of condominium ownership, or declaration of conditions, covenants and restrictions, this is the most important instrument. When recorded, it legally establishes the project as a condominium. It also, among other things, authorizes residents to form an operating association and describes individual units and commonly owned areas.

• *Bylaws*. These spell out the association's authority and responsibilities, authorize the making of a budget and the collection of various charges, and prescribe parliamentary procedures. They may empower the association to hire professional managers or contain other special provisions. The bylaws may also set forth insurance requirements and authorize the imposition of liens against the property of owners who fail to pay monthly charges, although these provisions may sometimes be included in the condo's enabling declaration.

• *House rules*. They state what owners can and can't do. Any restrictions on pets, children, decorations, use of facilities and such will be found here. The rules may be incorporated in the bylaws or set apart in a separate document.

• *Other papers*. These could include a copy of the operating budget, a schedule of current and proposed assessments, a financial statement on the owners' association, any leases or contracts, a plat or drawing of the project and your unit, and an engineer's report if one was done. One of the financial documents should show how much money has been reserved for unforeseen or emergency outlays, an important consideration. A few states require developers to give each potential buyer a prospectus that details all the important facts about the offering. Read it carefully; information that may be buried in small print or obscured by legalese in the other papers may be readily understandable in the prospectus.

You and your lawyer should take the time to evaluate all of this material before deciding whether to buy, no matter how onerous a job it is. There would be a lot less grief if condominium buyers were more careful.

Not only are there charges and assessments, but you could also be tapped for a share of any future deficits incurred by the association. Without competent management, costs can skyrocket, outstripping the budget in a matter of months. Elevators, interior hallways and extensive grounds can be especially expensive to keep up.

Insurance. Condominiums built before 1974 may be inadequately covered. Insurance companies lacked experience with condos and hadn't yet developed special policies for them. Your own unit and its contents as well as the development itself should be insured. You should also be protected from claims arising from damage to others, as could occur if, for example, water from a leak in your kitchen seeped into the apartment below.

If you become a director of the association, you will need liability insurance in case negligence or damage suits are brought against the board.

Consumer protection. Some states, including New York, Virginia, Florida, Michigan and California, plus the District of Columbia, regulate condo sales as such, and broader consumer-protection measures in others may apply (antifraud statutes, for instance). Your state may not require the delivery of documents to prospective buyers before a contract is signed. Even so, you should insist on time to examine these papers. For information about condo regulation in your state, contact the attorney general's office, a real estate board or a consumer protection agency.

Those, then, are the major caveats. Don't let them get you down. Making a wise condo purchase may be less formidable than it sounds. The thing to do is to be careful, take your time and never, never act impulsively.

8

Mobile homes

For millions of people, a mobile home offers a chance to own low-cost housing in a chosen environment. For retired couples especially, it offers a way to settle in with others of similar age, financial condition, likes and dislikes.

But you must recognize that entering a mobile-home community usually means changing your life-style and consenting to have your activities controlled in certain ways by park management on the one hand and a group of your neighbors on the other.

Two kinds of parks. There are "open" and "closed" parks. In an open park a mobile-home owner rents a small piece of property and has his manufactured house installed at his own expense. A written lease may or may not be involved. There generally are rules and regulations, but they are not always presented to the tenant in writing. Usually, the mobile-home owner simply rents the space on a month-to-month basis. Though he may pick up and leave when he wishes, he and his home stay there at the pleasure of the landlord.

New parks and those still under development are often promoted on the basis of amenities—swimming pools, shuffleboard courts, recreation halls—that are not yet in existence. And the landlord may let the amenities wait while funds and space are devoted to developing more sites for homes. An entrance fee of several hundred dollars may be charged, but some states have made entrance fees illegal.

In the closed park, on the other hand, the park management is also a mobile-home dealer, and you can get into the park only by buying a home from park management.

This arrangement is not necessarily sinister. It is one way a conscientious management can enforce strict standards for the homes that go into its park. You may be told that for the lot you have chosen to rent or lease you can choose from a fairly large listing of models, perhaps produced by a number of different manufacturers. You will be shown complete catalog and price information, and in some parks the management will encourage you to go to the factory to "custom design" your own home.

Prominent among the closed parks are those designed specifically for retirement living. Thousands, good and not so good, are scattered around the country, but they're concentrated in Florida, California, Texas and Arizona.

Who owns the land? There is a small but growing number of communities where mobile-home owners can buy rather than rent their own sites. In some places you can buy into "parkaminiums" that are, for all practical purposes, condos. However, in most areas the mobile-home owner-tenant lives in a peculiar state of vulnerability: He is the owner of a valuable piece of personal property located on the land of another person.

In a dispute with the landowner he may have no recourse but to sell his home or have it moved at great expense, assuming he can find a place to move it to. It costs quite a bit to move the typical 70-foot singlewide, even a short distance. Including necessary disassembly and reassembly, it can cost thousands to move a luxury doublewide less than 50 miles. Because of the expense and the damage that can result from vibration and road shock, such a doublewide is rarely moved. Generally it is sold, possibly at a loss, and the former owner buys another elsewhere.

Finding a good site. There are seven important steps for making an intelligent start on mobile home life.

1. Decide first on the geographic location of your new home; then select a community that best represents the life-style you seek. Stay a few days as a guest if the management can accommodate you. This will give you an opportunity to sample mobile-home living as it really is. Check on the security system, fire protection, trash collection, availability of emergency and routine medical care, access to nearby shopping centers, and religious and recreational facilities. Then visit other parks and compare.
2. Study the paperwork involved—the lease, the rules and regulations, and any other pertinent documents.
3. Never sign anything before checking it with an attorney.
4. Nose around the place. A good park should be full of tenants who are proud of the selection they have made.
5. Remember that the complexion of the park could change. Its very nature could be suddenly transformed by a new management or ownership.

As a tenant you have only certain legal protections against change. You must know what protections the local ordinances and state laws provide in order to make a happy and financially safe decision.

6. Unless you're buying a home already on a site, you should select an actual lot in a particular park before you buy your mobile home. Each must be suited to the other. A good management will work carefully with you on this to provide a combination that will be satisfactory for the foreseeable future.

7. Remember that a mobile home is *not* mobile. Once they are set in place, only about 2% are ever moved again.

FINANCING THE PURCHASE

Most mobiles are financed like motor vehicles—with chattel (personal property) loans. Interest rates are higher and payoff periods shorter, as a rule, than for mortgages on site-built houses. Down payment requirements are sometimes proportionally larger.

Mobil-home dealers, like car dealers, often will arrange financing. They sell insurance, too, giving buyers the convenience of a "simple one-step, one-payment transaction," to quote one industry source. But, as in car buying, you may pay a premium for the dealer's package, so check your other options. You may be able to get a government-backed loan, a credit union loan, even a conventional real estate mortgage loan. There is a trend, in fact, toward purchasing mobile homes with mortgage-type loans.

When you find a unit you like and know how much you want to borrow, ask as many lenders as possible about rates and terms. A few phone calls just might save you a lot of dollars.

Mobile home loans are subject to the federal truth-in-lending law, which means you must be informed in writing of the finance cost expressed as an annual percentage rate (APR). If somebody quotes you an unusually low figure, it's probably an "add-on" or "discount" rate, neither of which reflects the true cost. Always insist on being told the APR, as the law requires, and make sure that it is the figure in the contract.

When shopping for mortgage-type financing for a mobile home, check with all possible sources.

HUD and FHA loans. The Department of Housing and Urban Development's Federal Housing Administration insures loans made by approved lenders to purchasers who are able to make a small down payment. The unit must be used as your principal residence, and you must have an acceptable site for it, either owned or rented. The unit must be at least 40 feet long and meet HUD Minimum Property Standards. FHA can insure loans for up to 20 years on single units, 30 years on double or multisection homes. Applications can be obtained from participating banks and other lenders.

VA loans. For eligible veterans the Veterans Administration will guarantee up to 50% of a loan or $20,000, whichever is smaller. The loan can run 15 years on a singlewide unit, 20 years on a doublewide, and can be obtained for just the mobile home itself if you already own the property, or for the home in combination with a piece of property.

Other sources. The Farmers Home Administration has authority to include mobile homes in rural areas in its mortgage insurance and guaranty programs, but has yet to do so.

Many conventional real estate lenders such as savings and loan associations will finance mobile homes with mortgages, and their number is increasing.

PART THREE

PROTECTION AGAINST CATASTROPHE

9

Sorting out your insurance coverage

You buy insurance, regardless of type, for one of two reasons. It's either to protect you and your family from the consequences of a financial loss—affecting your health, your car, your home, your belongings or your life—or to make good on your obligations to others who might suffer injury or loss traceable to your person or property.

What you get for your money is a promise to pay if the event you hope never occurs, does occur. If the dreaded event never comes to pass, about the only tangible thing you have to show for your money is the policy document.

The policy is probably pockmarked with legalese. Sentences and paragraphs may be studded with terms like "incontestability period" and "nonforfeiture values." The reason for such prose is that the policy is a legal contract. Court interpretations over the years have attached specific meanings to certain terms and, taken together, those terms spell out your rights and obligations as well as those of the insurance company. Unless your policy expressly calls for the payment of a certain benefit upon the occurence of a given event, you won't be paid, no matter what a salesman or other representative may have told you. If the fine print takes away what the big print seems to bestow, that's your tough luck.

It is for this reason that, difficult and time-consuming though it may be, you should do to your policies what most insurance buyers fail to do: Read them. Read each and every one from front to back with a dictionary at your elbow and perhaps the phone numbers of your agents near at hand. In recent years some insurance companies have undertaken laudable campaigns to make their policies more understandable. But mostly you're on your own. Here's a rundown on how typical policies are organized and the kinds of insurance coverage available.

LIFE INSURANCE

Whether it's a form of whole life (meaning you're covered by a death benefit as long as you continue paying premiums, which generate a cash value that can be borrowed on); some kind of term coverage (temporary protection to a certain age or for a span of years, generally with no cash buildup); or an endowment (a plan that pays the face amount to you, if you live to a stated age or for a given time period, or to your survivor if you don't), a life insurance policy can be broken down into three parts.

The summary. This gives the essential details of the two-way deal between you and the company. For your part, you agree to pay, on a regular basis, a stipulated premium based primarily on your age. If the policy was issued on a participating basis, you'll receive dividends at regular intervals; if not, you won't. In return for your premiums the company promises to pay the face amount, less any unpaid loans and interest, to someone you have named, provided the policy is in force at your death. This section also commonly describes two additional benefits you may or may not have elected— waiver of premium (the company itself pays the premiums if you become totally disabled) and an accidental death rider (the benefit usually doubles if you die as the result of an accident).

The details. Here you'll learn about such things as the due date (when premiums are to be paid); the grace period (how long you have, usually a month, to pay the premiums without penalty); lapses (how soon the policy expires if you don't pay); reinstatements (how you can put the policy back in effect); nonforfeiture and surrender values (the money you have coming under a cash value policy, if you give up or lapse the protection); extended term and reduced paid-up options (ways you can use the cash values to provide continuing coverage without further payments); and settlement options (how you or the beneficiary can choose to have the proceeds paid).

The application. This section reflects what you told the company about yourself when you applied for coverage—age, occupation, health, other life insurance you carry and whether the activities you engage in could be considered dangerous—and how you wish to exercise the rights you have under the policy. For example, if you haven't assigned ownership to someone else, you can change the beneficiary arrangements, and you can determine how the dividends and cash values are to be used. Dividends can be taken in cash, used to reduce your premiums, left with the company at interest or used to buy more coverage; cash values can be earmarked to reimburse the company for any premiums you fail to pay.

If you are insured by a solid company and pay your premiums on time, there isn't much that can go wrong with a life insurance policy. Note, though, that if your age is misstated on the application, the company may pay whatever death benefit would have been called for by the correct age. While the suicide clause is in effect, usually during the first two years, the beneficiaries of those who take their own lives are entitled only to a return of premiums.

HEALTH INSURANCE

Because they are written in many dissimilar forms, health insurance policies can't be readily categorized. The major types are *hospital / medical / surgical* coverage (the basic protection that pays, up to specified limits, for room and board in a hospital, and the services of physicians and surgeons while you are a patient there); *major medical* (backup coverage that provides substantial reimbursement for the costs of a lengthy illness, often up to catastrophic amounts); *catastrophic medical* (protection that picks up where other coverages stop for serious illnesses involving long confinements); and *disability income protection* (policies that pay a percentage of your regular income when you are unable to work because of illness or injury).

Some policies contain far more liberal language than others, and that fact can determine whether your particular problem is covered or not. Here are a couple of examples of the difference a few words can make, cited by Herbert S. Denenberg when he was insurance commissioner of Pennsylvania.

• If, in defining which sicknesses are covered, a policy

says this means "sickness or disease which is first *manifested* after the effective date of this policy," you must have had symptoms or known you were ill when the policy took effect for the coverage to be denied. By contrast, if it is defined as "sickness or disease *contracted* and commencing after the policy has been in force not less than 30 days," it is necessary only that you had the disease when the policy took effect— whether you knew it or not—for your claim to be disqualified.

If injury is defined as "bodily injury sustained *directly and independently of all other causes*" rather than "accidental bodily injury sustained while this policy is in force," it increases the chances that the company will be able to deny the claim on the grounds that the injury was related in some way to other causes, such as medical condition.

AUTO AND HOME INSURANCE

Most automobile and homeowners policies are set up along similar lines.

Declarations. This section gives the personal information you supplied to the agent, such as your name and address, as well as a description of the coverage you have purchased. It spells out how long the policy is to run, the premiums and the deductible amount that applies. (The deductible is the sum you have to pay before the insurance cuts in.) The location of your dwelling or a description of the vehicle being protected is included in this section, along with a rundown on the kinds of coverage you have chosen: benefits to replace the house, other structures and personal property following a loss, money to help tide you over in temporary quarters, personal liability coverage and medical payments coverage for others under homeowners plans; liability, medical expense, uninsured motorist, collision, comprehensive, rental expense, total disability and accidental death indemnity insurance under auto policies. The dollar limits for each kind of coverage are also specified.

In your auto insurance policy, be careful to differentiate between *single* and *split* limits. Under single limits, the policy pays up to a total amount for all claims resulting from a single accident. Split coverage provides separate limits per accident for injuries to each individual, a total amount for bodily injuries and yet another sum for property damage.

Insuring agreement. To be covered, the event involving loss usually must be listed in this section, which is the company's promise to pay. This promise, however, is very broad, and payments for some mentioned occurences may be limited by the language in other parts of the policy.

Exclusions. Some risks—such as damages or injuries a policyholder inflicts intentionally—are not covered at all, and they are listed in this section. Other risks are only partially excluded, giving you the right to limited coverage under certain circumstances. In still other cases, a particular risk is considered to be so out of the ordinary that it is thought best to have it covered by a special endorsement rather than have all policyholders pay for it under a standard contract. One exclusion under auto policies prohibits coverage of a car while it is hired or used to carry people for a fee (shared-expense car pools don't come under this ban).

Conditions. This section clarifies the rights and obligations of both the policyholder and the company.

Some of the provisions tell what you must do following a loss in order to get paid. For example, if you're involved in a hit-and-run accident, you may have to report it to the police or the motor vehicle department within 24 hours and file a statement made under oath with the company within 30 days. If you fail to notify your agent within 30 days after trading in your car for another one, the new car may not be covered.

Endorsements. These attachments are used to tailor the broad policy format to individual needs, perhaps by adding boat trailer and boat coverage to auto insurance or extensive protection for jewelry and furs under a homeowners plan. However, the policy and its endorsements are considered as a unit, the latter having as much heft as the former. Make sure that the endorsements don't unduly limit or reduce the coverage spelled out in general terms elsewhere.

With that quick tour of insurance policies under your belt, you're ready to concentrate on getting the most coverage for the least money. The next four chapters are designed to help you with that task.

10

Insurance on your life

There is one sure test of whether you need life insurance: If your death would cause economic hardship for your spouse, children, parents or someone else you want to protect, then insurance is a sensible way to fulfill your obligations. But even in those cases, you should take the degree of need into account. Consider three different situations:

• *Little or no need.* You're a student, 22, unmarried, with parents who are financing your education. Viewed from a strictly economic standpoint, your death would create no problems. An enterprising insurance agent might nevertheless remind you that your parents would have to pay funeral and other final costs. They would not have to pay your school expenses, though, so that's not a convincing reason for buying the insurance.

The agent's strongest argument may be that you should buy a policy now while you're young and rates are low. It's true that younger people pay lower rates. But the agent's figures may not take into account the amount of interest you could earn by saving your money instead of spending for insurance premiums. Moreover, those low rates simply reflect the fact that you're less likely to die in your younger years, and thus less likely to collect on the policy.

• *Moderate need*. Consider a husband and wife with no children and each earning $19,000 a year. The death of either spouse would not be financially catastrophic; each could presumably survive on $19,000. Still, there might be a strain. Perhaps they own a home that can't be maintained on a single income, or have big debts. Also, there would be funeral costs. It could be argued that this couple needs insurance, but a modest amount would probably suffice.

• *Great need*. A husband and a nonworking wife have two young children. This is the stereotypical insurance situation. There are three people dependent on the husband for their total support, so insurance is vital. And if the wife should die, the husband would have to pay for daycare for the children—a very expensive proposition that argues for insurance on her life, as well.

HOW MUCH DO YOU NEED?

Recognizing that you need insurance is one thing. Figuring our *how much* you need is another. Many people just pluck some figure out of the air that seems reasonable and let it go at that. But you really should take an approach to the problem that is at least slightly more scientific.

Without getting too technical, you can arrive at a reasonable estimate of your life insurance needs like this:

Estimate the income your dependents would need to maintain their standard of living if you were to die tomorrow. Then subtract from that figure the income they could expect to receive in social security survivor's benefits (to find out how to calculate that, call the Social Security office listed in your local telephone book), salaries they now earn or could earn, investments and other sources. The difference is the amount your life insurance must provide.

Clearly, you have to make a number of assumptions in doing this, and they are complex assumptions that scare most people away from the task. For instance: What rate of inflation should you use when projecting that needed income into the future? Will the family live on the earnings generated by the proceeds of the policy and leave the principal alone, or should they expect to gradually use up the capital as well? What rate of interest can you safely assume the money will be able to earn? Will your spouse take a job, if he or she doesn't have one now? Will that require a period of training? How much can he or she realistically be expected to earn?

You can see what makes this task so difficult. Insurance companies will be happy to perform the calculations for you; most have developed computerized programs for the purpose. These can be helpful, but they amount essentially to broad, educated guesses, particularly in these days when costs are changing so quickly.

In practice you will have to pick some total insurance figure that seems a reasonable compromise between what you'd like to have and what you can afford, using the companies' estimates for reference. The key point to remember is that what you buy today will be worth less and less in purchasing power as the years go by.

TWO KINDS OF POLICIES

Insurance company actuaries and marketing executives are forever dreaming up ostensibly new policies that differ in some way from those offered by competitors. Actually, they merely play with variations of two types of life insurance—term insurance and cash value insurance (also called "permanent" or "whole life" insurance).

Term Insurance. This is the simplest kind. You insure your life for a fixed period—one year, five years or more—and pay an annual premium graded according to your age at purchase. If the policy is renewable, as most are, you can continue the insurance for another period, paying the higher premium for your age. The older you get, the more it costs.

Many companies won't sell term policies that run past a certain age, say 65. But a growing number now issue policies that go beyond such limits.

Term policies have no savings features, so for any given purchase age the term premium is usually the lowest rate available.

Term insurance comes in several varieties.

• *Level term.* The face amount remains fixed for the life of the contract.

• *Declining, decreasing, or reducing term.* The face amount periodically drops according to a fixed schedule over ten, fifteen, twenty or more years. Mortgage insurance policies, which pay the loan balance when the homeowner dies, represent a common form of decreasing term.

• *Term riders.* These policies are sold as supplements to cash value policies.

• *Convertible term*. The policy can be converted (for a higher premium) into a cash value policy without your having to meet medical standards. Most companies offer policies that are both convertible and renewable up to specified ages or for fixed periods.

Cash value insurance. In its basic whole life form, the cash value policy works this way: You pay a fixed premium, based on your age at purchase, for as long as the policy remains in force. The premium exceeds the company's cost of insuring your life during the early years. The surplus and interest it earns go into a reserve. After one or two years your reserve begins to create a cash value that you can draw on. The total cash value builds up slowly because the company uses part of the fund to pay the agent's commission and administrative costs.

You may borrow against the cash value (usually at 6% or 8% interest) while the policy stays in force, or take out the money if you surrender the policy. When you die, the company pays your beneficiary the policy's face amount (less any policy loan balance), *not* the face amount plus cash value.

Insurance companies offer cash value policies in a bewildering variety of forms, ranging from the standard whole life policy to specially designed contracts in which the premiums or face amounts change according to a set schedule.

WHICH KIND SHOULD YOU BUY?

When you purchase life insurance from an agent, the odds are he will steer you to a permanent policy. Rarely is term suggested as a first choice, although virtually all insurers sell both term and permanent policies. (One reason may be higher commissions paid to agents for sales of cash value policies.) Term may be shrugged off as temporary insurance, good for filling the gap until you can afford to buy a permanent policy or for supplementing a permanent policy.

Despite insurance company concentration on permanent policies, public demand has been tilting toward term for some years. Insurers have long sold term in various combinations with permanent policies. "Family income" plans, for example, combine a whole life policy with a decreasing term policy in such a way as to provide beneficiaries with a fixed income for a certain period. Such package plans have been losing favor, but sales of separate term policies have more than made up the difference.

Many insurance experts and company executives believe that continued inflation is certain to accelerate the term trend. As prices and incomes rise, you need more and more insurance to provide beneficiaries with the same amount of purchasing power. Whatever the relative costs of the two types of insurance over the long run, many people can't obtain enough insurance these days unless they start with term. Inflation also undermines fixed savings programs, such as the permanent policy's cash value accumulation.

If you're stretching to buy enough insurance, term should be your first choice. The primary purpose of life insurance is to provide dependents with income they would lose by your death. *Term gives you the most protection for your money.*

Term premiums can be extremely high in your later years, but the need for insurance late in life is sometimes exaggerated. At 70, for instance, it's likely that the only person depending on you will be your spouse. He or she will share in your pension, social security and other sources of income, so you should be able to reduce or drop your insurance then. In any case you can leave your options open by starting with a term policy that is convertible as well as renewable.

If you want a guaranteed right to continue the face amount until death (or for at least as long as you are able to pay premiums) and an assured level premium, you will probably feel safer with a permanent policy.

You can always compromise by buying both term and permanent, either separately or through a package plan, such as the family income policy mentioned earlier. Another way to add term to your permanent insurance is to purchase one-year term additions with your policy dividends. Many companies allow you to buy an amount equal to the current year's cash value. Some let you buy as much as the dividend will cover.

FINDING THE
LOWEST-PRICED POLICIES

The most obvious way to compare costs of various life insurance policies is to compare the premiums charged by different companies for the same coverage. Unfortunately, it's not that simple. Dividends, cash values, interest you could have earned elsewhere and the number of years a policy is kept in force also play an important role in determining the actual cost.

Insurance industry analysts have managed to incorporate all these considerations into a formula that yields something called the "interest adjusted surrender cost" of policies kept for various lengths of time. Insurance companies can, and in many states are required to, provide prospective buyers with these figures. When you have them, you have a means for comparing the true costs of different policies within the same company and among different companies.

Interest-adjusted costs vary according to the type of policy and your age at purchase. Also, the formula assumes that the policy will be surrendered for its cash value, if any, after a certain number of years, and the result varies with the period selected.

Ask the agent right from the start for the 10- and 20-year-interest-adjusted surrender costs per $1,000 of face amount for the specific policy he is recommending. Ask him also for comparable data for the same kinds of policies issued by two other companies. Insurers are under no obligation to furnish information on competitors' policies, but the agent should be able to obtain approximate figures for some companies from manuals widely used in the insurance business. If the agent won't or can't help, call other companies yourself.

Knowing the comparative interest-adjusted costs of a couple of policies will show you immediately which one is cheaper. But you'd have no way of knowing how they compared to policy costs in the industry as a whole. A survey of a large group of insurance companies conducted by the Wisconsin Insurance Department a couple of years ago can help you there. The tables on page 161 how the median interest-adjusted cost per $1,000 of coverage for a $50,000 policy in several different forms. The top table shows the cost for participating ("par") and nonparticipating ("nonpar") whole life policies issued to a male 25, 35, 45 or 55 years old and kept in force for 10 years or 20 years and then surrendered for its cash value. The bottom table shows the same figures for five-year renewable term policies kept the same lengths of time. If the interest-adjusted cost figures you get for policies you're considering are somewhere around these numbers, you're probably getting a reasonably fair deal. Lower figures, of course, would be better. And note that the figures are for policies covering men. Policies issued to cover women the same age should cost less, because women live longer, on the average, than men.

MAKING SURE WHO WILL COLLECT

Most people don't run into beneficiary difficulties with their life insurance, perhaps because their lives generally follow the anticipated course. A husband designates his wife as beneficiary; he dies; she receives the money as he intended. However, you can't be sure that even well-conceived beneficiary arrangements won't

$50,000 whole life policy for a male

		COST PER $1,000	
issue age	surrendered after	par policy	nonpar policy
25	10 yrs.	$ 4.47	$ 4.63
	20 yrs.	3.18	4.24
35	10 yrs.	6.03	6.28
	20 yrs.	5.11	6.71
45	10 yrs.	10.18	10.84
	20 yrs.	9.76	12.40
55	10 yrs.	18.97	20.82
	20 yrs.	19.76	24.48

$50,000 5-year renewable term policy, male

		COST PER $1,000	
issue age	surrendered after	par policy	nonpar policy
25	10 yrs.	$ 3.11	$ 3.33
	20 yrs.	3.47	3.76
35	10 yrs.	4.30	4.56
	20 yrs.	5.93	6.32
45	10 yrs.	8.86	9.19
	20 yrs.	13.39	13.65
55	10 yrs.	20.80	21.07
	20 yrs.	25.19	25.24

be upset by later events. To avoid problems, take stock of these essential points.

Naming beneficiaries. A policy owner can name anyone he chooses as beneficiary—relative, friend, business associate, charity. You can also change beneficiaries unless you have previously named someone as the irrevocable beneficiary. In that case, you must obtain the beneficiary's permission. Irrevocable designations develop most often from divorce and separation settlements.

Customarily, beneficiaries can be changed merely by filling in a company form and sending it to the company. Some older policies require that the change be made on the policy itself.

If you die without having recorded a living beneficiary with the company, the proceeds will be paid into your estate or sometimes to surviving children, depending on the terms of the policy.

Setting an order or precedence. The normal procedure is to name a primary beneficiary and a secondary or contingent beneficiary in case the primary should die before you do. You can select a third beneficiary to receive the money in case both the primary and secondary beneficiaries don't survive you.

If you name two or more beneficiaries in the same rank, the funds will be divided equally unless you provide otherwise. Two primary beneficiaries for example, will each receive 50%.

Leaving it to your spouse. To avoid confusion, a wife or husband should be identified by his or her given name. Mrs. John Nelson, for example, should be described as Mrs. Jane Nelson or Jane Nelson, wife of the insured. For further specification, her premarital surname could be added—for example, Mrs. Jane Smith

Nelson. If a woman has kept her premarital surname, the policy should use it, of course.

Leaving it to the kids. "My children" or "children of the insured" or some similar collective designation usually suffices because it usually covers all present and future children, including adopted children. However, a broad description might have to be modified to cope with a specific situation, such as stepchildren.

Per capita, per stirpes. These Latin terms refer to two significantly different ways of distributing insurance proceeds, as well as other estate payments.

Under a per capita plan, all beneficiaries share equally. A per stirpes arrangement distributes according to family lines. Assume a mother names her two sons as the beneficiaries of $120,000 in insurance. If both survive her, each will receive 50% (unless she specifies otherwise).

However, the mother wants to be sure that if either son dies before she does, shares will be distributed to his children. Suppose that son B dies, leaving three children. Then the mother dies. If she stipulated that the proceeds were to be allocated to her issue per capita, the figures on the left show how much each would receive. A per stirpes arrangement would produce quite a different result, as shown by the figures on the right. The example assumes that son A has no children at the time of his mother's death.

PER CAPITA		PER STIRPES	
son A	$30,000	*son A*	$60,000
grandchild 1	$30,000	grandchild 1	$20,000
grandchild 2	$30,000	grandchild 2	$20,000
grandchild 3	$30,000	grandchild 3	$20,000

Payments to minors. When you name a child as beneficiary, legal problems may arise if the proceeds of your insurance have to be paid while he is still a minor. To protect itself against future claims, the insurance company will want a valid receipt for payments, and a minor may not be considered legally qualified for that purpose. State laws vary considerably, but in some cases the court may decide to appoint a guardian to receive and take care of the funds.

To avoid those difficulties, you can appoint a trustee to accept the insurance money and administer it for the child's benefit while he is a minor. The trustee could be directed in the trust agreement to pay the child any funds remaining at the time he reaches his majority. You can also appoint a successor trustee to take over if the first becomes unable to serve.

The tax angles. A beneficiary receiving the death proceeds of a life insurance policy is given four substantial tax breaks:

- No income tax generally has to be paid on the money.
- The funds don't have to go through the time-consuming and possibly expensive probate procedures required for assets transferred by a will.
- A surviving spouse is permitted to exclude from taxable income some of the interest earned on the proceeds. (See the discussion of installments on page 166.)
- The state may exempt part or all of the money from death taxes.

Life insurance proceeds may not be completely tax-free because the money is included in the estate of the insured when estate taxes are figured. But life insurance may be taken out of an estate. One way is to assign to the beneficiary all "incidents of ownership," including the right to surrender the policy for its cash value or to change the beneficiary. Another method is to transfer ownership of the policy to an irrevocable living trust (a trust set up while you are living and whose terms normally can't be changed).

By taking either of these steps, you in effect make a gift of the insurance to someone else (the beneficiary or the trust) and may have to pay a gift tax (see chapter 25).

If you think you need estate tax planning, don't try doing it on your own with ready-made forms. Consult an experienced attorney.

If you both die. Somewhere in the beneficiary forms you should find mention of "common disaster," a situation in which both the husband and wife die in the same accident or later from the effects of the accident.

Common disasters sometimes create tax and legal difficulties when one spouse survives the other briefly. This is something to think about when you are deciding about a settlement option. An option providing for the insurance company to keep the policy proceeds and pay them to the primary beneficiary—the wife, for example—as she wants them, with any funds not drawn out by her going directly to her husband's contingent beneficiaries upon her death, would be one way to meet the problem of a common disaster. Ask the agent for a detailed explanation of the plans suggested by his company.

HOW SHOULD THE PROCEEDS BE PAID?

Life insurance proceeds are usually paid out in a lump sum. But insurance companies also offer several alternative arrangements known as settlement options. As a policy owner, you can select one of those plans for your beneficiary. If you make no choice, the beneficiary can elect one within a certain period after your death. These are the options commonly available:

• *Interest only*. The funds are left on deposit with the insurance company, which guarantees a minimum rate of interest but normally pays more. Interest is paid to the beneficiary, who can be given the right to withdraw principal as desired.

• *Installments for a fixed period*. The funds are distributed in periodic installments over a selected period. Interest is paid as above.

• *Installments in fixed amounts*. The proceeds are paid out in equal amounts for as long as the money lasts. Again, the company usually adds extra interest to its guaranteed rate.

• *Life income*. The beneficiary is guaranteed a lifetime income based on his age and on the amount of the proceeds. The company may allow the beneficiary to use the proceeds to buy one of its regular annuities at a discount.

In the case of installment and life income arrangements, a surviving spouse is entitled to exclude from income taxes up to $1,000 of interest a year received from the company as part of the installment payments. Interest earned when the proceeds are simply kept on deposit with the company is taxable, just as it would be if the money were put in a savings account.

Installment and annuity plans may be useful in providing for a beneficiary who doesn't have the experience to manage a large sum. But it may not be wise to choose a settlement option for your beneficiary in all cases. A beneficiary often needs cash immediately for burial and other expenses. Furthermore, the beneficiary can probably invest the money safely at a better rate than the insurance company offers.

SHOULD YOU INSURE YOUR KIDS?

Just about anyone with any knowledge of life insurance will advise you that insuring your children is not a very good idea. Whatever money you have available for premiums should be spent on insurance for breadwinners, those whose death would reduce the family income. Until they are adequately insured, why should you buy policies for the kids?

Year in and year out, though, parents insure their children for billions of dollars, often in mistaken solicitude for the child's welfare.

Insurance on juveniles is one of those gray areas where what is generally true may not apply to your specific situation. To be sure you are not overlooking one possible way of helping your child, consider the pros and cons and the kinds of insurance available. The arguments for insuring kids go like this:

"It costs relatively little to insure a child, so you would not really be burdening your budget."

Counter argument: One reason you pay less for children, of course, is that the chance of death in the near future is low. In the case of a whole life policy, insurance companies have a longer time to accumulate the reserve fund needed to cover the heavier mortality costs of the later years.

Of course, you need not spend much to insure a child. You could settle for a small amount of protection and buy a term policy. The starting premiums for term are much lower than those for cash value policies.

"By buying a policy for a child at an early age, you lock in the low premium rate, thereby making it easier for him to carry the policy later. Moreover, you might pay less in premiums over a long period."

Counter argument: Consider the last column in this cost tabulation for a hypothetical $10,000 nonparticipating policy, the type that does not return part of your premiums as dividends:

age at purchase	annual premium	premium payments through 65
16	$102.20	$5,110
20	115.40	5,308
24	130.90	5,498

The premium payments through age 65 *appear* to indicate that you get several years of insurance coverage for nothing because the 16-year old wouldn't pay as much as the 24-year old. To see the gap in that reasoning, let's add another column showing the amount you would accumulate by 65 if you merely deposited the annual premiums in a 5¼% savings account instead of giving them to the insurance company:

age at purchase	equivalent savings through 65 at 5¼% interest
16	$24,413
20	22,036
24	19,884

In effect, the extra interest you could earn on the early-age premium payments would go to the insurance company. It stands to reason that the company must charge something for insuring your child's life for those years.

"The policy's cash value will provide your child with a nest egg for education expenses or other purposes."

Counter argument: Cash values could add to your financial resources, but insurance is usually a poor way to save. Cash can be drawn out of the policy's cash value fund in only two ways: You can get the entire cash value by surrendering the policy, thereby terminating coverage the child might need later. Or you can borrow against the cash value and keep the policy in force. However, any unpaid loan balance will be deducted from the face amount if the youngster dies. To keep the face amount up, the loan will eventually have to be repaid, just like any other loan.

Still another drawback of saving through life insurance is this: You should be able to beat the interest paid by the companies on cash values by investing on your own.

"Later in life your child might take a job or suffer a health impairment that would make him ineligible for insurance or for insurance at regular rates. You can guard against that danger by insuring him now."

Counter argument: Relatively few people are turned down by insurance companies or charged a high-risk premium. The last survey conducted by the American Council on Life Insurance, a public relations organization for insurance companies, showed that 91% of the people who apply are accepted at regular rates and 6% at extra-risk rates. Only 3% are rejected by the companies for various reasons.

Those figures cover applicants of all ages, including the older years when people are more likely to have health problems. Your child will probably be buying insurance in his late twenties or early thirties. The odds strongly favor his being able to get all the protection he wants at standard premiums.

"A child's policy will help defray burial expenses if he dies prematurely."

Counter argument: The overriding problem in a serious illness is not the burial but the potentially catastrophic cost of medical treatment. The money spent on a life insurance policy might better be used to beef up medical coverage.

Conclusion: The decision to insure a child must overcome several impressive objections before it becomes justifiable. But in considering ways to help your children, you don't want to limit yourself to cold economic calculations. What seems unwarranted on a cost basis might make sense when viewed as a gift.

That doesn't mean you must accept all the claims made for juvenile insurance or buy any kind of policy. If you want to build up an education fund, you'd still be wiser to save on your own.

On the other hand, as child-insurance proponents maintain, you can accomplish some important long-term objectives by insuring your child early in life.

- You can start off his or her adult career with a low, out-of-pocket expense for life protection that he is bound to need. The lifetime premium cost may be more, but that extra cost represents your present to your child.
- You can protect him against the risk, however small, of not being able to buy insurance at standard rates.
- By carefully selecting the kind of insurance you buy, you can give him a base on which to build his own insurance program later. With inflation constantly

eroding the value of each dollar of insurance bought now, he will need a good start.

MAIL-ORDER INSURANCE

Mail-order sellers of life insurance say their marketing techniques can produce cost savings not obtainable when policies are marketed through individual agents. But how the insurance is sold influences the policy terms and premiums, and the techniques differ significantly.

Some mail policies are sold to professional, fraternal and trade associations, and corporate-sponsored groups, such as the depositors in a savings and loan. Associations may use sales commissions from their insurance programs to raise funds instead of passing those savings on to members through lower premiums. A sizable number of all plans are set up and administered by insurance brokerage firms that specialize in mail-order sales of life, health and other types of insurance.

If you buy directly from the insurance company, you get an individual policy, just as you would if you bought one from an agent. If the insurance comes through an association or sponsored group, you are covered only through the seller's master contract with the insurer or the broker. That distinction has two very important ramifications for the buyer.

First, individual policy rates are guaranteed. Association and group-plan rates are not. All term policies are renewed periodically, and rates are stepped up in line with the policyholder's age. Renewal premiums for individual policies can't be increased further than that. With association plans the insurer reserves the right to raise the rates beyond those normal increases. Of course, your premium might never be increased, but you can't be sure of that.

Second, if the individual policy is automatically renewable each year, as most are, you can keep the insurance in force up to the ultimate termination age by paying the premiums. With association and group plans the insurance normally stops if you leave the group and the coverage can be maintained only by converting the term policy into a higher-premium cash value policy.

Mail vs. regular rates. Putting aside those considerations for the moment, do the claimed economies of selling by mail actually produce savings for the buyer?

A definitive answer would require a huge study because of the number of mail-order plans on the market and the problems of matching them with agent-sold plans. A few random comparisons indicate that you do better sometimes by mail, sometimes by buying through an agent, For example, here are the annual premiums for two $20,000 term policies sold by Bankers Life & Casualty Company late in 1980. The direct-mail policy is renewable to age 70 and convertible into cash value insurance up to age 65. The policy sold by the company's agents is renewable to age 100 and convertible to age 85. The agent policy rates do not include the available discounts of 10% for nonsmokers and 5% for people considered preferred risks. No discounts are offered for the mail-order plan.

age (men)	direct mail	agent policy
30	$ 57.28	$ 71.22
35	68.72	81.62
40	103.12	113.42
45	160.40	159.42
50	263.48	224.22
55	423.88	316.42

The mail-order policy is cheaper for men in lower age groups but more expensive for those in the higher age groups. The same pattern shows up in a comparison of two policies sold by MONY, the Mutual Life Insurance Company of New York. One is marketed through a fraternal organization, the other by MONY's agents. A MONY actuary says medical screening by mail tends to be less effective for older applicants than for younger ones, so the premium rates are correspondingly higher.

Medical qualifications. The insurance discussed so far is subject to medical qualifications. The application form requires answers to a few questions that the company uses to evaluate your acceptability. Your replies will probably be cross-checked against data that may be on file with the Medical Information Bureau, through which companies swap information. You may be asked to have a medical examination at the company's expense.

However, some plans are sold without any medical conditions—you are guaranteed acceptance if you pay the premium. To avoid being swamped by high-risk applicants, the insurers employ several safeguards:

- The policy may be offered only during limited enrollment periods.
- The total amount of insurance is fairly modest.
- The full face value isn't paid for deaths that occur during at least the first two years the policy is in force. Old American Insurance Company, for instance, has offered by mail an individual cash value policy that pays the full amount during the first three years only if the person dies as a result of an accident. For deaths from natural causes the policy pays 25% of the face amount if the death occurs in the first year, 50% in the second year and 75% in the third.

• The premium may be set considerably above rates for medically screened plans sold through agents. You can't bank on mail-order insurance being a bargain merely because no agent commission is involved. The insurance companies set premium rates on the basis of sales costs, as well as actuarial considerations. Only 1% to 2% of the people solicited by mail actually buy the insurance, and that is often regarded as a good return. Therefore, the rates have to take into account the costs of mailing to the other 99% or 98% who fail to respond to the first solicitation. Association plans may produce a higher response because of the sponsor's endorsement, but the insurer has to figure in fees to brokers and others involved in the deal.

The lack of premium and other guarantees in many mail-order policies indicates that it's best to regard them as potential supplements to your individual insurance, not as the core of a family protection program.

Plans for which there are no medical qualifications must be hedged and priced to cover the additional risks the companies assume, so there's no point in buying that kind of policy until you're sure you need it. Try first to obtain regular insurance, either by mail or through agents, at standard premiums.

CREDIT LIFE INSURANCE

Two things can be said immediately about credit life insurance: As sensible as it sounds, you may not need it. And as affordable as it sounds, it probably costs too much. Credit life is one of several kinds of insurance sold through lenders—banks, auto dealers, finance companies, retailers—in connection with their loans and charge accounts. (Others are credit accident and health insurance, which covers your payments if you become disabled, and credit property insurance, which covers the items you buy on credit.) The credit insurance controversy has focused on credit life because it has the highest volume and thus the greatest potential for abuse.

Though it's usually legal for a creditor to require you to have insurance as security for a debt, state laws generally make it illegal for the creditor to require you to buy it from him or from someone else he names. You have the option of pledging an existing policy or buying coverage elsewhere. If the lender requires the insurance and you buy it from him, its cost has to be included in the loan's finance charge and annual percentage rate.

If the insurance isn't required but you decide to buy it anyway, the lender doesn't have to include its cost in the finance charge. Instead, the charges will be set out in a separate statement you're required to sign and date, acknowledging that you're buying the coverage voluntarily. This arrangement allows and even encourages lenders to pressure their customers to buy credit insurance (or at least suggest that they buy it) without actually requiring it; that way, they don't have to reflect the cost of the insurance to the consumer in the annual percentage rate. The price of credit life, which is usually decreasing term coverage, is generally expressed as cents per $100 of initial coverage per year of the loan. (Credit life is offered on loans of up to ten years' duration.)

Every state except Alaska sets a maximum rate, which tends to become the market price. These range from a high of $1 per $100 in Alabama and three other states to less than 40 cents in California, which has a sliding scale. (To justify such a disparity actuarily, the mortality rate in Alabama would have to be more than double the mortality rate in California.) Most states' maximums fall between 60 cents and $1.

One big catch in computing what a borrower pays for credit life is that the premium is usually added to the loan and financed at the same rate, so you end up paying to insure not only the loan principal but also the insurance premium and all finance charges. You are actually insuring the insurance.

Let's say that you're borrowing $6,000 for four years at 13% and that credit life costs 75 cents per $100 of coverage. You'd end up buying insurance not on $6,000 but on $8,036.01. That breaks down like this:

loan principal	$6,000.00
interest on loan	1,725.60
credit life premium	241.08
interest on premium	69.33
total coverage	$8,036.01

This decreasing term policy would cost you $310.41, or $6.47 a month. (When credit accident and health premiums are added in, as they usually are, the insurance charges will be two to three times higher.)

In contrast, at the time those figures were compiled, Bankers Security Life Insurance Society could offer a 35-year-old man an $8,000 five-year, level-term policy for $4.41 a month; for $6.47 he could buy $16,893 worth of coverage. Age makes a difference here, though; a 50-year old man would pay $9.09 for a similar policy.

Is credit life ever a good insurance buy?

• Not if you're in your twenties or thirties and eligible for other kinds of life insurance at better rates.
• Not if you're single with no heirs to worry about. Credit life is supposed to protect your surviving family from claims against your estate; if you have no family, you end up protecting the creditor.

- Not if you already have enough insurance to cover the debt.
- And not if your main reason for wanting more insurance is to beef up your overall coverage. Depending on your age and health, you can usually buy long-term policies in large enough amounts for a much smaller unit cost than you can buy credit life.

If you're interested only in insuring a small, short-term loan—say $2,000 for two years—credit life may be your only source. Some creditors deal with more than one insurer, so rates may vary.

Credit life also might be a reasonable buy if you can't meet the health requirements for other insurance coverage; if you live in a low-rate state, such as California or Maine, or if at your age other policies cost even more than credit life.

The best deal on credit life is offered by credit unions, which traditionally have provided the insurance at no extra charge. Even when the borrower pays, CUNA Mutual, the insurance affiliate of the Credit Union National Association, offers policies at comparatively low rates.

A GLOSSARY OF BASIC
LIFE INSURANCE TYPES

Annuity. A policy that guarantees its owner a specified lifetime income in return for a payment to the insurance company. The payment may be all in a lump sum or can be spread out over a period of years.

Convertible term. A term policy that can be converted into a whole life policy or other cash value type of plan without a new medical check. Most insurance companies offer term policies that are both convertible and renewable.

Deferred annuity. An annuity paid for with annual premiums instead of a lump sum.

Endowment policy. A policy designed to pay off after a certain number of years, rather than at death. Endowment policies are usually employed as a savings vehicle to assure the availability of money for a specific purpose at a specific time, such as college or retirement.

Participating policy. A policy that pays annual dividends that can be taken out as cash, used to reduce premium payments, left in an interest-earning account or used to buy small, additional amounts of insurance. The "dividends" are actually refunds of excess premium amounts paid by policyholders.

Reducing or decreasing term. A term policy whose face amount is reduced in stages over a prescribed period. The reduction is usually scheduled so as to leave enough face amount at any point to pay off a debt, such as a mortgage or installment loan, or to provide a certain minimum income to the beneficiary.

Term insurance. A policy that insures your life for a specified number of years and then must be renewed to be kept in force. Term sells for considerably lower premiums than whole life. It does not normally accumulate cash values, and the premium increases at each renewal in step with your age. The policy can't be renewed beyond the age stipulated by the issuing company.

Variable annuity. An annuity based in part on an investment by the insurance company in a securities fund. The monthly payments from the annuity policy vary with the performance of the stocks.

Whole life insurance. A policy for which you pay premiums, ordinarily the same amount each year, for as long as you live. Whole life policies accumulate cash values, which you can borrow against while the policy is in force or withdraw if you surrender the policy. Whole life and other types of cash value policies are sometimes referred to as permanent insurance.

11

Insurance on your health

Having enough health insurance protection should be one of your top priorities. What would happen to your financial well-being if you or someone in your family came down with a serious illness? If you were underinsured, how quickly would those snowballing medical bills wipe you out?

BASIC KINDS OF COVERAGE

Questions like these make it obvious that you should have as much health insurance as you can reasonably afford. And between any group plan that may be available where you work and the various policies offered by private carriers, chances are you can put together enough coverage to give you peace of mind.

You'll find these basic protections offered by group and individual policies:

Hospitalization. This will cover you for daily room and board and regular nursing services while in the hospital. You'll also be covered for certain hospital services and supplies, such as X rays, lab tests, and drugs and medication.

Surgical. This coverage pays for certain surgical procedures in and out of the hospital.

Medical. It covers you for doctors' visits in and out of the hospital. Some plans also cover such services as diagnostic tests and various laboratory tests.

Major medical. Although this is geared to take over where your basic coverage leaves off, you can also buy it as part of a comprehensive policy if you have no basic coverage. Levels of protection and benefits are higher than those found in basic policies.

Excess major medical. This coverage protects you from the risk of a long-term serious illness. If both you and your spouse had severe heart attacks, for instance, the protection generated by an excess major medical policy could keep your family afloat financially. If you already have health insurance, this permits you to increase your coverage without changing current policies.

Disability. Disability insurance is designed to offset earnings lost because of an accident or sickness. You can get coverage for both long-term and short-term disability in the form of salary continuation at work or disability insurance, or a combination of the two.

HOW POLICIES PAY OFF

Having the right types of protection doesn't necessarily mean that you are well covered. Most every policy you own, no matter how good it is, has a limit to the amount of benefits it will pay. The trick is to make sure the benefit limits you choose keep pace with the ever-rising cost of medical care.

There are two basic types of policies as far as benefit payouts are concerned.

• *Actual costs*. For each insured service this type pays a percentage of the fee that is "usual, customary and reasonable" for the community. Some services may be fully covered within these guidelines, others only partially covered. For example, 100% of your hospital bills may be paid but only 75% of your medical and surgical costs. And if your doctor's fee should be above the usual range for your area, you'll have to make up the difference. Benefits are paid directly to the doctor or hospital.

• *Predetermined costs*. An indemnity or scheduled type of policy pays specific dollar amounts for each covered service according to a predetermined schedule or table of benefits. These schedules tend to become out of date even before the ink is dry on the policy. That means you could wind up digging deeper into your pocket to make up the difference between what the insurance company pays and what the doctor or hospital charges.

With either type of policy you can't be sure that you're adequately insured unless you know exactly what's covered, and that may not be completely clear to you. The health insurance companies are trying to use plainer language in their policies, but there are still cases in which you'll want the company to spell out exactly what a term means.

For instance, what does coverage for a preexisting condition really mean? Are you covered for a preexisting condition you didn't know about when you took out the policy or just for known conditions that the insurance company agrees to accept? In disability insurance, are you covered if you can't perform any job your education or training prepared you for, or only if you can't perform your normal job?

DEDUCTIBLES AND LIMITATIONS

Conceivably, you could buy health insurance to pay for aspirin when you need it or to cover the expense of bandaging a cut thumb. But who needs that kind of insurance? You can foot those bills yourself. Insuring such commonplace and financially insignificant needs or even routine visits to your doctor would only make your health insurance more expensive.

Catastrophic illnesses are something else. You want insurance to help you pay for dire eventualities precisely because you couldn't manage to pay for them yourself. And naturally you want that protection to be as cheap as possible because the cheaper the protection is, the more protection you can afford.

That's why health insurance is sold with a system of deductibles and coinsurance. A *deductible* is the amount you pay—say $250 or $500—before the insurance company makes any payments. *Coinsurance* is the amount of the bill you pay above the deductible, with the insurance company picking up the rest of the tab up to the policy limits. For instance, you may pay 20% to 30% in coinsurance up to $2,500 or so, after which the company takes over up to the maximum.

Deductibles and coinsurance are usually found in major medical policies. The higher they are, the lower your premium. A general rule is to match the deductible of your major medical policy to the limits of your basic coverage. That way your major medical policy will pick up right where your basic policy leaves off.

Deductibles can vary within a policy, with certain services having higher deductibles than others. Deductibles that apply to the family as a whole are preferable to individual deductibles for each family member. With the former, once one or two members have met the family deductible, any illness befalling other family members is covered immediately.

Various limits and exclusions are written into the policy, too. For instance, there is a limit to how many days you can stay in the hospital and still be covered. There is also a limit to how long deductibles can be combined to reach the point at which the insurance begins to pay off. If you don't reach that point within a stated time, you have to go back to square one and start counting toward the deductible sum all over again.

Similarly, there is usually a limit to the benefits payable. You may have either a maximum limit for each cause of illness or a lifetime maximum for all illnesses. Some plans also limit the hospital or doctor you can go to, but most cover you anywhere in the United States.

You are excluded from coverage for care in government hospitals and for illnesses and accidents covered by workers' compensation.

With disability insurance, there's an "elimination period" between the onset of disability and the first payment by the insurance company. The elimination period can range from one day to two years; generally, the longer it is, the lower the premium. The amount of money you can collect in disability payments is also limited. The limit is usually about 40% to 60% of your gross earnings, but payments may be partially or completely tax-free.

Another point worth particular attention is policy renewability. A group plan is renewable as long as your employer pays the premium and the insurance company chooses to keep the policy in force, but you have to be careful about the renewability terms of an individual policy.

Your best bet is a guaranteed-renewable policy. That means the company can't refuse to cover you as long as you pay your premiums and no acts of fraud are involved. Premiums can be raised only if the entire class to which you belong gets a premium increase. However, some companies switch to optionally renewable policies, which gives them the right to end coverage when your policy period is over.

MAKING SURE YOU HAVE ENOUGH

How much basic protection should you have? There are a variety of opinions about this. A study conducted in 1979 by Pracon, Inc., a research firm, under a grant from Roche Laboratories, concluded that the "minimum adequate benefit package" should cover hospital care and medication for at least 15 days; physicians' services, including hospital, office, and home visits; X rays and laboratory work; prenatal care; inpatient psychiatric care; outpatient services; and nursing home care. The insurance should pay 80% of the costs except for psychiatric care, for which any inpatient benefit was considered adequate.

By those standards, 85% of the protected population is adequately insured for hospital and psychiatric care, about 90% for X rays and lab work. But fewer than two-thirds have adequate coverage for maternity care; only about half have enough for physicians' hospital visits. Even fewer people than that are compensated for the cost of doctors' office and home visits and for nursing home care.

What should you have in the way of major medical? For individuals the Pracon study recommends coverage that would pay at least $250,000 in benefits over your lifetime and also provide stop-loss, or cost-sharing, protection, an all-important safeguard that puts an annual limit, often $1,000, on your share of costs. The

Health Insurance Institute says most experts are in accord on the $250,000 figure, which is the most common limit in Blue Cross/Blue Shield plans.

About 142,000,000 Americans are protected to some degree against catastrophic costs, and the majority of them have a benefit limit of $250,000 or more. About half of those covered by employee group plans are eligible for benefits up to $1,000,000 or more, and for nearly a third there is no benefit ceiling at all.

Nonetheless, most of these people could still incur ruinous expenses because, as mentioned earlier, insurance rarely pays all costs. Most major medical is "80/20"—the company pays 80% and the policyholder pays 20% of costs above a deductible, which is also paid by the policyholder. Deductibles range from $100 to over $1,000.

As health care costs spiral upward, so do those out-of-pocket expenses. Once, if insurance covered 75% of your costs, that seemed adequate, but today it's very easy to run up a $20,000 hospital bill. With 75% coverage you'd have to pay $5,000.

But not if you have stop-loss protection. No matter how high the bills run up, or for how long, you pay no more than the stipulated amount in any one year.

Here's how one plan works: After the policyholder pays a $100 deductible, the insurance company pays 80% of the first $5,000 of covered expenses during a five-year benefit period. The company pays 100% of any additional expenses up to $1,000,000. The policyholder's obligation would be capped at $1,100 per benefit period—the $100 deductible plus 20% of $5,000.

Insurers offer various choices of stop-loss limits. As with deductibles, the higher the limit, the lower the premiums.

A POLICY YOU CAN AFFORD

Choosing an affordable policy, either basic or major medical, that best meets your needs is not the simplest of tasks. Here are some guidelines:

- Since group insurance is usually cheaper than individual policies, find out whether you're eligible for a group plan through membership in a club, professional or fraternal society, or other organization. If you are not, consider joining some group that offers a group plan.

- If you leave a job that provided insurance and aren't soon to be covered under new employment, see whether the coverage can be converted to an individual policy.

- Try to mesh your basic protection and major medical so that there are few gaps. If you're shopping for both, you may get better coordination and service by buying from one company.

- Avoid duplicating or overlapping coverages. Coordination-of-benefit clauses may prevent you from collecting from more than one policy.

- Don't be unduly influenced by ads emphasizing high benefits levels, such as $1,000,000. Pay close attention to the stop-loss protection. You want to keep your expenses within reason.

- Try to get a guarantee that you can renew the policy either indefinitely or until you qualify for medicare. This is a decided plus.

The more policies you examine and compare, the better your chances of finding a good buy. Note carefully all conditions, restrictions, exclusions, waiting periods and other terms. Be sure you understand just what is covered and what isn't. Get as much protection as your budget will allow.

For a list of companies that sell major medical to individuals, write to the Health Insurance Institute, 1850 K Street, N.W., Washington, D.C. 20006.

JOIN AN HMO?

One of these days your employer may offer you the option of switching from a health insurance plan to a health maintenance organization. A company with 25 or more workers and a health insurance plan is required to offer a prepaid group option if it is approached by an existing qualified HMO. The employees must be given a reasonable explanation of how the HMO works and how it compares with the company's plan.

The trouble is, those who do the explaining may not be able to fill you in on everything you need to know, so you ought to educate yourself on the pros and cons of HMOs before you have to make a decision.

What is an HMO? With conventional health insurance you go to your doctor when you have a medical problem. He may decide you should see one or more specialists or go to a lab or the hospital for special tests. All this means setting up appointments in various locations. It also means filling out insurance forms so you can be reimbursed for your payments.

An HMO does away with medical trekking and the irritation of filing claims for every episode of illness. The idea is to make services easily available, mostly under one roof, and to encourage you to come in soon enough to prevent a minor condition from becoming serious and costly. Since you pay in advance for guaranteed care, HMO proponents say, you won't put off visits at the expense of your health, and this kind of vigilance not only keeps you fitter but also results in lower costs for health care.

A number of studies seem to support the claim that HMO care is more economical. Though the figures are not the last word, they do show that HMO members' health care bills are 10% to 40% smaller on the average and that members tend to go to the hospital one-third as frequently as patients under traditional care and lose less time from work.

The notion of doctors joining together and offering a variety of prepaid services is not new. One such organization with a famous name—the Kaiser-Permanente Medical Care Program of California—is already middle-aged. HMOs with successful track records flourish in New York City, Minneapolis, Seattle and Washington, D.C.

HMOs are available to more people than ever and their members are increasing. After an uneven start in the early 1970s, the number of prepaid medical practices has grown by more than 100% and now totals over 200, with some 8,000,000 members.

Recently, HMOs have started or expanded to serve the employees of such large companies as American Can Company, IBM, Ford, Honeywell, U.S. Steel and the Bell System. Blue Cross and Blue Shield plans sponsor HMOs. By 1988 the U.S. Department of Health and Human services expects there to be 442 HMOs serving more than 19,000,000 Americans at a savings of about 20 billion dollars in hospital costs alone.

The federal government has encouraged the growth of HMOs with millions of dollars in grants, loans and loan guarantees to help pay for planning and starting HMOs and to cover initial operating costs. Unions, consumer organizations and medical groups can apply for such funding provided they give assurance that the organization will deliver a broad range of health care services. An HMO can be operated on a not-for-profit or for-profit basis.

Should you join? If you have the option of joining an HMO, forget about the worry that you might have to deal with just any doctor who happens to be on duty when you have a medical problem. In an HMO you or members of your family will usually have a choice of which doctor you see first when you have a medical complaint. He prescribes treatment or refers you to one of the staff specialists and hospitalizes you when necessary, using one of the hospitals associated with the group. You may have to accept a stand-in in an emergency or if your own doctor is off duty, but this happens in private practice, too.

In a well-run HMO you are encouraged to come in for periodic checkups and to make doctor appointments whenever justified. Most plans completely cover routine visits, checkups, major illnesses requiring hospitalization, anthesia, lab work, X rays, and physician and surgeon services.

But details vary among plans. For example, congenital malformations are covered in HMOs in Washington, D.C., but two Minneapolis plans cover them only for family members born after the family signs up for the HMO.

Because of the economies achieved in HMOs through preventive medicine and cost control, there is additional cash, at least in some of them, to expand preventive and support services. These include courses in prenatal care, physical fitness, weight control and smoking cessation. Some groups provide guidance in reducing the risk of chronic ailments or controlling such disorders as high blood pressure and diabetes.

HMOs differ in how they are organized, and how

they deliver services and pay doctors. In one type, doctors receive a salary based on standards and qualifications other than how many patients they see. Because there is no incentive to give unnecessary service, it is reasoned, the organization incurs fewer costs and patients' premiums can be held down.

A second type of HMO is essentially a bookkeeping arrangement. If your doctor joins an Individual Practice Association (IPA), you can have the prepaid advantage of an HMO without having to change doctors. In an IPA the monthly premium does away with bills and insurance forms, just as in a regular HMO, but because care is usually not centralized, you and your doctor still have the obligation of locating medical facilities as they are needed.

IPA physicians are paid from premium income, usually 80% of their standard fee. The other 20% goes to cover the plan's expenses. If sufficient economies are realized, the cash pool or parts of it may be returned to participating doctors. Ideally, if the plan runs short of cash, payments to physicians are reduced so that members don't have to make up the deficit with higher premiums. About half of HMOs are of the IPA type.

How much would you pay if you belonged to an HMO? In 1980 family premiums averaged about $120 a month, with a low of $68 and a high of $162. Some employers require employees to pay the difference if the HMO premium is higher than coverage for workers under conventional insurance. Unlike conventional insurance, most HMOs have no deductible, but to discourage misuse, some require members to pay a dollar or two per visit.

Criticisms of HMOs. HMOs can have their drawbacks. An HMO could fail and leave members unprotected. Critics charge that an underfinanced HMO could easily scrimp on care and that group prepaid practices can take on the atmosphere of a clinic, with reception rooms that are crowded and long waiting periods for appointments.

Comparisons of the quality of prepaid care versus traditional medicine abound, but until recently nobody bothered to put the results together. But researchers from the Johns Hopkins School of Hygiene and Public Health, in an evaluation of 27 studies found that 19 of them considered HMO care better than that provided by doctors working primarily for fees. Care was comparable or findings inconclusive in eight others, but in no case was HMO care judged to be inferior.

A separate five-year study failed to bear out the suspicion that HMO patients wait longer for doctor appointments. Indeed, women seeking sessions with obstetricians and gynecologists waited an average of 12 days, compared with 14 for fee-for-service patients.

Waiting time to see a general practitioner, pediatrician or general surgeon was generally the same in both forms of care, according to Mathematica Policy Research of Princeton, New Jersey. When it comes to internists, things tipped a bit the other way, with HMO patients waiting about ten days compared with eight for traditional care. Once patients were in the office, though, they waited about 18 minutes to see HMO doctors; patients of conventional doctors waited about 20 minutes.

What about gripes in general? The seven HMOs that compete vigorously for business in the twin cities of Minneapolis and St. Paul have enrolled more than 300,000 people, yet a special state office established to oversee HMO operations says it gets only 20 to 30 complaints a month. A poll taken by General Mills of 1,600 workers covered by HMOs in the same area showed that 95% of those responding approved of the quality of their care.

Before you join. Attractive as they seem, HMOs are not for everyone. You may not be eligible for HMO protection as part of a benefits package offered by your employer or a group. If so and the HMO idea appeals to you, find out whether the HMO accepts single applications. Some do, but only during a once-a-year open enrollment period.

Eligibility for medicare could affect your benefits under an HMO. Not all HMOs accept medicare patients. Those that do could fill in the gaps in your coverage. Check this out carefully.

If your employer offers the HMO option, listen to the explanation, read the written information and try to find out whether joining would be a good idea. Pinning down the benefits you can count on is important, but you should also find out whether you can get back into your company's conventional insurance program without loss of coverage if you become disenchanted or the HMO collapses. An agreement should exempt you from the organization's bad debt if it gets into trouble.

Here are some additional tips.

• *Know what you're giving up.* Going into an HMO should be a family decision. If members now see several physicians and have good relationships with them, switching will mean severing ties and starting over with the HMO doctors. Be sure everyone understands the rules. In some cases an HMO might not be the best deal. One family opted to stay with its regular indemnity plan because it paid for treatment by a trusted asthma specialist in another city and the HMO available had no similar reimbursement arrangement. Remember that the main idea is to centralize facilities. HMOs cover emergency out-of-town hospitalization, but after the emergency passes, reimbursement varies.

• *Consider the convenience*. Most HMOs tend to be concentrated in metropolitan areas. Be sure the HMO you're thinking of joining is within a reasonable distance of your home or office.

• *Understand the complaint network*. Usually, a staff member is assigned to handle members' complaints or problems. If no settlement is reached, there should be a formal grievance procedure, which may include a review of the complaint by the board of directors. If the HMO is federally qualified, the grievance procedure has met requirements set up by the government. Your employer should be able to tell you whether there are any major complaints outstanding against the HMO it is doing business with.

• *Check out the plan's health*. Ask the HMO for the names of members you can call for an evaluation. Be suspicious of any HMO that refuses your request. To get and keep its label of "federally qualified," an HMO must provide a specified range of services and meet established standards for staff and facilities. About half of all HMOs are federally qualified, but lack of such designation is not reason by itself to rule out a plan. Reliable prepaid practices existed long before the government got into the act. Also, a plan may be in the process of seeking federal approval, or its organizers may have decided to develop privately without federal funds.

Comparing the number of days members generally spend in the hospital can be a good clue to efficiency. If hospital days per 1,000 members range between 350 and 525, you can be reasonably sure that the HMO has a commitment to economy. Such information should be readily available from the HMO.

Either too many or too few members can affect care adversely, so you should ask about the current size and stability of the membership. An annual growth rate of 8% is good. If you live in an area with a fairly steady population and the dropout rate is high in comparison with HMOs that are nearby, find out why before turning over your self and your dollars to the organization.

SPECIAL KINDS OF HEALTH INSURANCE

Stop-gap policies. If you lose your job, you'll also lose your employer-sponsored health insurance, and buying that protection on your own will be costly. Fortunately, most group plans include a grace period that extends your coverage for a month or so after you leave the job. Check with your employer to find out when your coverage will lapse if you find yourself in such a situation. Also ask whether you can convert from a group plan to an individual policy with the same insurance company, picking up the premium payments yourself. An individual policy won't offer as much protection as the group plan.

Several companies offer interim insurance plans for people who don't qualify for group coverage but expect to in the near future. Such policies are offered for 60, 90 or 180 days. Contact insurance agents to see what's available. The premium will vary according to the coverage, where you live and the size of your family. It could easily amount to $100 or more per month.

Dread-disease insurance. These policies cover only specified ailments, such as cancer or multiple sclerosis. Individual cancer policies have been banned from sale in several states on the grounds that they provide minimal economic benefits. Often, dread disease policies merely duplicate coverage already being paid for in comprehensive health insurance policies. In no case should such policies be purchased as anything other than a supplement to a broad health insurance package, and then only after careful review and cost-comparisons with excess major medical policies.

Dental insurance. More and more Americans are able to handle some dental care costs through a dental insurance or prepayment plan. Right now the number covered is over 60,000,000.

Keep in mind that dental insurance is different in principle from medical insurance. When you buy coverage for medical bills, you're paying for protection against the unlikely event—a medical disaster that could mean bankruptcy. Basic dental policies cover the recurrent and predictable, such as exams, cleanings and troublesome cavities that nearly all of us have at one time or another. So dental insurance is more a way of preventing small problems from becoming large ones than it is of guarding against the unexpected.

Virtually all dental policies are sold to groups, such as company employees, members of unions and associations and school groups. In every group some participants are bound to need little dental care, some a lot. Sharing the risk in this way helps control the costs. If the choice of whether to sign up were left to individuals, those with known problems would more likely be customers than those with sound teeth.

Can you buy individual coverage? Not easily. Most insurers believe individual coverage is a bad deal for them because there is no spreading of the risk and patients with individual policies tend to use the benefits heavily. So about the only way you can get individual protection is to buy it in the form of an expensive rider on another health policy.

Dental coverage is becoming available in some HMOs, but don't assume all dental work is free after the premium is paid. Like regular dental insurance, HMO coverage stresses improvement in oral health. That means that preventive care such as examinations, cleaning and flouride treatments are usually covered in full to encourage their use. More extensive work—fillings, caps, and the like—often require you to shell out a deductible before benefits start. Orthodontic benefits have lifetime limits; in one big HMO this is $500. Plans also have annual limits for all types of dental care.

Medigap insurance. Since medicare pays only about 40% of their health care costs, most people 65 and over must obtain insurance on their own or risk financial disaster if a serious illness strikes. To protect themselves, an estimated two-thirds of those under medicare buy medicare supplement, or "medigap" policies.

Tragically, some buyers are gouged or defrauded. High-pressure selling and other abuses amount to a national scandal, according to the Select Committee on Aging of the House of Representatives. Medigap contracts differ enormously in price, terms and benefit limits, and a paucity of consumer information makes it difficult to pick the right one.

There is a federal law designed to help with the problem. It calls for a voluntary federal certification program to begin in the summer of 1982. Only plans that meet minimum standards will be awarded the government's seal of approval:

• The policy must supplement both part A and part B of medicare.
• It must be written in easy-to-understand language.

- It cannot exclude coverage of a preexisting health condition for more than six months.
- It has to permit cancellation within 30 days without financial loss.
- It must offer reasonable economic benefit in relation to the premium charged.

The U.S. Department of Health and Human Services (HHS) will design an emblem for display on federally approved policies.

In addition to establishing the certification program, the new law takes aim at medigap abuses by making it a federal crime for agents to use certain sales practices. It will be illegal, for example, to knowingly sell a policy that duplicates coverage an individual already has from medicare or another private policy. It will also be a crime to claim falsely that a policy has been approved by the government or for a company to offer a mail-order medigap policy in a state unless the policy has been approved by the state's insurance office.

Law or no law, you'll still have to do your own shopping for a good policy. You can get some help from the HHS "Medicare/Private Insurance Checklist." This four-page work sheet shows the limits of medicare coverage and gives you space to chart the terms and benefits of supplemental policies you are considering. You can get copies of the checklist free from the office that handles your medicare.

12

Insurance on your car

A car insurance policy is not what you would call interesting reading. But if you're concerned or merely curious about what you are entitled to for your insurance premiums, the policy constitutes the best single source of information.

The following explanations of the major parts of the typical policy should help you pick your way through the legal thickets so common to insurance contracts.

LIABILITY PROTECTION

It's this part of the policy that provides help when your car hurts people or damages property.

To illustrate how liability insurance works, assume an accident for which you are clearly responsible: You run through a red light, strike another car and injure the driver.

Under the liability section of your policy the company agrees to defend you—in court, if necessary—and pay claims to the other driver for bodily injuries and car damage. The company, take note, does not compensate you for damage to your car or any of the injuries unless they are covered by other parts of the policy.

Assume now that you are involved in an intersection collision and there are no witnesses or evidence to pin the blame on either driver. Here, too, your insurance company is obligated to defend you against any proceedings the other driver may take against you. The family automobile policy, one of the standard auto policy forms, makes that point clear in these words: ". . . and the company shall defend any suit alleging such bodily injury or property damage and seeking damages which are payable under the terms of this policy, even if any of the allegations of the suit are groundless, false, or fraudulent. . . ."

The company limits its liability payments to the amount of coverage you select. If you buy a policy with $10,000/$20,000/$5,000 liability limits (often abbreviated 10/20/5), the company will pay up to $10,000 for bodily injury suffered by one person, up to $20,000 for all people hurt in the same accident, and up to $5,000 for property damage resulting from that accident. However, the company may exceed the limit for an accident in another state that requires more liability insurance than your state if you bought only enough to satisfy your state's minimum.

Alternatively, the company may use a single liability limit that applies to total payments for both property and bodily injury claims arising from the same accident.

The company's expenses for defending you against liability actions are not included in the liability limits; they're an extra benefit. You're also entitled to money for bail bonds (usually $100 to $250) and the cost of attending hearings and trials, and often a daily allowance ($25 to $50) for earnings lost during those periods.

How much liability protection should you carry? You aren't forced to buy more than your state's minimum, but that's likely to be fairly modest.

Given the high level of medical and repair costs and the likelihood of further increases, it's apparent that the state minimums don't come close to covering a serious accident. Remember that you personally are responsible for paying claims that exceed the liability limit stated in the policy. Moreover, many policies free the company from any obligation to continue your legal defense for sums above the amount it has to pay.

Insurance company representatives point out that you can substantially increase liability coverage for a small extra premium. It may be a sales pitch, but it's a suggestion worth considering. If you're paying, say, $60 a year for $10,000/$20,000 of bodily injury liability, you should be able to buy $100,000/$300,000 for about $125 a year. If your $5,000 of property damage liability costs $70 a year, $25,000 may be available for about $80.

COLLISION PROTECTION

Liability coverage cuts two ways. Just as someone can sue you, you can sue others you believe were responsible for an accident. Why, then, protect your car with collision insurance, which is optional (although it may be necessary in order to qualify for a new-car loan), expensive and subject to a deductible that makes you pay for small losses? Here are the more obvious reasons.

- Despite the most careful driving, you may cause an accident, or at least be held responsible for one. In that case you can't collect for damage to your car by taking action against the other driver. Collision coverage will pay for the damage, even when you're at fault.

- It may take a long time to collect if the other driver's insurer contests your claim. With collision coverage you can have your company repair the car and take over your claim against the other driver (a procedure known as subrogation). Your company is ethically bound to fight for enough money to pay you back part or all of the deductible.
- The other driver may have no liability insurance. Suing him could very well enmesh you in a protracted, fruitless legal tangle. As you will see later, the uninsured-motorist coverage of the auto policy does not necessarily help in these situations. Collision will.
- When your car strikes a tree or a lamppost or runs through a barrier or overturns, there is no one to take action against. Only collision will pay for the damage to your car.

The amount of collision coverage your policy provides depends on the type of car and its age. You can only vary the total by buying a smaller or larger deductible. How much you will be paid for an accident depends on the nature and extent of the damage, whether new or used parts are used and so on. However, you should be aware of one special restriction: The company is not obligated to pay more in repairs than the car was worth before the accident, minus the salvage value of the damaged vehicle.

For example, say the car was worth $2,000 before the accident and $500 for salvage afterward. The company does not have to pay more than $1,500 in repairs. If the repairs would exceed the amount, the company can take the damaged car and give you the $2,000.

MEDICAL PAYMENTS

Collision, unlike liability protection, entitles you to compensation from your own insurance company. Medical payments coverage operates on the same principle.

You and family members who live with you qualify for reimbursement of medical costs resulting from auto accidents while in your car or someone else's car or while walking or, in some cases, bicycling. Guests also qualify if they are injured in your car.

Generally, companies won't sell less than $500 of medical payments insurance or more than $10,000, and it costs relatively little to raise the coverage. If $500 requires a $10 annual premium, $10,000 should cost about $30 a year.

The company will reimburse a wide range of expenses, including funeral costs, subject to varying conditions. One policy may pay expenses only for the first three years, another might extend payments to five years provided you buy more than a stipulated amount of protection. Payments can be reduced to the extent you receive or are entitled to receive compensation from other parts of the policy or from other sources. In certain situations the company may pay only expenses that exceed the compensation obtainable from other insurance.

Medical payments insurance is no longer sold in some states because of the introduction of no-fault systems that also allow you to collect medical expenses, as well as other benefits, directly from your own insurer.

UNINSURED MOTORISTS

There are a lot of people driving without any liability insurance. The uninsured-motorist section of your policy will provide some financial relief if you or family members who live with you are hurt by one of those drivers while you're in your car, walking or, in some policies, bicycling. Guests qualify if they are hurt while in your car. The insurance also applies when you are struck and injured by a hit-and-run driver, and, in some cases, by a driver insured by a company that becomes insolvent.

The other driver must be responsible for the accident. In most states, when who's to blame is in doubt or the amount payable is contested, you and your insurer have to submit your differences to arbitration.

In the great majority of states this kind of insurance covers only costs arising from bodily injuries. In those states in which property damages are included, claims may be reduced by a deductible.

Generally, companies are obligated to pay claims up to the same minimum amount fixed by your state for liability insurance. But often you can purchase higher limits for an additional premium. Most states require insurance companies to offer uninsured-motorist protection.

COMPREHENSIVE COVERAGE

A combination of liability, collision, medical payments and uninsured-motorist insurance would seem to take care of all conceivable risks. Yet none of that insurance would necessarily cover losses from these hazards: theft of the car or some of its contents, glass breakage, missiles, falling objects, fire, explosion, earthquake, windstorm, hail, water, flood, malicious mischief, vandalism or riots. Comprehensive insurance will handle those losses, either in full or subject to a deductible.

You are also entitled to some compensation for renting a car if yours is stolen. Insurers usually allow $10 a day starting 48 hours after you report the theft to the company, up to a maximum of $300.

NO-FAULT INSURANCE

As indicated earlier, liability insurance constitutes your main financial defense against catastrophic accidents—those that result in long hospital stays, permanent physical impairments or extensive property destruction.

However, liability insurance is flawed by the crucial requirement that one person must be to blame for an accident in order for another person to qualify for compensation. And proving fault—which is not always possible—can lead to payment delays and expensive legal action.

Over a decade ago a broad-based effort to take the fault out of liability got under way. The objective was to have the losses incurred by accident victims paid by their own insurance companies, regardless of who was to blame for the accident, thereby eliminating the need for liability actions.

Attempts to obtain a national no-fault law have so far failed, but plans that reduce the fault element in some way have been enacted in a number of states, including Colorado, Connecticut, Florida, Georgia, Hawaii, Kansas, Kentucky, Massachusetts, Michigan, Minnesota, New Jersey, New York, North Dakota, Pennsylvania and Utah. Other states—Arkansas, Delaware, Maryland, New Hampshire, Oregon, South Carolina, South Dakota, Texas, Virginia and Washington—have adopted "add-on" plans that increase the benefits you can obtain from your own insurance company but do not restrict your rights to pursue a liability claim. No-fault laws vary greatly, but they follow a general pattern.

- Your insurance company has to pay you and others covered by your policy for medical bills, wage losses, the cost of hiring people to do household tasks you are unable to perform as a result of injuries and funeral expenses up to specified limits. Michigan, New Jersey and Pennsylvania provide for unlimited medical expenses

- Property damage is excluded from the no-fault insurance drivers must buy. (Property losses remain covered by other parts of the policy.)

- No-fault benefits do not include compensation for pain and suffering claims. For those, you have to depend on a liability action.

- You can't usually take action against others on a liability basis until expenses of the type covered by the no-fault insurance exceed a certain amount. And conversely, you are immune to suits by others until their costs exceed that limit. In Florida, Michigan and New York liability actions are prohibited except for serious injuries or death. To protect themselves against fault-based suits permitted under no-fault regulations, drivers must continue to buy traditional liability insurance. But liability payments may be reduced by compensation received under the no-fault provisions. The add-on plans generally provide benefits similar to, but less generous than, the no-fault programs.

HOW YOUR RATE IS SET

The amount you pay for auto insurance is the product of a complex process that begins when you first apply for a policy. At that point you are screened by a company underwriter who decides whether the company wants to insure you, and if so, in what general category to fit you.

One large company, for example, separates drivers

into three underwriting categories: preferred, standard and nonstandard. Its rates for preferred applicants generally run 15% under standard rates. Nonstandard policyholders are surcharged 35%, 50% or 75%, depending on the number of traffic violations and accidents.

If you're considered a high-risk driver, you might be rejected and eventually forced into a state assigned-risk plan that requires a regular insurance company to give you protection, albeit at a price that may be 50% more than other drivers are charged. Alternatively, one of the regular companies might shunt you into a subsidiary company that specializes in high-risk drivers. Those "substandard" insurers, as they are known in the business, also charge higher premiums.

Once you are accepted for insurance, whatever the plan or premium level, the company then has to determine precisely how much you will pay relative to other policyholders for the same amount and type of insurance. To see how that's done, you have to back up a bit in the premium-making process.

Each company periodically computes the premium income it needs in each state in which it operates. It wants money enough to pay for claims and expenses and a margin for profits and contingencies. The total state premium is then allocated among the various territories into which the state is divided for rating purposes. The boundaries are supposed to demarcate areas with significantly different loss records.

The exact relationships vary from one state to another, but according to one study people in central neighborhoods of small metropolitan areas (100,000 to 400,000 population) generally pay less than the state average; their counterparts in big cities (over 1,000,000) pay substantially more. Small-city suburbanites are charged less than the state average; big-city suburbanites are charged somewhat more.

The company establishes in each territory a set of base premiums for the individual coverages that make up auto insurance—bodily injury liability, comprehensive (fire, theft, vandalism), medical payments and so on. Those base rates customarily pertain to a particular stereotype: an adult male with a standard car used only for pleasure. Everyone else pays more or less, depending on the company's evaluation of his relative risk potential.

In effect, you are assigned to a group defined according to characteristics that are believed to predict the group's chances of creating insurance losses. Although classification plans differ, the companies employ for the most part these basic criteria: age, sex, marital status, accidents and traffic violations, whether the young driver has taken a driver education course, whether he is entitled to a good-student discount, the number of cars, the models, use of the cars (pleasure, commuting, business, farm) and the mileage.

Each characteristic is assigned a numerical weight based on its tendency to increase or reduce the probability of loss. All the factors that apply to you are combined to fix your position on the company's premium scale. A 100 ranking indicates that you pay 100% of the base premium. With a 90 ranking you pay 90% of the base—which means you are getting a 10% discount. If you're pegged at 225, you are charged 225% of the base.

Many companies follow a plan developed by the Insurance Services Office that applies the same weight factors to all parts of the auto policy—bodily injury liability, property damage liability, and so forth.

Despite a few attempts at simplification, risk classification systems have tended to become more complex over the years. Michigan's insurance bureau once estimated that the possible combinations of rating factors in some plans exceeded the number of people insured.

FINDING THE BEST DEAL

This complicated rating system has come under increasing criticism over the past several years and is probably due for some changes in a number of states. In the meantime, it's up to you to search out opportunities for reducing your premium. Here are possibilities you may not have been using as extensively as you could.

Learn the ins and outs. Posing as ordinary buyers, investigators of the Pennsylvania Insurance Department visited 186 insurance agencies in three cities. Of the 92 Philadelphia agents contacted, fewer than 30% volunteered information on discounts and deductibles that could have reduced premiums 20% to 40%.

If that experience is in any way indicative of conditions elsewhere, it's best to arm yourself with as much information as you can before approaching agents.

Ask your state insurance department for any material it may have published. Check the experience of friends and neighbors. And read through your present policy carefully so that you're sure of the kind and amount of protection you have.

Contact several companies. Every fresh survey confirms that auto insurance companies often charge greatly different premiums for the same coverage. In a Missouri study, rates for a St. Louis couple with an 18-year-old son and one car ranged from $405 to $2,086.

Rates may not vary as widely in your area, but the odds are you will discover substantial differences if you take the time to get premium quotations from a number of companies.

Manage your youngsters' driving. Remember, they're charged the highest rates, and those rates govern what you pay if they are on your policy. If possible, avoid allowing them to become the principal driver of a car. That pushes up the premium even more. Make sure they take driver education so they qualify for that discount. Some companies offer a discount for students with above-average grades. You may also be entitled to a reduced rate if your children spend part of the year at an out-of-town school.

Check your car's rating. Several years ago insurers introduced surcharges for "muscle" cars. That practice of gearing rates to specific makes and models has been spreading ever since. Allstate offers discounts on collision and comprehensive coverage for several models and surcharges others. State Farm does the same.

Before you buy your next car, it might pay to check on such differentials with the insurance company. Incidentally, a surcharge does not constitute a judgment of a car's quality. The rate variations reflect repair costs, accident frequency, theft losses and other factors.

Consider larger deductibles. An unmarried man under 21 might be able to save about $50 a year on collision coverage by raising the deductible to $250 from $100. He can lower his premium bill for comprehensive by $15 to $40 if he buys a $100 deductible policy instead of one providing full coverage.

Whatever your situation, you can save something by accepting a larger deductible and thus transferring part of the risk from the company to yourself. It's not an ideal solution, but it's one of the few cost-cutting opportunities that are readily available.

Use the same company for all cars. You are not charged the full rate for the second and successive cars covered by the same policy, so it's usually more economical to put all your cars on one policy.

Avoid installment payments. The company tacks an extra amount onto your premium when you pay in monthly or quarterly installments.

MAKING THE INSURANCE COMPANY PAY

Just about every driver knows how exasperating it can be to try to collect on an auto insurance claim. The adjuster who does not return telephone calls, the misplaced records, the company that disclaims responsibility, the body shop that argues the job can't be done right at the company's estimate—all these and other such annoyances can make the aftermath of a minor accident as upsetting as the accident itself.

There are millions of accidents every year. Maybe 90% of them are covered by insurance. Some of those never reach an insurance company because the policy deductible wipes out the claim or the person at fault elects to pay the damage to avoid cancellation of his policy or an increase in premiums.

When claims are filed, the companies usually settle them reasonably well. Still, a survey commissioned by the American Insurance Association, a large trade group, found that about 25% of the licensed drivers contacted were lukewarm to negative about their companies' claim performance. That finding is supported by the steady stream of complaints to state insurance departments and the fact that many states have adopted rules on unfair claims practices.

The proper strategy for you to follow depends on the issue in dispute, the circumstances of the accident, and so on. Here are several pointers that may prove useful.

• *Know your rights.* If you're dealing with your own company, look for support for your position in the policy, which constitutes a legal agreement between you and the company and spells out its obligations to you. When you're seeking compensation from another company, your agent and friends with experience in similar situations may have an idea of what you can reasonably demand.

• *Take names.* Companies range from the large to the colossal. State Farm, the leading auto insurer, covers about 21,000,000 cars and has more than 10,000 claims employees. Allstate covers about 11,000,000 cars. To avoid getting lost among the thousands of claims the company is processing each day, record the names and telephone numbers of people you've contacted, take notes on important conversations (don't forget the dates) and make copies of letters and other material affecting your claim.

• *Don't let them rattle you.* Rarely does a government agency offer such sage counsel as in this excerpt from the automobile insurance guide of the Washington State Insurance Department:

"Unfortunately, no one can ever be fully compensated for all the trouble and expense that an accident causes. A certain amount of running around is often unavoidable, and petty frustrations sometimes result. Accepting these difficulties is sometimes the only solution, and knowing this in advance may help make a bad situation bearable."

Those words should not be taken as a suggestion to submit gladly to unfair treatment. Anticipating an accident's inevitable inconveniences helps channel your anger into purposeful action.

Be assertive. Quietly tell the other person how you feel and what you need, without derogatory terms that will only harden his opposition. If you want a new bumper and the adjuster insists on a rechromed one, state—don't argue—your position: "My bumper was in good condition before the accident. I feel I'm entitled to a new one. I need my car. How can we settle this matter?"

The adjuster is hardly likely to concede immediately. Continue asserting your position calmly and firmly and throw the burden of finding a solution on him. If he won't budge, ask to speak to his superior and resume presenting your interests. It may be a transparent tactic, but assertive behavior can work where blustering and name-calling won't.

• *Don't rush to subrogate*. It's a convenient alternative when the company insuring the driver who you believe caused the accident balks at settling. But there are potential drawbacks.

1. Your company reduces its payment by the collision deductible. If it succeeds in settling the case with the other insurer, you may be refunded only part of that amount, depending on the sum recovered and the expenses incurred.
2. If your company loses its case, you might be judged liable for the accident and become subject to a premium surcharge.
3. You may not be entitled to car rental expenses when the claim is covered by your company, as you might be when you take action against the other company.

Check out those possibilities with the agent before you turn over the claim to your company. If you have a strong case against the other driver, it may be better to push the claim with his company before you try subrogation.

• *Complain to the state*. Very few states have complete authority to order an insurance company to pay a disputed claim or increase the settlement. Still, state insurance regulators do have influence.

A General Accounting Office report last year found that nearly all state insurance departments respond to complaints and often contact the insurance company about them. Moreover, a majority of states have adopted a model law that specifically prohibits several unfair claims practices, including these:

• Failing to acknowledge and act promptly on communications relating to insured claims.
• Failing to provide a reasonable explanation of policy conditions or laws under which a claim is denied or a compromise offer is made.
• Delaying settlement of one part of a claim in order to influence settlement of another. (This would apply if the company resists paying car damanges to pressure you into settling on bodily injury costs.)
• Not attempting to make prompt, fair and equitable settlements in cases in which liability has become clear.
• Forcing people to start legal action by making unreasonably low settlement offers.

Your state insurance department may have someone designated to handle consumer complaints. If not, write to the insurance commissioner. Keep a copy of the letter and any important material you enclose.

• *Consider hiring an attorney*. If you're injured in an accident, you might want to hire an attorney, even if only for guidance. The decision depends on the extent of the injury and the type of claim.

Attorneys usually charge a percentage of the recovered amount in personal injury cases. The standard fee is about a third, but you might also have to pay court costs if the case goes to trial. Relatively few go that far.

Look for an attorney with experience in injury claims. If you can't find someone through personal contacts, call the legal referral service in your area. It may be listed in the Yellow Pages.

The available evidence indicates that attorneys obtain larger settlements for their clients than claimants get on their own. However, a study made by insurance companies suggests that the net payment after fees may be less in some cases than unrepresented claimants receive. The study assumed a uniform fee of 35½%.

• *Consider paying your own claim.* This seems to defeat the purpose for which you bought insurance. But by facing facts as they are, not as they should be, you may find that it costs less in the long run to cover a small loss yourself.

Most insurance companies use merit rating plans that raise premiums when you violate certain traffic laws or cause an accident that results in physical injuries or damage over a certain amount, usually $200. When you take out the policy, you are assessed penalty points for each incident during the preceding three years, and further points are imposed for accidents and violations occurring while the policy is in force. All the drivers who regularly drive you car are covered, so you will be surcharged when your spouse or youngster is responsible. Generally, each point sticks on your record for three years.

The premium increase varies with the policy's base premium and the company's surcharge schedule. Just one point might be enough for a 30% hike in the base premium for the collision, liability and comprehensive coverages in your policy. Two points could lead to a doubling of the premium.

Suppose that you scrape the side of the car against a post in a parking lot and the repairs come to $225. If you have a $100 deductible, the company will pay you $125. But if you have already received payment for other small claims, you can be charged with a point that will jump the premium for the next three years by considerably more than $125. You might be better off paying the $125 yourself and saving your points for a big claim.

You're on less certain ground, though, when the accident involves another car or person and you are or could be considered responsible. The other person might accept your check but come back several weeks or months later with a claim for hidden damages or personal injuries. You would then be forced to refer the case to the insurance company, and the company might be reluctant to accept liability. It could argue that you failed to observe the policy clause requiring prompt reporting of accidents. Whether it would actually refuse the case would depend on company policy and the circumstances. Conceivably, it might take a tough position if the delay resulted in the loss of key evidence. Thus, you might add to your problems by paying a claim.

In a survey conducted by the American Insurance Association, 27% of the drivers contacted said they had been in accidents in which they or the other person had not filed an insurance claim out of fear their policies would be cancelled or their premiums increased.

Ask your agent for a copy of the company's merit rating provisions. If the figures suggest that it may be advantageous to pay for small losses yourself, you might also consider raising the deductible on your collision policy. That way you will at least save something on the premium.

13

Insurance on your home

Insuring your home year after year becomes so routine that you have to be particularly careful to avoid two potentially costly errors:

- Assuming that all homeowners policies are alike. Actually, policies come in several varieties, and company versions of those varieties differ.
- Taking it for granted that your insurance company charges about the same premium as others. Prices, in fact, sometimes differ by astonishingly large margins.

To make sure you buy the right protection for your property, review the basic aspects of homeowners policies described in this chapter. They're important to know for another reason, too. Homeowners coverage extends over so many fields, some of which seem so unrelated to house insurance, that you may have been neglecting to submit claims for insured losses.

The basic characteristics of the six major types of homeowners policies are summarized on the table spread across pages 220 and 221. The descriptions are based on standard forms that have been gradually introduced in a majority of states during the past few years. Companies usually phase in the new policies when the old ones are renewed. You may not notice the difference because the fundamental elements haven't changed.

Each policy type is identified in the table by number (HO-1, etc.) and, in parentheses, by the name often used in the insurance business. One or the other designation should appear somewhere on your policy.

Observe that the policies combine two kinds of insurance:

1. Property protection. These policy clauses pay you for losses to the house and other property. Included is reimbursement for credit card, forgery and counterfeit-money losses, and for additional living expenses or loss of income incurred when you or someone renting part of your house has to move temporarily because of damage to the living quarters.

The standard amounts payable on losses other than the house itself are generally figured as a percentage of the insurance bought on the house. For instance, with HO-1, -2, -3, and -5 your personal property is automatically insured for 50% of the house amount. (More coverage is available on many policies—see the discussion of "replacement cost" for household contents on page 224.) That 50% is in addition to the house insurance, not part of it. With renter and condominium policies the loss limits are geared to the amount of personal property insurance bought.

You can increase some coverages without raising the building amount by paying an additional premium. The special limits of liability that are listed in the table represent the maximum paid for those specific items. Usually, jewelry, furs, boats and other items subject to special limits have to be insured separately if you want more coverage.

2. Liability protection. These parts of the policy—the comprehensive personal liability, damage to property of others and medical payments—pay others for injuries or damage caused by you or by an accident around your home. Under the comprehensive liability clause, the company is obligated to pay claims when you are considered legally liable for the injury and to provide a legal defense if necessary. You would be covered, for example, if a visitor fell into an inadequately safeguarded hole in your walkway or if you struck someone accidentally with a ball on the golf course. The other two clauses don't require a presumption that you are legally responsible for the injury.

HOW POLICIES DIFFER

At first sight the house policies (the HO-1, -2, -3 and -5) appear to offer much the same protection. And they do on most points. The crucial difference lies in the number of perils insured. Not to be forgotten when you buy a homeowners policy is that you're entitled to compensation for house and personal property losses only for damage caused by a peril against which you are insured. With the HO-5 you are insured against any hazard not excluded in the policy.

Other parts of the policies may not apply unless an insured peril produces the loss. For example, the policies pay for emergency repairs to protect the house after an accident but on the condition that the damage to the house resulted from an insured peril.

GUIDE TO HOMEOWNERS POLICIES

These are the principal features of standard homeowners policies. The policies of some companies differ in a few respects from the standard ones. Policy conditions may vary according to state requirements.

You can usually increase insurance for some items by paying an additional premium. The special limits of liability refer to the maximum amounts the policy will pay for the types of property listed. Usually, jewelry, furs, boats, and other items subject to special limits have to be insured separately if you want greater coverage.

	HO-1 (basic form)	HO-2 (broad form)	HO-3 (special form)	HO-4 (renters' contents broad form)	HO-5 (comprehensive form)	HO-6 (for condominium owners)
PERILS COVERED (see key below)	perils 1–10	perils 1–17	perils 1–17 on personal property except glass breakage; all risks, except those specifically excluded, on buildings	perils 1–17	all risks except those specifically excluded	perils 1–17
STANDARD AMOUNT OF INSURANCE ON house and attached structures	based on property value, minimum $15,000	based on property value, minimum $15,000	based on property value, minimum $20,000	10% of personal insurance on additions and alterations to unit	based on property value, minimum $30,000	$1,000 on owner's additions and alterations to unit
detached structures	10% of amount of insurance on house	10% of amount of insurance on house	10% of amount of insurance on house	no coverage	10% of amount of insurance on house	no coverage
trees, shrubs, plants	5% of amount of insurance on house, $500 maximum per item	5% of amount of insurance on house, $500 maximum per item	5% of amount of insurance on house, $500 maximum per item	10% of personal property insurance, $500 maximum per item	5% of amount of insurance on house, $500 maximum per item	10% of personal property insurance, $500 maximum per item

personal property	50% of insurance on house; 10% for property normally kept at another residence, minimum $1,000	50% of insurance on house; 10% for property normally kept at another residence, minimum $1,000	50% of insurance on house; 10% for property normally kept at another residence, minimum $1,000	50% of insurance on house; 10% for property normally kept at another residence, minimum $1,000	based on value of property, minimum $6,000; 10% for property normally kept at another residence, minimum $1,000
loss of use, additional living expense; loss of rent if rental unit uninhabitable	10% of insurance on house	20% of insurance on house	20% of insurance on house	20% of insurance on house	40% of personal property insurance
SPECIAL LIMITS OF LIABILITY	Money, bank notes, bullion, gold other than goldware, silver other than silverware, platinum, coins, and medals—$100. Securities, accounts, deeds, manuscripts, passports, tickets, stamps, etc.—$500. Watercraft, including their trailers, furnishings, equipment, and outboard motors—$500. Trailers not used with watercraft—$500. Grave markers—$500. Theft of jewelry, watches, furs, precious and semiprecious stones—$500. Theft of silverware, silver-plated ware, gold-ware, gold-plated ware, and pewterware—$1,000. Theft of guns—$1,000.				
CREDIT CARD, FORGERY, COUNTERFEIT MONEY	$500	$500	$500	$500	$500
COMPREHENSIVE PERSONAL LIABILITY	$25,000	$25,000	$25,000	$25,000	$25,000
DAMAGE TO PROPERTY OF OTHERS	$250	$250	$250	$250	$250
MEDICAL PAYMENTS	$500 per person	$500 per person	$500 per person	$500 per person	$500 per person

Key to perils covered

1. fire, lightning
2. windstorm, hail
3. explosion
4. riots
5. damage by aircraft
6. damage by vehicles not owned or operated by people covered by policy
7. damage from smoke
8. vandalism, malicious mischief
9. theft
10. glass breakage
11. falling objects
12. weight of ice, snow, sleet
13. collapse of building or any part of building
14. leakage or overflow of water or steam from a plumbing, heating or air-conditioning system
15. bursting, cracking, burning, or bulging of a steam- or hot-water heating system, or of appliances for heating water
16. freezing of plumbing, heating, and air-conditioning systems and domestic appliances
17. injury to electrical appliances, devices, fixtures, and wiring (excluding tubes, transistors, and similar electronic components) from short circuits or other accidentally generated currents

Not all the policies that insure against a particular peril necessarily provide the same degree of protection. The HO-1 payments for broken windows are limited to $50. The HO-1 won't pay for damage to the garage by a car driven by you or someone who lives with you. The HO-2, on the other hand, will pay you in that situation for damage to the garage but not for damage to a fence, driveway or walk. The HO-3 and -5 will pay for all those losses.

Despite restrictions here and there, the HO-1 gives you a great deal of protection. But security-minded owners will undoubtedly feel more comfortable with the HO-2, which generally costs only 5% to 10% more. If you're considering the still more expensive HO-3 or -5, check whether the risks you are concerned about are covered. Neither the HO-3 nor the -5, for instance, takes care of damage caused by flood or settling, problems that often concern homeowners. When you're selecting a policy, also consider the possibility that you might do better by buying additional insurance for such items as pictures, antiques, and musical instruments, than by purchasing a homeowners form with more blanket coverage.

Compensation methods. The insurance companies compute payments for homeowners policy losses in two ways. One, replacement cost, usually applies only to the building. The other, actual cash value, is for personal property.

Stripped of technicalities, the replacement cost provision works this way:

If at the time the damage occurs the amount of insurance on the house equals 80% or more of the cost of replacing the structure, the company will pay the cost of repair or replacement without any deduction for depreciation. The payment remains subject, however, to the policy deductible.

If you're carrying less than 80% insurance, the company is obligated to pay only the depreciated value—the "cash value," as it's called in the policy—of the damaged part of the house or a proportion of the replacement cost, whichever is more. The proportion is based on the relationship between the actual amount of insurance and the sum needed to meet the 80% criterion. Thus, if you have $40,000 of insurance but need $60,000 to come up to 80%, the company will pay two-thirds of the loss. You would receive only $4,000 for a $6,000 loss, $6,000 for a $9,000 loss, and so on.

Insurance agents have access to cost-index figures to help update the replacement value. Many companies have instituted plans for periodically increasing the amount in line with inflation. When you compute the required amount of insurance, remember to eliminate the value of the land, excavations, foundations, underground pipes and similar building components not likely to be damaged.

Most accidents involve only parts of the house, so you will be entitled to the full replacement cost even if you insure for only 80%. But what if the house is completely destroyed? Then the company will pay only up to the face amount of insurance, leaving you to foot the other 20%. That's why you should consider insuring for 100%

Insurance for older homes. Good as it may be for ordinary homes, the replacement cost system presents problems for old houses that might cost more to restore to their original condition than they could be sold for. If you insure a house with a sales value of $34,000 for 80% of its $60,000 replacement cost, or $48,000, the house is in effect overinsured.

The insurance companies have developed three new plans to cope with that situation (but some companies sell them subject to different conditions, and some don't sell them at all):

1. A homeowners policy that pays for repairs with lower-cost, commonly used materials instead of those originally employed (a parquet floor, for instance, might be replaced with carpeting over a plywood base).
2. A policy that pays the actual cash value, which might be interpreted by the company as the current market value or as the replacement cost minus depreciation.
3. An endorsement—a policy addition—that allows you to insure for less than 80% without giving up your right to replacement cost for partial losses.

For furniture, appliances, awnings, outdoor equipment, clothing and other personal property, the company usually need not pay more than the cash value. If your couch goes up in flames, the claim is adjusted for wear and tear.

Replacement cost coverage for contents. A number of companies have begun selling an endorsement that extends replacement cost coverage to personal property. Aetna charges an extra 15% of the policy premium for its plan, which also increases the total for personal property from 50% of the insurance on the house to 75%. The Aetna endorsement excludes fine arts, antiques and other items that are expected to appreciate. It also limits payments for other items to a maximum of four times the cash value. Allstate, State Farm and other large insurers also offer replacement cost endorsements to their homeowners policies.

Shopping around. You can expect to find companies

offering the same policy at substantially different premium rates. A 1978 Missouri State Insurance Department report revealed that one company was charging twice as much as the company with the lowest price for comparable coverage on homes in Kansas City. In Independence the high-premium company was charging two and a half times more. A New York City study made a few years ago turned up 50% and 60% differences.

Of course, you can't survey all the companies selling insurance in your area, but contacting just a few might produce some savings.

There's still enough uniformity among the companies' policies that you can use the standard forms to compare premiums. Companies sometimes modify the standard provisions, but it's not always easy to tell whether the changes broaden or narrow your protection. For example: The standard forms provide $500 for credit card, forgery and counterfeit-money losses.

You're usually entitled to a lower rate for a brick home than for a frame structure. Also, you might qualify for a discount if your house is new or only a few years old, or if you have installed smoke alarms or antitheft devices. However, discount plans are not as common for homeowners insurance as they are for auto policies.

If the insurance agent computes the replacement cost of the house on the basis of square footage, be sure to check his figures.

PART FOUR

INVESTMENTS FOR TODAY AND TOMORROW

14

Investing in times like these

THE CHOICES YOU FACE

What's a level-headed investor to do these days? Only a few short years ago, the answer seemed simple. If you wanted a source of steady income, you bought high-quality corporate or government bonds, sat back and collected your interest. If you insisted on keeping your capital close to home, the natural thing to do was to stick it in a passbook savings account. If you wanted capital gains and were willing to wait a while to get them, you put your money into common stocks.

Or so it was said. But high inflation, a long period of sluggish stock market movement and increasingly common forecasts of impending economic calamity have wreaked havoc with traditional American notions of saving and investing. Anyone who hopes to survive the years ahead with his capital intact—let alone to make it grow—has long since reconsidered the options.

What should you be doing with the money you are setting aside for the future—for college bills, retirement, the down payment on a house? If you're like a lot of others, you've been putting much of that money into short-term propositions that offered a chance to take advantage of high interest rates. And in fact, concentrating on certificates of deposit, Treasury bills and money-market funds has proven to be a pretty good strategy—so good that you may have forgotten the long-range benefits of a more diversified approach to investing.

Today there are three principles on which most investment advisers would probably agree; 1) No one kind of investment works best all the time; 2) Diversification of your invested funds offers the best chance for finding profitable opportunities and avoiding major reversals; and 3) Liquidity—the ability to change a substantial portion of your asset mix quickly—is the key to survival in an uncertain investment climate. If you have committed most of your funds to one particular investment approach, now might be a good time to think about developing a long-range plan that covers a broader range of investments.

Diversification does not mean dividing your money equally among stocks, bonds, real estate and so forth. You have to find investments that are by their nature suited to your objectives and then mix them in combinations that are suited to market conditions.

Theoretically, that should be fairly easy because there are investments suited to practically every purpose. The next six chapters will discuss many of the choices in detail, ranging from ultraconservative, supersafe instruments such as Treasury bills to frankly speculative markets such as options and futures. Some of these investments you wouldn't want to touch with a ten-foot pole, and that's as it should be. Stick to what feels comfortable.

Take note of where you stand. At regular intervals—say, once a year—sit down and add up the value of all your investments, including the equity in your home. (The forms in chapter 1 will help you do this.) To get a picture of your asset distribution, compute each type of investment—stocks, bonds, real estate, gold and so forth—as a percentage of the total. Does the result surprise you? If you haven't already achieved a suitable asset mix, you now know which parts have to be increased, which cut back. As the years go by, the percentage mix of your investments will change without your lifting a finger, as some parts of your portfolio rise in value and others fall. This is what makes a periodic review so important.

Stay in your risk zone. The standard approach among professional investment counselors is first to determine their client's risk tolerance. How much risk you are prepared to assume dictates the kinds of investments you should have and the return you can expect. You can get by nicely most of the time by observing two commonsense rules:

• Don't invest in anything that still leaves you uneasy after you have investigated its strengths and weaknesses.

• Don't buy anything you don't know how to sell.

Adopt a clear-cut strategy. Reading brokerage house reports and financial publications is a reliable way to get an idea of how contradictory investment advice can be. The same factors used to explain today's drop in stocks may be advanced as the reason for tomorrow's rise. While one broker urges buying utility stocks and selling steel, another may be advising his clients to sell utilities and buy steel. It's the unpredictability of the future, not lack of expertise, that creates such seemingly absurd contradictions. In fact, security analysts produce a vast amount of useful information. But don't depend on them for a surefire investment program. They can help you pick securities if that's what you want. But you have to formulate your own strategy. It needn't be very elaborate, but it should be specific. For example, three different investors might devise strategies like these:

"I believe that common stocks are by their nature too unstable for me, and I will limit my stock investments, even during rising markets, to 15%."

Or, "Real estate, despite occasional setbacks, offers the best chance of long-term gain. I will try to keep 50% of my assets in real estate and divide the remainder between major growth company stocks and short-term debt instruments."

Or, "I plan to be a passive investor, spreading my funds across a wide range of investments in the hope that gains in some categories will eventually exceed losses in others. I will try to invest 20% in growth company shares, 30% in bonds, 10% in convertible bonds, 30% in money-market funds and certificates of deposit, and 10% in shares of a real estate investment trust."

Be prepared to change. From time to time you will have to adjust your investments to stay within your limits. You may occasionally want to revise your strategy as your situation changes. Retirement, for instance, may suggest a switch from equities to fixed-income securities.

You can modify your asset mix by allocating new investment money from savings, dividends and interest to the category you want to increase. But market shifts sometimes dictate selling off big chunks of your assets. Abrupt changes expose you to a whipsaw action: A stock drops, you sell and switch to bonds, the stock recovers and the bonds decline.

Only clairvoyance will unfailingly tell you the correct moment to sell or buy, so resign yourself to mistakes. Institutional investors aren't necessarily any better at timing portfolio revisions than you are, despite all their expert help.

Some investors try to avoid the problem by selling on the basis of fixed gain-and-loss limits. They sell when the price increases or declines by predetermined amounts. A broker can arrange this sort of approach for you.

You can control the distribution of your investment assets more easily with mutual funds than with individual stocks or bonds. Each fund's shares give you a stake in a diversified portfolio of similar securities. You can move from one no-load fund to another without incurring any commission costs. And many of the load fund groups permit you to exchange shares in one fund for another in the same group without paying an additional sales charge. (See chapter 17 for more on this.)

Don't expect too much. How much you make depends on not only what you buy but also when you buy it and when you sell it. The potential gains are easy to exaggerate by looking back only at an investment's most favorable period for buying or selling.

Keep in mind the trade-off between risk and return. The conservative investor sacrifices potential gain to limit his potential losses. The more aggressive investor sacrifices safety to raise the potential gain.

INVESTING IN THE YEARS AHEAD

Although no one can predict the future in much detail, there are a number of strong trends in the works that should create investment opportunities.

Population growth is one of them. By 1990, the population will be approaching 250 million—roughly 10% higher than in 1981. That means about 20 million more people creating demand for additional goods and services.

More important than the total, however, is the mix. The population will be undergoing significant shifts in the years to come.

- The single largest adult age group will be the 25- to 34-year-olds. They constitute a prime market for homes and the things that go in them. Sellers of such products should do a brisk business throughout the decade.
- The number of new 18- to 24-year-olds will shrink, easing the need for the job market to create entry-level positions for new workers. The result should be a lower unemployment rate as the decade proceeds. At the same time colleges and other institutions that have depended on young adults as their primary clients will have to widen their appeal or suffer the consequences.
- The growth in practically every other age bracket will mean shifting tastes in the things people buy. Older adults, further along in their working lives, have more money to spend than the youngsters who constituted the major marketing target of the 1960s and 1970s. They represent a potential boon to businesses that serve them.

Changes of this magnitude involve millions of people. By 1990 there will be some 4,000,000 fewer 18- to 24-year-olds than now, though there will still be 25,000,000 of them. There will be 10,000,000 more 35- to 44-year-olds, 3,000,000 more 45- to 54-year-olds. Numbers like that translate to major markets for business.

Changes of this magnitude also translate into promising long-term investment opportunities.

Stocks. Difficult as it is to select individual companies that stand to benefit most from developments in the 1980s, it is possible to anticipate the industries that seem most likely to gain. When stock market prognosticators talk about good investments, three categories crop up again and again in their forecasts: technology, communications and national defense.

• *Technology*. Many market analysts believe that we are in the early stages of a technological revolution equal to any that has gone before. If they are right, the key to that revolution will likely be electronics or, more precisely, electronic miniaturization. Companies are still discovering new uses for microprocessors, integrated circuits and other technological wonders that have already brought us pocket calculators, home computers and "intelligent" typewriters and telephones. Although it is difficult for small, emerging firms to finance the kind of research that leads to major breakthroughs, several have been successful in devising new applications for components developed by others.

• *Communications*. Much effort in the future will be in an area some analysts have begun to call "telematics," a linking of computers with telecommunications instruments, such as TV sets and telephones. Those games you play on your TV screen are examples of telematics, as are the experimental hookups in some places that permit consumers to order from catalogs, vote in opinion polls and talk back to broadcasts on their home TV sets. Business applications of telematics should provide a lucrative market for makers of products that save time and travel costs through inter-office connections for data retrieval, word processing and instant copying. The leading companies in this area will have easily recognizable names—IBM, AT&T—but investors will also be on the lookout for smaller companies with good ideas and marketing know-how.

• *Defense*. Congress and the President alike seem determined to infuse the U.S. military with billions of additional dollars over the next several years. This means that companies making things the military buys should benefit from increased orders. But scout out these firms with caution. Shares of the major defense contractors have benefited already from talk of the increased spending.

• *Other promising areas*. There are other, smaller industries in good position to profit during the 1980s. Manufacturers of furniture, appliances, carpets and rugs should find fast-growing markets for their products. Makers of synthetic fibers, such as acrylics, polyesters, vinyls and nylons, should prosper. The home entertainment industry—television sets, record and tape players, video recorders—looks strong. In the energy field, coal mining seems poised for some solid growth. Among the service industries, financial, insurance and real estate companies should do well.

These industries will be some of the laggards in the 1980s: leather goods, cigarettes and tobacco, candy, highway construction, dairy products and printing. They are expected to grow only a little or not at all.

Real Estate. Certainly one of the best investments anyone could have made in the past several years has been a house. That should continue to be the case in the decade ahead. A study done for the National Association of Home Builders projects that housing prices will rise 9% to 10% a year throughout the 1980s. According to the study, the median price of a new house in 1987 will be $118,000. That sounds like a whopping price, but incomes are expected to keep up, and the demand created by the large number of 25- to 34-year-olds setting up housekeeping should help keep pressure on the market.

You have probably read more than one report about how the average family can no longer afford to buy a house. To keep such reports in perspective, note this: About two-thirds of American households already own their homes. As prices rise, homeowners are the chief beneficiaries, and many eventually decide to invest their equity in more expensive homes. That fact, coupled with population growth, should assure a steady demand for housing throughout the 1980s. Town houses and condominiums will make significant inroads in the market, but most buyers will still want single-family dwellings.

The outlook for commercial real estate investments is less certain. The market has been clobbered before—most recently in 1974–75—and could be again. The best investments will be in the fastest-growing areas, primarily the principal cities in the sunbelt region of the South and West. The Pacific Coast will gain more than any other region; the Census Bureau estimates that about 4,000,000 more people will be living there by 1990. One trend you shouldn't count on too heavily in the 1980s is the move back to the cities. With the exception of some areas of a few cities, the strongest lure for newcomers to a region will still be the suburbs.

How do you cash in on the investment opportunities that lie ahead? That's what the next six chapters are about.

15

Ins and outs of common stocks

After several years of turning up their noses at common stocks, small investors are growing increasingly interested in owning equities again. So reports the New York Stock Exchange, which surveys patterns of stock ownership every few years. The stock market still hasn't quite regained its most-favored status in the hearts and portfolios of American investors, but it has come a long way back.

The number of individuals owning shares of stock actually peaked in 1970 at about 31 million. By 1975 that number had dwindled to just over 25 million, no doubt a reflection of the frustrating performance of the stock market in the intervening years. But by 1980 the shareholder population had recouped all but a million of its numbers, climbing back up to the neighborhood of 30 million.

A number of factors have contributed to this renewed interest in owning stocks. For one thing, the number of people holding shares in the companies they work for through Employee Stock Ownership Plans nearly doubled between 1975 and 1980 to 12 million. Also, the growing ranks of working women began acquiring investment portfolios in the 1970s. Then, in 1978, Congress voted a substantial reduction in the capital gains tax, an act that probably stimulated more interest in owning stocks.

The people who run the stock exchanges read those numbers a different way. They like to think Americans are regaining their traditional faith in the stock market as a sensible and promising place to put their money.

Certainly there is no shortage of cheery prognostications for the long-range future of stock prices. And judged by historical relationships, such as the ratio of share prices to company earnings, many common stock issues do appear to be bargains.

In short, if you wanted to construct a convincing case for investing in common stocks, you could. But as an individual investor, the general trend of the stock market is not necessarily your primary concern. What you have to do is pick the right stocks—the ones that will repay your faith with solid profits.

HOW TO PICK STOCKS

Most of the information and advice you need to analyze securities and develop an investment strategy are available free. But ironically, the very abundance of investment advice and material may make your task even more difficult. During any given week brokers and analysts suggest hundreds of individual stocks. You want to buy just a few. By employing the proper analytical tools, you should be able to identify the stocks most likely to meet your special needs. As a start, learn the basic methods for gauging security values.

Earnings per share. For the ordinary investor EPS constitutes that "bottom line" you hear so much about because it distills all the company's financial experiences into a neat, easily understood figure.

Simply defined, earnings per share is the company's net income (after taxes and funds are set aside for preferred stock dividends) divided by the average number of common stock shares outstanding. EPS figures are sometimes refined to differentiate between income produced by regular operations and income resulting from unusual transactions, say the sale of a subsidiary.

Customarily, when a company is described as growing at a certain rate, it's the EPS that's being used as the measure.

Price-to-earnings ratio. Divide the current price of a stock by its EPS for the last 12-month period and you have the price-earnings ratio—or the multiple, as it is often called. The P/E is probably the single most widely used analytical tool. What makes it so important is that it mirrors investors' opinions of a particular stock compared with the stock market as a whole.

The fact that investors are willing to pay 12 times earnings for stock A and only seven times for stock B tells you instantly that A is more highly regarded than B. Presumably, investors feel more confident that company A will be able to increase its earnings, or increase them faster, or pay higher dividends—an especially significant consideration during bear markets, when dividends help offset losses in stock prices.

Multiples change constantly. Any company's P/E doesn't provide an investment clue until it's compared with P/E values of the same company over past years, the P/Es of other companies in the same business and the P/E based on stock indexes representing the market as a whole. (The *Wall Street Journal* publishes the average multiple of the Dow Jones industrial-stock index on Mondays. Standard & Poor's 500-stock index average multiple can be found in S&P's weekly publication, *The Outlook*, which may be available at a large library.)

To see why relative P/E figures must be used, consider this case: Eastman Kodak's multiple plummeted from 36 times earnings in 1972 to an average of about nine in 1979. But Polaroid, Kodak's prime competitor, and the S&P index as a whole, also suffered large losses during the same period. The Eastman Kodak drop was therefore not as catastrophic as it appeared standing alone (although the decline did produce heavy losses for Kodak shareholders).

The link between earnings and multiples may seem to suggest a strategy of buying high P/E stocks on the assumption that faster growth will ultimately lead to still higher prices. Actually, one study found that low P/E stocks resulted in better returns, at least during the 14-year period studied.

Whatever the stock you intend to buy, you want to get it at the lowest possible P/E. As other investors begin to recognize the stock's potential, they may bid up the multiple, thereby giving the stock additional price momentum as the company's earnings per share rise. That is your hope, but reality doesn't always oblige. In depressed markets a rise in earnings per share may actually be accompanied by a drop in the multiple.

Book Value. Shorn of technicalities, book value—or stockholders' equity, as it may be referred to—is based on the difference between a company's assets and its liabilities. Dividing that figure by the number of outstanding shares gives you the book value per share.

Theoretically, book value represents the amount

stockholders would receive for each share they own if the company were to sell all its assets, pay all its debts and go out of business. Few companies whose shares are widely traded ever do shut their doors. Still, stocks are often recommended as cheap because they are selling below book value or very little above.

Those relationships could prove significant, but you should have more information to go on before you start buying. At one point, stocks of all five of the major tire companies were selling at 47% to 75.5% below their book values. But investors saw little reason to pay more at that time, and for good reason.

The tire industry's financial situation had deteriorated seriously as a result of auto production cutbacks and a drop in car usage. Indeed, it was about then that a smaller producer, Mansfield Tire & Rubber Company, filed for protection under the federal bankruptcy law.

Return on book value. A company's total net income, expressed as a percentage of total book value, measures how much the company earns on the stockholders' stake in the enterprise. Return on book value, also called return on equity, varies greatly among companies and fluctuates with economic conditions. The top 25% of insured banks had 15.6% or higher return on equity in 1978; the lowest 25% reported 6.2% or less. From 1936 through 1978 the return on equity of the 30 companies in the Dow Jones industrial-stock index ranged from a low of 6.9% in 1938 to a high of 15.8% in 1950.

Total return. Stockholders tend to think of gains and losses in terms of price changes rather than dividends. Bond owners focus on interest yields and may ignore price changes.

Compartmentalizing price changes and income often makes sense. If your objective is to maximize current income, you're interested primarily in dividend and interest yields. On the other hand, you may prefer a stock with a low dividend but a lot of price potential if you want the income tax break you get for capital gains.

Nevertheless, both price changes and current income should be taken into account to evaluate investment performance. Together, they show your total return, which makes it possible to compare stocks with bonds, preferred stocks, Treasury bills and other alternative investments. You can roughly approximate a stock's total return by adding (or subtracting) the price change and the dividends for the past 12 months and then dividing by the price at the start of the period.

Volatility. Some stocks' prices move slowly and within a relatively narrow band; others roll and pitch about. The freewheeling stocks naturally involve more risk because when they go down, they may go way down. Analysts have developed a special measure of price volatility called *beta,* which tells you how much a stock characteristically moves in relation to a change in the S&P 500-stock index. A 1.10 beta stock, for instance, historically rises or falls more than the index. A .98 beta stock is less volatile than the index—it would be expected to go up 9.8% if the market rises 10% or down by 9.8% if the index falls 10%.

Unfortunately, this convenient indicator isn't usually available to ordinary investors. Your broker might be able to obtain some of the figures, though, from research prepared for institutional clients. You can estimate volatility for a given period on your own by using this shortcut formula:

$$\frac{\text{high price} - \text{low price}}{\text{average of high} + \text{low price}} \times 100 = \text{volatility \%}$$

The volatility percentage you calculate this way for any single stock has to be measured against similarly computed figures—not the actual betas—for other stocks you are considering.

Professional analysts employ a number of other evaluation techniques, many of which rarely show up in reports for public distribution. David L. Babson & Company, a Boston-based advisory firm that manages about four billion dollars in investments, uses a 15-point scale to rate companies. Here's an abbreviated sample analysis of Schlumberger, Ltd., a leading oil-field service company showing the factors Babson considers important and how Schlumberger fared.

Babson score	factors
2+	Growth in sales, adjusted for inflation, 1973–78.
1.5+	Relative control over costs and pretax profit margins.
2+	Pricing flexibility.
2+	Ability to finance growth internally.
2+	Consistency of earnings growth.
1+	Leading position in its key product lines.
1+	Conservative, understandable accounting; earnings and assets not seriously distorted by inflation or acquisitions.
1+	Limited exposure to environmental, social and political pressures.
2+	Annual dividend growth relative to cost-of-living increase.
14.5+	

Schlumberger's near-perfect score explains why the stock was owned by about 500 banks, investment companies and insurance companies at the time the score was compiled.

Technical analysis. From time to time you may come across buy or sell recommendations that reflect what is known as technical analysis. Technicians try to forecast price movements by examining previous price changes, shifts in margin debt, the ratio of advancing to declining stocks, the volume of short sales, and a wide and sometimes bewildering range of other statistical material. To technicians these factors, often plotted on charts, reveal the basic forces that they believe raise or lower prices.

Technicians speak their own language, particularly when referring to chart patterns they feel have special significance—heads and shoulders, channels, saucers, wedges, pennants, double bottoms.

Although critics may scoff at such apparent mumbo jumbo, technical analysis commands respect among n any in the investment business. And committed adhe rents of fundamental analysis, the opposite school, often check a stock's technical position before acting.

DEVISING AN INVESTMENT STRATEGY

About 4,000 stock issues are traded on the various exchanges. Another 3,000 or so trade over the counter in the NASDAQ network of the National Association of Securities Dealers. Countless other issues are bought and sold elsewhere.

You can't by yourself sort through that huge collection for the relatively few stocks you intend to buy. Once in a while you may come across an interesting company through business or personal contacts. For the most part, though, you have to look for investment prospects among the recommendations of the brokerage firms and financial publications. Sifting through their leads will be much easier if you first take the time to decide on an overall investment strategy.

Buy and hold? Typically, investors in this category prefer to hold their stocks a long time—three, five, ten years or more. They are prepared to ride out market declines in the hope that the inherent strength of their companies will ultimately reward them with higher earnings, dividends and prices.

Buy-and-hold investors often favor such prominent companies as IBM, Procter & Gamble, Minnesota Mining & Manufacturing, Coca-Cola, Merck & Company, American Home Products, Johnson & Johnson, Xerox, Halliburton, Lubrizol and Burroughs. Many of those huge corporations have consistently raised per-share earnings at high rates. Johnson & Johnson increased earnings per share at an 18.6% annual compound rate for 1968–78; Burroughs, 16.8%; IBM, 13.2%. Some investors look for smaller companies with high annual growth rates.

The big growth company stocks were the darlings of the market in the 1950s and 1960s, when some were bid up to lofty price-earnings multiples. They fell out of favor in the early 1970s but turned around again late in the decade.

Over the past few years many long- and short-term investors have been searching for the IBMs and Xeroxes of the future among high-technology firms— big corporations on the order of Texas Instruments and Memorex, as well as smaller companies like Medtronic, Advanced Micro-Devices and California Microwave. However, a growth company may pop up in any field.

A buy-and-hold strategy does not necessarily imply growth stocks. Some people feel more comfortable with General Motors, American Telephone & Telegraph and other giants that are so integral to the economy that they must prosper—so the theory goes—as the nation grows.

If you're essentially a conservative buy-and-hold investor who wants to keep some assets in stocks at all times, ask your broker to suggest a few favorably priced big companies with consistently high earnings and a record of increasing dividends. In the trade they are often referred to as the quality companies.

Move with the tide? Ideally, you should be able to improve your returns by anticipating or at least moving with the ups and downs in the economy. If you anticipate an upturn, it would be logical to concentrate on industries that should benefit most—retail stores, entertainment companies, machinery producers, autos and so on. You sell them as the economy starts to top off, and you shift into issues that tend to resist recessions—household-supply manufacturers, distillers, retail food chains, life insurers and others, referred to as "defensive" issues.

Bet on one industry? Individual industries are always pushing to the forefront of the investment field as a result of economic or social changes, technological developments and marketing innovations, and sometimes for obscure reasons that seem no more weighty than market fads. New marketing concepts can create whole new businesses—discount chains, fast-food franchises, hospital administration companies. Technological advances, such as the miniaturization of electronic parts, may spawn a host of new products and services.

Your hope to capitalize on such trends lies in picking stocks in the industry before the boom starts or while it is in its early stages. For maximum effect, look for what the analysts call "pure play" companies, those that specialize in the field and so stand to gain most. Many big corporations are so highly diversified that gains in any one product may not substantially increase total profits.

In most cases you should plan to sell a stock when its price appears to be reaching a plateau. If you're lucky, one of the companies could turn into a growth leader that you can hold for the long pull.

Executives may be better placed than outsiders to spot opportunities in their own industries, so look first in your own field. Trade journals sometimes provide good clues, and many professional analysts read them religiously.

Should you speculate? When you're taking a flier, the long-term qualities of the stock aren't as important as the near term potential. You're looking for issues that will jump rather than crawl: Companies selling stock to the public for the first time, corporations likely to be bought out by another company or to buy out another company, "concept" companies promoting some new product or service, or turnaround stocks that have been severely depressed and are expected to snap back.

You can speculate with any stock by the way you trade it. Buying on margin (financing part of the purchase with a loan from the broker) and selling short (selling borrowed shares in the hope of replacing them later with shares bought at a lower rate) increase the risk and the potential return. Options and futures, described in chapter 19, are favorite tools of speculators.

Another speculative approach involves betting on relatively short term swings in the market. When the market appears ready for a rise, you buy high-volatility stocks, the ones with high betas, because they should go up more than the market as a whole. When prices are topping off, you cash in everything and put the money into a more neutral investment—perhaps money-market instruments—to wait for the next upswing.

Should you diversify? Committing all your funds to one or a few of even the most conservative issues could expose you to greater losses than owning a flock of speculative stocks.

J. Russell Holmes, who delved into stock returns produced over a 107-year period, concluded that one of the three keys to succeeding in the market was to "think in terms of portfolios, not individual issues." The other two, according to Holmes, are taking time to select issues with growth potential and holding stock for the long term (ten- to fifteen-year periods).

How many stocks it takes to diversify properly depends on several technical factors. One study indicates that you need a minimum of ten separate issues if you're dealing with high-quality companies. Another way to spread the risk would be to buy just a few individual issues and buffer them with shares in mutual funds, whose portfolios will ordinarily hold no fewer than forty issues. Mutual funds are the subject of chapter 17.

CUTTING THE COSTS
OF BUYING AND SELLING

Ordinarily the last thing you worry about when you choose a stock is the commission you'll have to pay to buy and sell it. But commission costs can't be easily ignored. For some time now, they have been heading upward, so shopping around for the best rates can pay off.

Unfortunately, commission rates can be difficult to compare. A businessman with more than $100,000 in the stock market complained to the *New York Times* not long ago that when he tried to get commission schedules from several large brokerage firms, his requests were mostly ignored. One firm claimed to have no published schedule. Another said he could get the rates from an account executive if he were preparing to place an order. Among the schedules he did receive, some were so complicated that they were practically indecipherable.

If you have a good working relationship with a broker, and if he provides valuable help in making your investment decisions, then probably commissions aren't much of a concern. Most people select a brokerage firm for reasons that have nothing to do with commissions, anyway—perhaps its office is conveniently located, its research reports are useful or the account executive is helpful. Factors such as these can easily compensate for the commissions, especially for relatively modest investors.

However, if you don't want or don't need such services, or if you make a sizable number of trades during the course of a year, then the easiest way to save is to use a discount broker. These were mostly bare-bones "pipe rack" operations when they first started to appear in the early 1970s. They shaved overhead costs by doing without large sales and research staffs and spiffy offices, passing along the savings in lower commission rates. Discounters also tended to be local operations, not big national chains.

But the discount brokerage business has changed over the years. Today there are about 100 such firms, some of them members of the New York Stock Exchange with offices in several cities around the country. A few provide research reports, but most are set up only to execute buy and sell orders for investors who make their own decisions. Most have toll-free telephone numbers for distant clients or will accept collect calls. Discounts, depending on the size of the transaction, can amount to as much as 80% of what you'd pay a full service broker, although 20% to 30% is a more representative saving.

It is simple enough to open an account with a discounter by calling or writing for an application. But before you sign on, find out if there is a minimum commission charge. Some firms set a $25 or $30 minimum fee regardless of the size of the trade. On small trades, that could wipe out the savings you might be anticipating. Also ask about annual service charges. Some firms, wishing to limit their business to well-heeled investors, levy an annual fee to keep the small ones away.

Here is a listing of some well-established discount brokers. All are members of the Securities Investor Protection Corporation, meaning customers' accounts are protected up to $500,000 against the possibility of the firm's failure. Some of the firms have offices in more than one city. For them, the address of the headquarters office is given. Toll-free numbers are for out-of-state calls. If the firm has a toll-free number for long-distance calls within its state, that is listed second.

C. D. Anderson & Co.,
   Inc.
Suite 440
300 Montgomery St.
San Francisco, Calif.
   94104
800-227-4216
800-622-0875 (Calif.)
800-227-3033 (Alaska &
   Hawaii)

Brokers Exchange, Inc.
8580-A Laureldale Drive
Laurel, Md. 20810
800-492-1278
301-490-9200 (Md.)

Brown & Co. Securities
   Corp.
7 Water St.
Boston, Mass. 02109
800-225-6707
1-800-392-6077 (Mass.)
     742-2600 (local)

Burke, Christensen &
  Lewis Securities, Inc.
120 S. LaSalle St.
Chicago, Ill. 60603
800-972-1633
312-346-8283

W. T. Cabe & Co., Inc.
1270 Ave. of the
  Americas
New York, N.Y. 10020
800-223-6555
212-541-6690

Columbine Securities,
  Inc.
2020 Prudential Plaza
1050 Seventeenth St.
Denver, Colo. 80265
303-524-3344

Discount Brokerage
  Corp.
67 Wall St.
New York, N.Y. 10005
800-221-5088
943-8500 (local)

Fidelity Brokerage
  Services, Inc.
161 Devonshire St.
Boston, Mass. 02208
800-225-2097
800-882-1269

Icahn & Co., Inc.
25 Broadway
New York, N.Y. 10004
1-800-221-5735
212-422-5937

Kenneth Kass & Co.
301 Main St.
Chatham, N.J. 07928
800-243-4549
800-922-7288 (Conn.)

Kashner Lodge
  Securities Corp.
10 S. Adams Drive
Sarasota, Fla. 33577
800-237-9631
800-282-9420 (Fla.)

Letterman Transaction
  Services, Inc.
19742 MacArthur Blvd.
Irvine, Calif. 92715
800-854-3564
800-854-0307 (Alaska &
  Hawaii)
800-432-7008 (Calif.)
  752-0070 (local)

Odd Lots Securities,
  Ltd.
60 E. 42nd St.
New York, N.Y. 10165
800-221-2095
800-442-5929 (N.Y. state)
  661-6755 (local)

Ovest Securities, Inc.
76 Beaver St.
New York, N.Y. 10005
800-221-5713
212-425-3003

Andrew Peck
  Associates, Inc.
32 Broadway
New York, N.Y. 10004
800-221-5873
212-363-3770

Quick & Reilly, Inc.
120 Wall St.
New York, N.Y. 10005
800-221-5220
800-522-8712 (N.Y. state)
    943-8686 (local)

ReCom Securities, Inc.
644 IDS Tower
Minneapolis, Minn.
  55402
800-328-8600
800-292-7923

Rose & Company
Board of Trade Bldg.
Chicago, Ill. 60604
800-621-3700
800-572-3188 (Ill.)
    987-9400 (local)

Royal Investors Group,
  Inc.
120 Wall St.
New York, N.Y. 10005
800-221-9900
212-635-0880

Charles Schwab & Co.,
  Inc.
One Second St.
San Francisco, Calif.
  94105
800-227-4444
800-227-3020 (Hawaii &
  Alaska)
800-648-5300 (Calif.)

Muriel Siebert & Co.,
  Inc.
77 Water St.
New York, N.Y. 10005
800-221-4206
212-248-0618

Source Securities Corp.
70 Pine St.
New York, N.Y. 10005
800-221-5338
212-422-6000

Springer Investment &
  Securities Co., Inc.
6060 N. College Ave.
P.O. Box 20395
Indianapolis, Ind. 46220
317-255-6673

Stockcross
One Washington Mall
Boston, Mass. 02108
1-800-225-6196
1-800-392-6104 (Mass.)
   367-5700 (local)

Thrift Trading, Inc.
223 Northstar Ctr.
Minneapolis, Minn.
  55402
612-335-4206

Tradex Brokerage
  Service, Inc.
82 Beaver St.
New York, N.Y. 10005
800-221-7874
212-425-7800

DON'T MAKE THESE
INVESTMENT MISTAKES

It has been said that the winners of tennis matches, football games, even battles, are those who make the fewest mistakes. Or, to put it another way, the winners are those who manage not to lose. The same could be said for the stock market. One major requirement for successful investing is to keep mistakes to a minimum.

What are the most common ways investors go wrong? *Changing Times* magazine has examined this question over the years and has discovered 10 recurring mistakes you would do well to avoid.

1. *Not having an investment plan or philosophy*. This error takes various forms. Without the guidance of a long-range objective, you fail to decide in advance what type of company you want to own stocks in— long-term growth companies, cyclical or speculative ones. You don't decide whether you want current income or capital gains. You shoot from the hip. If by

chance you do have a plan, you abandon it when the market is bursting with optimism or sulking with pessimism.

2. *Being optimistic at the top and pessimistic at the bottom.* Optimism and bullishness are infectious, as are pessimism and bearishness. Thus, even when the market is high by such standards as the ratio of prices to earnings, people go right on buying. They do it because everyone seems to be buying or because they extrapolate recent trends and assume that what has been happening will continue to happen or because they mistakenly think there is an exact correlation between the stock market and level of business. Conversely, people grow increasingly pessimistic as the market drops and tend to reach the bottom of the pit when stocks are cheapest. This is when they should be buying, or at least holding on to what they have.

3. *Not taking the trouble and time to be informed.* One broker says that many investors prove to him that colleges still don't teach practical economics. "Some customers," he says, "don't know the difference between a stock and a bond."

Failing to get information about the company they invest in is another variation. Says one adviser, "They don't read the annual report or look up the company in the financial manuals. In some cases they don't even know what the company makes or whether its products have any future at all."

4. *Not getting the best advice.* Many investors don't check on a broker or adviser before doing business with him. They don't investigate, for example, his educational background, how long he has been in business or been handling other people's money, how well he has done. They don't ask to see sample accounts.

In the words of the manager of a large mutual funds

complex, "Following the advice of a mediocre broker is known as a 'cut flower' program. The broker keeps picking flowers and selling them to you. When one bunch withers, he sells you another. It's not like having your own garden."

5. *Investing money that should be set aside for another use.* Too often people tie up money that should be available for emergencies or for purchase of a new car or some other predictable expense. If you invest what should be emergency funds in stocks, you may be forced into selling stocks at a time not of your own choosing. Fate often decrees that this will be a period of low prices when you must take a loss.

6. *Buying on the basis of tips and rumors.* There's hardly any chance that the average investor will get advance or inside information about any company whose stock is publicly held. And even if he does, there is very little chance that it will do him any good. Remember, there are professional speculators watching the Dow Jones broad tape all day long. This tape prints business news as it happens minute by minute. Then there are the specialists who make a market in each stock listed on the various exchanges. At any rumor about a company or any unusual change in the volume of trading, the specialist calls up the company's management and gets the pertinent facts.

So no matter how hot a tip you hear, remember: Someone knew it before you did.

7. *Buying low-priced stocks on the theory that they will show the largest percentage gains.* A low-priced stock may be a bargain, but not necessarily because it is low priced. The price of a stock is what the marketplace believes a company to be worth divided by the number of shares outstanding.

8. *Becoming sentimental about a stock or an indus-*

try. Some investors become as fond of their stocks as they do of their pets. As a result, companies can be held long after they have lost their potential for growth and profit. A similar mistake is for an investor to fail to sell a stock because he hates to admit he was wrong in buying it.

9. *Selling the winners and holding the losers*. Investors tend to hold stocks in which they have a loss in the hope, often vain, that they will come back. On the other hand, they tend to "nail down profits" by selling stocks in which they have a capital gain. In this way investors sell the best stocks and keep the worst.

10. *Failing to learn from mistakes*. Bernard Baruch, who made a fortune in the stock market and gained public acclaim for his years of service as a high-level adviser to U.S. presidents, knew how to avoid this trap. "I began a habit I was never to forsake—of analysing my losses to determine where I had made my mistakes," he wrote. "This was a practice I was to develop ever more systematically as my operations grew in size. After each major undertaking—and particularly when things had turned sour—I would shake loose from Wall Street and go off to some quiet place where I could review what I had done and where I had gone wrong."

16

Bonds and other fixed-income investments

Buying fixed-income securities was once considered a humdrum approach to investing, suitable mainly for retired people or those with a steady need for ready cash. But several developments in the later years of the 1970s and the early months of the 1980s changed that perception drastically. The stock marked turned in a mostly dreary performance over that period, and would-be stock investors began to look with more favor on the guaranteed return offered by bonds. Then, as inflation heated up, interest rates creeped up, too, making new bonds even more attractive in the face of a persistently sluggish stock market.

But as inflation persisted, bonds issued at what seemed like high rates actually lost value as time went by. Potential buyers weren't willing to pay full face value for bonds yielding 10% when they could easily obtain, say, 12% elsewhere. Thus, the 10% bonds had to be sold at a discount, meaning a loss to the seller. For those who elected to hold on, that 10% return started to look pretty puny when inflation topped 13%. And eventually inflation worked the same whammy on buyers of those 12% bonds. Breathtaking swings in interest rates dealt quick losses to fixed-income investors unlucky enough to have bought at or near the bottoms of the swings.

So it is clear that the sedate image of fixed-income investing is a thing of the past, another of inflation's victims. The bond markets, and markets for other fixed-income instruments, are tricky territory these days. And they will remain that way until inflation settles down into a slower, more predictable track.

Still, the temptation is there: With bond rates running so far above their historical highs, wouldn't it be smart to buy some in anticipation of the time—maybe several years away—when interest rates could be running closer to their traditional patterns? An unequivocal answer to that question requires an ability to predict the future, and thus is impossible. If interest rates do indeed fall significantly in the next few years, then bonds issued today could pay off handsomely if owners are able to sell them at a premium over their face value or hold onto them and collect the interest. But if rates go higher, bonds available at today's prices will become cheaper, and those who buy them will lose.

Fortunately, investors drawn to fixed-income securities aren't limited to the choice of whether or not to buy bonds. The marketplace is wide and diverse, and it contains opportunities to hedge inflation, trim taxes, even secure capital gains that are virtually guaranteed. This chapter will discuss those and other opportunities.

A PRIMER FOR INCOME INVESTORS

In their basic form, *bonds* and other credit instruments, such as *notes, bills,* and *commercial paper,* bind the issuing organization to pay a fixed amount of interest each year and repay the full face amount of the instrument on its maturity date, which is set when the bond is issued.

Corporations and governments regularly finance their operations by selling credit instruments. *Agency securities* are issues of various U.S. government agencies, such as the Farm Credit Banks or the Federal National Mortgage Association. *Municipals,* also known as tax-exempts, are issued by state and local governments.

Secured bonds are backed by a lien on part of a corporation's plant, equipment or other assets. Unsecured bonds, known as *debentures,* are backed only by the general credit of the corporation.

General obligation municipal bonds are secured by the full taxing power of the issuing organization. *Revenue bonds* depend on revenues from a specific source, such as bridge or road tolls. Some municipals are secured by revenues from a specific tax.

Corporations also pay a fixed annual amount on *preferred stock,* when their profit permits, but preferred shares represent an ownership stake in the corporation, not a debt. However, because of the fixed return, the price of preferred stocks tends to fluctuate more like bonds, in response to interest rate changes, than like common stocks.

Some bonds, debentures and preferred stocks are *convertible* into the corporation's common stock at a fixed ratio—a certain number of shares of common stock in exchange for a certain amount of bonds or preferred shares. Convertibles may sell at lower yields than nonconvertibles because of the possibility that the owner can make a profit on the conversion.

Denominations. The standard face value for bonds is $1,000 or $5,000. Some are issued in larger denominations; smaller denominations are less common.

Forms of ownership. Bonds and notes usually can be registered with the issuing organization in the name of the owner, just like common stock. *Bearer securities* are unregistered and thus presumed to be the property of whomever has possession of them. Bearer bonds are accompanied by coupons that must be sent to the paying agent in order to collect the interest. Sometimes ownership is in *book entry* form, meaning the issuer keeps a record of buyers' names but no securities actually change hands. Treasury bills are normally issued this way.

Schedule of interest payments. Most bonds pay interest semiannually. Many mutual funds and unit trusts invested in bonds pay dividends monthly as a convenience to shareholders. *Discount securities,* such as U.S. Treasury bills, pay interest immediately by deducting it from the sales price.

Terms of maturity. "Short" term refers to securities maturing in two years or less; "intermediate" term means maturities of up to ten years; and "long" term means securities maturing in ten or more years. Many bonds have been issued with 25- to 30-year maturities. *Notes* usually run about seven years. The lines separating the categories aren't hard and fast, however, so it's important to check the actual number of years to maturity for any security you're considering.

Call options. Issuers often retain the right to "call," meaning redeem, a bond at a specified date before the scheduled maturity. It has been customary to pay owners of called bonds a small premium over the face value.

Sinking funds. Some bond issues are retired gradually in installments under a "sinking fund" plan. The bonds are selected for redemption by lottery or bought on the open market.

Tax considerations. Interest and capital gains on corporate credit instruments are normally subject to federal, state and local income taxes. Income from Treasury and agency securities is subject to federal income taxes. All Treasury and some agency securities are exempt from state and local income taxes.

Interest on municipal bonds is exempt from federal income taxes. Most state and local governments exempt interest on their own bonds but tax income on securities issued by other states. Because of their tax advantage, municipals pay a lower interest rate than taxable bonds.

What's the yield? The *coupon rate* is the fixed annual interest payment expressed as a percentage of the face value. A 10% coupon bond, for instance, pays $100 a year interest on each $1,000 of face value. The rate is set when the bond is issued and does not change as the bond's price fluctuates.

- *Current yield* is the annual interest payment expressed as a percentage of the bond's current market price. Thus, a 10% coupon bond selling for $900 has a current yield of 11.1% ($100 interest divided by $900 price × 100).
- *Yield to maturity* takes into account the current yield and the eventual gain or loss it is assumed the owner will receive by holding to maturity a bond selling at a discount or a premium. If you pay $900 for a 10% coupon bond with a face value of $1,000 maturing five years from the date of purchase, you will earn not only $100 a year interest, but also an additional $100

five years later when the bond is redeemed for $1,000 by its issuer. That $100 of extra income may qualify for a tax break as a capital gain. By the same token, if you buy that bond for $1,100—representing a $100 premium—you will lose $100 at maturity. That $100 represents a capital loss. (The loss, however, could be more than offset by the extra interest earned on a premium-priced bond because its coupon rate presumably exceeds the current yield available on comparable securities. Tax considerations could also make the capital loss worth taking.) For bonds selling at a discount, the yield to maturity probably provides the best measure of total return.

- *Yield to call* is computed the same way as yield to maturity except that it is assumed the bond will be redeemed at the first call date for the face value plus the call premium. For a bond selling at a premium, it might be wise to use the next call date in calculating yield.

Effect of interest rate changes. Because the amount of interest paid on a credit instrument normally remains fixed for the life of the issue, the bond adjusts to interest rate movements by changes in price.

To see how that works, consider a newly issued $1,000 bond with a coupon interest rate of 10%—$100 a year. If interest rates rise to 11% after the bond is issued, you can sell your 10% bond only by offering it at a price that will deliver an 11% current yield to the buyer. So the price becomes whatever $100 represents 11% of, which is $909. Thus, you lose $91 if you sell. By the same token, if interest rates decline to 9% while you're holding your 10% bond, you can sell it for whatever $100 represents 9% of, which is $1,111. That's a $111 capital gain.

These examples oversimplify the relationship, since in the actual marketplace prices are also strongly influenced by the time remaining to the bond's maturity or possible call. But the underlying principle is the same: As interest rates rise, bond prices fall; as interest rates fall, bond prices rise. (More on this in the discussion of discount bonds later in the chapter.)

How prices are quoted. If you look them up in the financial pages of a newspaper, you'll find bond prices identified by the abbreviated name of the issuer, the coupon rate and the maturity date. The more common price lists give only the current yield, but your broker can get the yields to maturity and call for you. Prices are reported as a percentage of $100. To get the actual price, multiply the decimal equivalent of the percentage by 1,000. Thus, a Commonwealth Edison Company 8% bond maturing in 2003 might be reported as "ComwEd 8s03 89 3/4," meaning the issue is selling at the time of the listing for $897.50 per $1,000 face value, a fairly hefty discount.

WHAT DO BOND RATINGS MEAN?

When you set out to buy bonds, it is tempting to look for the highest possible yields. But yield figures can be misleading unless you also take into account the quality of the bond itself. If there is any doubt about the ability of the bond issuer to pay off on time, high yield could be poor compensation for the risk. That's why ordinary investors should stick to high-quality bonds. But what is high quality? And how high is high enough?

From top to bottom. At the top of the safety scale stand all those issues for which the U.S. government has a direct obligation to meet interest and principal payments. The government, after all, is the only borrower on the market that can print money to pay its debts if necessary.

Below that lofty level lie a vast array of securities issued by U.S. agencies, corporations and local government units—states, counties, cities. There you will find bonds ranging from those that are almost as solid as U.S. government issues to those close to or already in default.

Fortunately, you can quickly check a bond by its credit, or quality, rating. Most widely traded bonds are rated by at least one of the three agencies in the field—Moody's Investors Service, Standard & Poor's Corporation, and the lesser-known Fitch Investors Service. Their judgments can be valuable provided you know what they mean and how they affect market prices.

These are the rating categories used by the two major agencies:

	S&P	Moody's
investment grades	AAA	Aaa
	AA	Aa
	A	A
	BBB	Baa
speculative grades	BB	Ba
	B	B
	CCC	Caa
	CC	Ca
	C	C
	D	

Standard and Poor's AA, A, BBB, BB and B ratings are sometimes supplemented with a plus (+) or a minus (−) sign to raise or lower a bond's position within the group. Moody's may add the numeral *1* for tax-exempt issues in the A and Baa groups with somewhat stronger standings.

Ratings modified by *P,* for provisional, or *Con.,* for conditional, indicate that some condition has to be fulfilled before a final judgment can be made. For example, the bond may be backed by revenues from a project not yet completed.

The investment grades include the bonds that individual and institutional investors seeking stable income and safety ordinarily buy. BBB/Baa is the lowest rating that qualifies for commercial bank investments, but it's a borderline group for which, in Standard & Poor's words, "adverse economic conditions or changing circumstances are more likely to lead to a weakened capacity to pay interest and repay principal . . . than for bonds in higher-rated categories."

Below BBB/Baa you're in speculative territory. Bonds in the C and D ranks are in or near default.

Moody's and Standard & Poor's don't always agree on a bond's rank. It's not unusual for them to rate an issue one grade apart.

The price of quality. Credit ratings play a big role in determining the relative levels of bond prices. Normally, you pay a higher price for bonds with each notch you move up the quality scale. A triple-A usually costs more than a double-A with comparable characteristics (maturity, coupon interest rate, etc.), a double-A costs more than A, and so on. Looked at another way, the higher the quality, generally, the lower the yield.

The risk premium—the extra yield on lower-rated issues—tends to increase during extended stock market declines and business recessions. Presumably, unsettled economic conditions encourage investors to concentrate on top-quality bonds. Riskier issues can be sold in those periods only if they offer an extra-high yield.

It is true that few investment-grade issues have ever

defaulted—at least not during the past three decades. But there have been enough notable cases—Penn Central railroad, for one—to reinforce the attraction of A and higher ratings.

Many institutional investors, such as pension plans and mutual funds, limit themselves to A or higher-rated issues either by choice or for legal reasons. Some institutional investors have developed their own rating programs or hired special services to grade issues with greater precision than the broad categories used by Moody's and Standard & Poor's.

The rating agencies are supposed to track the financial condition of issuers and update their ratings if necessary. In fact, many issues are either upgraded or downgraded each year, so you have to check current ratings when buying bonds that have been on the market for some time.

THE LURE OF DISCOUNT BONDS

A *discount bond* sells for a price below the face value at which the issuing company or governmental agency will ultimately redeem it from the owner. A *deep discount bond* is a bond selling at a large discount.

Sometimes bonds are issued at a discount. But the big discounts develop mainly as a result of changes in the general level of interest rates. As an illustration of how that happens, start with a 20-year corporate bond issued ten years ago at par—$1,000 or multiples of that amount—with a 6% coupon interest rate.

You wouldn't give the owner $1,000 for that bond today for obvious reasons. It still pays $60 a year interest because the coupon rate was permanently fixed when the bond was issued. Interest rates have risen substantially since then and you expect to earn about twice that amount for each $1,000 you invest in bonds now.

At what price would that 6% bond become a good buy? To judge discount bonds properly, you employ the three yield measures discussed earlier in this chapter.

• *Current yield.* This is the annual interest payment divided by the present price. Let's assume that the bond is selling for $720. The current yield, therefore, comes to 8.3% ($60 ÷ $720 × 100).

• *Yield to maturity.* As you scan bond price lists, you will see current yields of only 6% among bonds issued by corporations as reputable as those issuing bonds paying 9% at the same time. The reason for that seemingly illogical difference probably lies in the nature of the income the bonds produce for the investor.

The 6% bond used in our example will give you $60 a year, no matter what you pay for the bond. In addition, the company that issued the bond will redeem it in ten years for $1,000, which is $280 more than the current price. You won't realize the $280 for ten years, but assume for mathematical convenience that you can amortize the discount as equal installments of $28 for the ten years. The percentage figure that tells you how much you are earning from interest and the amortized discount is the yield to maturity. But don't simply add and then divide. It's more complicated than that. Bond dealers use bond tables and programmed calculators to compute yields, and some hand-held calculators can do it. But you can approximate the yield to maturity with the following shortcut formula:

$$\frac{\text{annual interest payment} \quad + \quad \text{annually accumulated discount}}{\text{average of par value and current price}} \times 100$$

$$\frac{60 + 28}{860} = \frac{88}{860} \times 100 = 10.2\%$$

The same formula can be used for bonds for which you pay a premium. In those cases you would subtract the annually accumulated premium from the annual interest payment.

• *Yield after tax.* Deep discount bonds attract many investors because of the tax advantage of the built-in capital gain. (As you will see later, the bonds also appeal to speculators betting on a drop in interest rates.) Only 40% of a long-term capital gain must be included in your taxable income for federal taxes. Capital gains qualify for that tax break if you own the security more than a year. (Gains that reflect your recovery of a discount given when the bond was first issued may or may not qualify, depending on some very complex tax regulations.)

The 40% rule drastically reduces the tax burden for high-income investors. If you're in the 49% bracket—that is, if you pay 49 cents tax on each additional dollar of regular income—then you have to pay only 19.6% (40% of 49%) on capital gains, or less than 20 cents on each dollar.

With a discount bond you receive both taxable interest and tax-favored capital gains. With a deep discount a substantial proportion of the return consists of capital gains. Even the $1,000, 6% bond used in the examples produces $280 in capital gains, plus $600 in interest income in the ten years to maturity.

The 10.2% yield to maturity of the 6% bond might, for that reason, prove more profitable than a new 10.2% bond issued at par, all of whose interest is taxable at the full rate. The new 10.2% bond has an after-tax yield of 5.2% for someone in the 49% tax bracket. The 6% bond yields about 6.2% after tax, if held to maturity.

You can roughly approximate the after-tax figure by adapting the shortcut formula used earlier. Subtract the income tax you would pay on the annual interest payment and the capital gains tax due on the annually accumulated discount and then proceed as before.

As you may have already surmised, deep discount bonds should be compared with state and local tax-exempt issues as well as regular bonds. However, keep this fact in mind when evaluating tax-exempt yields: Although all the interest received on a tax-exempt bond and any discount given buyers when the bond is issued are exempt from federal—and possibly state and local—income taxes, any capital gains are taxable. Therefore, discounts that develop *after* issue reduce the tax advantage of a tax-exempt bond.

When you compare taxable bonds, take into consideration one feature that makes deep discount bonds a particularly good vehicle for speculation. Deep discount bonds carry low coupon interest rates, and low coupon bonds fluctuate more widely than high coupon issues. The added volatility works to your advantage if interest rates fall after you buy the bond because its price should rise more than that of a higher coupon issue. It works against you if rates rise.

Buying tips on discount bonds. Your broker may not follow the bond markets, but the firm's research department should be able to suggest a number of worthwhile discount bonds. Here are a few general buying tips that will make it easier to select good bonds.

• *Update the credit rating.* A bond's quality rating may be revised after it is issued because of a change in the issuer's financial position. Edward A. Taber III, president of Rowe Price Prime Reserve Fund, points out that many discount bonds have been on the market a long time, so it's important to check current ratings.

• *Be sure you can bail out.* Although you may buy a bond firmly intending to hold it to maturity, it usually doesn't make sense to freeze an investment. Taber suggests that ordinary investors restrict themselves to bonds that can be priced and sold easily.

• *Time the maturities.* Often you can select bonds that will mature exactly when you need large sums—say, for college expenses or, at retirement, for reinvestment in bonds with high current yields to supplement your pension income.

U.S. GOVERNMENT SECURITIES

Because they can't be matched for safety, securities issued by the U.S. government and its agencies are the choice of many conservative investors concerned with preservation of their capital. The U.S. Treasury has been in the credit markets in such volume for the past decade or so that its debt instruments have found their way into other investors' portfolios as well. There are dozens of government issues to choose from—some, such as Treasury bills, readily salable in the open marketplace; others, such as U.S. savings bonds, less liquid. Yields on government issues usually run a little lower than on high-grade corporate issues because of the safety factor. Here's a rundown of the most widely held government debt instruments.

TREASURY BILLS. These are short-term issues, usually carrying three- or six-month maturities, which are auctioned off to investors weekly. Minimum purchase is $10,000. Some bills run for a year and are auctioned off only every four weeks. T-bills are sold on a discount basis, then redeemed at maturity for the full face amount. Thus, they pay the interest up front. If the rate is 10%, you pay $9,000 for a $10,000 bill, then collect $10,000 when it matures. This "auction," or "discount" rate actually understates the yield when compared with other securities, which are usually described in terms of their bond equivalent yield. To find that for a T-bill, calculate the relationship between the amount of interest paid and the cash you actually had to lay out to get it. In the example above, you're laying out only $9,000 in order to collect $1,000 in interest. Thus, assuming this is a one-year bill, your bond equivalent yield would be 11.1%.

In addition to their safety, T-bills, along with other Treasury securities, are exempt from state and local income taxes. They are issued in book-entry form, meaning you don't actually receive the certificates, just a notification that they are being held in your name.

If you live near a Federal Reserve bank or branch, you can stop by and pick up the forms for purchasing T-bills. Otherwise, you must write to a Federal Reserve bank or branch for instructions and an application form, return it with payment for the amount of purchase and wait for notification that a bill has been purchased in your name. For information on how to proceed and addresses of Federal Reserve banks and branches, write to the Bureau of the Public Debt, Dept. F, Washington, D.C. 20226. Commercial banks and brokers will make the purchase for you, but their fee, usually around $25, cuts into the yield.

TREASURY NOTES. Notes run for one to ten years. They are coupon issues in much the same way as corporate bonds. As with T-bills, you can purchase them directly through a Federal Reserve bank or branch, or you can have a broker or a commercial bank do it for you. Interest is paid semiannually, the notes are not callable prior to maturity, and the minimum purchase is $5,000 for two- and two-and-a-half-year notes, $1,000 for longer-term issues.

TREASURY BONDS. T-bonds carry maturity dates generally over ten years after issue. Most cannot be called in early by the Treasury. Minimum purchase is $1,000.

U.S. SAVINGS BONDS. Savings bonds now come in two varieties.

• Newly issued series EE bonds mature in eight years, accruing 9% interest compounded semiannually and payable upon redemption. For bonds held for less than maturity, the yield is reduced: After one year EE bonds pay 6%. After five years the yield works out to 8½%. Bonds can't be redeemed at all for six months after purchase, at which time they will return 4.04% if cashed in. EE bonds are sold at 50% discount in face value denominations of $50, $75, $100, $200, $500, $1,000, $5,000 and $10,000. Interest earned is exempt from state and local income taxes and federal income taxes may be deferred (see below).

The interest rate on series E bonds, Savings Notes and EE bonds issued before May 1981 has been improved so that they provide a yield comparable to EE bonds if held to their next maturity dates. There is usually no advantage to cashing them in early in order to buy EEs, and there may be a disadvantage due to the gradually increasing scale that piles up interest in a bond's later years.

• HH bonds sell at full face value, pay current income and mature in ten years. If they were purchased in or after November 1980, they pay a level interest rate of 8½%. Bonds purchased for cash—as opposed to being taken in exchange for matured E bonds—will suffer a reduction in interest if redeemed within five years of purchase. The 8½% interest is also paid on HH bonds issued from January 1980 through April 1981, effective with the first interest period beginning on or after May

1, 1981. The interest penalty for purchased bonds redeemed within five years of issue also applies.

Yields have been improved on outstanding H bonds, which are no longer issued, in order to bring them up to par with the HHs.

Do they make any sense? The 9% available from EE bonds doesn't look very attractive in today's market. Is there any reason to consider buying savings bonds? Patriotism motivates some people; the low rate allows the Treasury to borrow on the cheap. But most of the bond buyers are probably motivated by other considerations: safety, convenience and, in many cases, substantial tax advantages.

• *Safety*. There's no safer place to put your money. Savings bonds are backed by the full faith and credit of the U.S. government. Payment of the interest and principal is guaranteed. Lost, stolen, damaged or destroyed bonds can be replaced free. (For information about that, write to the Bureau of the Public Debt, Parkersburg, West Virginia 26101.)

• *Convenience*. Payroll savings plans sponsored by employers and bond-a-month plans available at banks make it easy to accumulate bonds. This convenience is attractive to savers who need an incentive to put something aside on a regular basis. Bonds can also be easily purchased at banks, savings institutions and other places.

• *Tax advantages*. Were it not for this feature, savings bonds would probably be much less widely held. To begin with, the interest is exempt from all state and local income taxes. And although the exemption doesn't extend to federal taxes (except for the dividend and interest exclusion of $200—$400 on a joint return—

in effect for 1981. Your various options for paying the federal tab create opportunities to increase your effective return considerably.

For E and EE bonds you can (1) pay the tax each year as the interest accrues, applying your exclusion or (2) postpone the day of reckoning until you cash in the bond or dispose of it (by giving it away, for instance) or until it reaches final maturity. You also have the option of exchanging your E and EE bonds for HH bonds and thereby continuing to put off paying tax on the accumulated E or EE bond interest until you cash in or dispose of the HHs or until they reach final maturity. Here's how investors in certain circumstances can profit from these options.

• *Investors with young children.* If you'd like to start, say, a college fund for a child, you can take advantage of the option to report the interest on EE bonds as it accrues. You simply purchase bonds in the child's name (list yourself as beneficiary in case something happens to the child, but don't make yourself co-owner). This will make the child liable for the tax. And since it will probably be several years before the child has enough income to incur any tax liability, the income from the bonds will accumulate, for practical purposes, tax-free.

You set this up by filing a federal income tax return in the child's name when you first start the program and stating on the return that your child will be reporting the interest yearly. Report all the interest earned up to then. This establishes your intent. No further returns are necessary until the child's bond interest plus other income reaches the level at which a return would be required by law. At that time the child need report only that year's interest. Previously accrued interest escapes tax.

• *Workers with an eye on retirement.* In this case taxpayers with high incomes can take advantage of the option that allows postponing the federal income tax on E or EE bond interest until the bonds are cashed. You will almost certainly drop into a lower tax bracket after retirement, and the difference can boost your effective return substantially.

Take another example. Say you belong to a pension fund financed in part by your own contributions. When you retire, your pension benefits may be tax-exempt until you've recovered your contributions. Cashing in your bonds during that period may permit you to escape all or most of the tax on their interest because your taxable income will be so low.

There's yet another choice: You could exchange your E or EE bonds for HH bonds, further postponing taxes on the accumulated interest until you cash in the HHs. In return you'd get semiannual checks for the interest on the HH bonds. You'd have to pay taxes on that interest, but you will have effectively beaten the tax on the E or EE bonds for as long as you hold onto the HHs.

Relatively few people choose the bond exchange route, however, possibly because HH bonds are much less convenient to own than EEs. They can be bought or redeemed only at Federal Reserve banks or their branches or through the Bureau of the Public Debt.

U.S. AGENCY SECURITIES. A number of U.S. government agencies and federally sponsored enterprises issue debt securities. They usually do not carry the full faith and credit of the government, but this difference may seem like quibbling to some since it is doubtful that the government would allow one of its agencies to default on an obligation. Nevertheless, the difference is usually reflected in the relative yields of agency vs.

Treasury debt instruments. Agency issues, being the "inferior" risk, pay a bit more. This is despite the additional fact that some agency securities—but not all—are exempt from state and local income taxes, just like Treasury issues.

A description of the various securities available would amount to a description of the functions of the issuing agencies. Each has its own financing needs, each goes to the markets to fulfill them and each pays the going rates. Some, such as the Federal Farm Credit System, the Federal Home Loan Bank System and the Federal National Mortgage Association, often issue short- as well as long-term debt instruments. Most float mainly intermediate-term issues. Minimum purchase requirements vary greatly, ranging from $1,000 to $10,000 or more. Purchases must usually be made through brokers, who can supply a listing of the securities available.

MUNICIPAL BONDS

High inflation and the progressive federal income tax tables have made municipal bonds popular with middle-income investors who once thought of them chiefly as havens for the rich. Municipals are described in detail in chapter 22.

CERTIFICATES OF DEPOSIT

There are several kinds of savings and investment vehicles commonly referred to as CDs. They range from so-called "time deposit" savings certificates, available in modest denominations at banks, savings and loan associations and credit unions, to negotiable certificates requiring minimum deposits of $100,000 or more. As long as market interest rates remain several points above the level financial institutions are permitted to pay on their long-term savings certificates, investor interest in them should remain tepid. It makes little sense to tie up money for several years in accounts paying in the neighborhood of 7% or 8%, especially when the terms of such accounts require you to suffer financial penalties if you have the audacity to want to get your money out before the certificate matures.

It is for this reason that most of the activity for the past couple of years has involved six-month money-market certificates and 30-month certificates that pay interest at a level closer to market rates.

• *Money-market certificates*. These are available at commercial banks, s&ls and mutual savings banks. They run six months to maturity and interest cannot be compounded. Minimum denomination is supposed to be $10,000, but many institutions get around that by accepting lower amounts and lending depositors the difference at favorable rates. This reduces the yield, but the CD buyer still comes out way ahead of passbook rates.

The interest paid on money-market certificates is ¼ of 1% higher than the average yield being paid on six-month Treasury bills, as determined by the latest weekly auction. If the T-bill rate dips below 9%, s&ls and mutuals can tack on an additional amount, up to ¼ of 1% higher than commercial banks, giving them a slight edge in the competition for depositors. But when the T-bill rate is 9% or above, no differential is allowed.

Don't automatically assume that the quarter-point differential makes these certificates a better deal than T-bills. The auction rate on which they are based is lower than the bond equivalent rate, as explained before. In states with high personal income tax rates, that difference, plus the fact that states don't tax T-bill interest but do tax certificate interest, can make T-bills the better bet, especially if you're in a high tax bracket.

• *Small-saver certificates*. These run for 30 months or more and pay a rate based on that being paid at the time of purchase by Treasury securities of comparable maturities. Savings and loan associations and mutual savings banks can pay the same as the Treasury rate, but commercial banks must pay at least ¼ of 1% below. For certificates issued prior to August 1, 1981, the maximum rate was 12% at thrifts and 11-¾% at banks, but that ceiling has been lifted by the Depository Institutions Deregulation Committee. Compounding is permitted, and it can boost the yield over the life of a 30-month certificate by nearly a point at institutions that compound daily.

• *Tax-exempt All-Savers certificates*. Available in denominations of $500 at banks and thrift institutions, these mature in a year and pay 70% of the 52-week Treasury bill rate at the time of issue. Up to $1,000 of interest earned from them ($2,000 on a joint return) is exempt from federal income taxes. You should know three things about these certificates. First, if you want one, don't delay. The law authorizes their issue only through 1982. Second, the interest exemption is a lifetime limit, meaning no more than $1,000 will be exempted for singles and no more than $2,000 will be exempted for joint returns. Third, if your tax bracket is lower than 30%, you could be better off buying the T-bills or some other security of comparable yield and paying taxes on the interest. The key in any individual case is after-tax yield.

As compensation to the Treasury for the tax revenue being lost to these certificates, Congress included in the 1981 tax bill a provision that reduces the overall dividend and interest exclusion available to everyone. For

1981, it is $200 ($400 on a joint return), but for 1982 and thereafter, it drops to $100/$200 and can be applied only to dividends.

Penalties for Early Withdrawal. The penalties imposed on savers who attempt to cash in their certificates before maturity should make you think twice before doing it. Actually, issuers can legally refuse to redeem certificates at all before they mature, although few have ever done so. Institutions are required to permit early withdrawals only if a depositor dies or is declared mentally incompetent, and then no penalties can be imposed.

Savings institutions are permitted—but not required—to waive all penalties when certificates used to fund tax-sheltered Individual Retirement Accounts or Keogh retirement savings plans are redeemed by an owner who is disabled or age 59½ or over.

Otherwise, federal regulations require that one of three minimum penalties be imposed for early redemption of certificates.

- *Penalty 1* can be applied only to certificates sold before July 1, 1979. It amounts to forfeiture of three months' interest, plus reduction of the interest paid for the remaining time to the rate paid on passbook accounts.
- *Penalty 2* applies to certificates issued, extended or renewed from July 1, 1979, through June 1, 1980—but issuers are permitted to apply it instead of Penalty 1 to older certificates. Penalty 2 is loss of six months' interest for certificates with maturities of more than one year, or loss of three months' interest for certificates with shorter maturities.
- *Penalty 3* applies to certificates issued, extended or renewed after June 1, 1980, though it can be substi-

tuted for Penalty 1. It's the same as Penalty 2 except that if insufficient interest has accrued to pay the penalty, the difference is taken out of the principal. There is also a special provision for certificates that mature in less than three months; the penalty on them is the amount that would have been earned at maturity.

When they adopted Penalty 3, federal authorities decreed that issuers should compute minimum penalties in simple interest on the principal, even though earnings may be calculated on a compounded basis.

Remember, all three penalties are minimums. Issuers can slap on stiffer ones, and some do. Others keep penalties as light as they can to avoid losing customers.

17

Mutual funds and other investment pools

If you haven't the time or the inclination to assemble and keep watch on your own investment portfolio, why not hire a professional investment manager to do it for you? At first the thought sounds expensive: Investment managers' fees can be steep. But if you could pool your investments with those of others and pay only your proportional share of the fee, then the cost of professional management wouldn't be so high.

That is precisely the idea behind mutual funds, closed-end investment companies and unit trusts. Odds are that somewhere among the hundreds of such pooled investment arrangements on the market today there is one that fits your particular objectives to a tee.

MUTUAL FUNDS

For investors operating on a modest scale, mutual funds offer a combination of services impossible to obtain any other way.

• *Small minimum investment*. Some funds will accept orders of as little as $25 or $50. A number have no minimums. Funds with large initial purchase requirements usually accept smaller amounts for subsequent purchases.

• *Diversification*. Each share of a mutual fund gives you a cross-section interest in a broad range of stocks, bonds or other investments of the type in which the fund specializes. Diversification does not by itself insulate you against market movements, but it does help dampen the impact of wide price fluctuations in individual securities.

• *Liquidity*. A fund always stands ready to buy back its shares when you want to sell.

• *Automatic reinvestment*. Most funds will automatically reinvest dividends earned plus any capital gains that may accrue to your account as a result of the fund's buying and selling of investments for its portfolio.

• *Automatic withdrawals*. Most funds will set up automatic withdrawal or retirement plans for shareholders who want regular income.

How they operate. Mutual funds use money from their shareholders to buy their portfolios. Most funds offer shares to the public continuously, either directly through advertisements that offer their prospectuses, or through stock brokers and other dealers.

• *Management fees*. Mutual funds are usually run by management companies that administer their day-to-day operations, provide their staffs and guide their investments. The management company may also sell the fund's shares through an affiliate. Many funds are managed by stock brokerage firms or investment counselors who serve other clients.

The management company is paid an annual fee, commonly one-half of 1% of the fund's average assets. The rate is often stepped down as the fund's assets increase—the larger the fund gets, the smaller the percentage. Some funds use an incentive system, periodically adjusting the fee according to the fund's performance compared with the stock market as a whole: the better the performance, the higher the fee.

• *Investment objectives*. The majority of funds invest in common stocks, but some buy gold or other kinds of assets. Some concentrate on only one industry or on particular types of securities, such as bonds and preferred stocks. Portfolios are geared to meet specific objectives—safety of capital, high income, moderate capital appreciation or fast growth. The most speculative funds may employ such techniques as short selling, buying on margin or investing in "letter" stocks (securities that have not yet been registered for general sale).

Investment policies, as well as other details of a fund's operations, are spelled out in a prospectus, which is available on request and must be given to each prospective buyer.

• *Net asset value*. The value of a fund share is expressed in terms of its net asset value—the fund's total net assets divided by the number of shares outstanding. Because net asset value rises and falls with the market prices of a fund's holdings, the funds calculate the figure each day. The price at which you buy fund shares or sell them back to the fund is based on the next calculated net asset value following receipt of your order.

• *Sales charges*. About half the mutual funds impose a sales charge, which is almost always figured on a sliding scale. A fairly typical schedule would start at 8.5% for investments up to $10,000 and then go to 7.5% for

$10,000 to $25,000, 6% for $25,000, and so on down to 1% for extremely large purchases. Note that this "load" is calculated on the gross amount of your payment. In effect, if you give an 8.5% fund $1,000, $85 will be deducted as a sales charge and $915 will be invested in the fund's shares. An 8.5% sales charge works out to about 9.3% of your net investment in such a case.

Some management companies administer two or more funds, a collection usually referred to as a "family" of funds. You are usually permitted to exchange shares in one fund for shares in another in the same family by paying a small service charge.

About 300 mutual funds charge no sales fee and are known as no-load funds. They have no salesmen, so you have to get in touch with them through the mail or by telephone. In other respects, they operate like the load funds.

Mutual fund prices published in newspapers and other periodicals show two quotations: the net asset value or "bid" price, and the "offering," or "asked" price at which you can buy a share. The offering price includes the maximum sales charge. With no-load funds the bid price is identical to the asked or offering price.

Both load and no-load funds redeem—that is, buy back—shares at their net asset values.

• *Minimum investments.* Although a few funds have no bottom limits on orders, general practice is to require a minimum amount for initial and subsequent investments. The starting minimums usually range from $100 to $500, but may be as much as several thousand dollars.

When you invest by dollar amounts, your purchase will probably include a fractional share. For instance, $1,000 will buy 61.728 shares of a no-load fund with a $16.20 asset value.

• *Fund income.* A fund derives its revenues from dividends and interest on the securities it owns and from capital gains made on the sales of those securities or other investments. Virtually all income left after payment of management fees and other expenses is distributed to shareholders.

How to pick a mutual fund. While a mutual fund may relieve you of the trouble of selecting the individual investments in a portfolio, it does not relieve you of the risks involved. If you choose a fund that performs poorly you take that loss just as surely as if you had chosen its portfolio yourself.

It is important, therefore, to know what you are getting into. Mutual funds are not all alike. Some, as mentioned earlier, take a conservative approach; others are decidedly risky; many fall somewhere in between. When setting out to select a fund, your first task is to formulate your own investment objectives. Then you can look closely at the funds that seem to match them. The following major groupings offer more options than most investors will ever use.

• *Maximum capital gain funds.* These strive for big profits, generally by investing in small companies and developing industries or by concentrating on volatile issues. One group, known as hedge funds, uses speculative techniques, such as trading with borrowed money and short selling. The greater the drive for high profits, the greater the risk. Examples of funds that try for maximum capital gains are T. Rowe Price New Horizons Fund, Oppenheimer Special Fund and Twentieth Century Growth Investors.

• *Growth funds.* These look for long-range capital gains by buying the stocks of companies that supposedly have unique characteristics that will enable them to grow faster than inflation. Growth-and-income funds, which form another group, have much the same objective, but they put greater emphasis on capital preservation and try to produce more current dividend income for their shareholders. Examples: D. L. Babson Investment Fund, Fidelity Fund, Penn Square Mutual Fund.

• *Income funds.* Designed to return a higher level of dividends than others, these funds invest in bonds, preferred stocks and high-yielding common stocks. Examples: Northeast Investors Trust, T. Rowe Price New Income Fund.

• *Balanced funds.* Assets in these funds, too, are generally distributed among common stocks, preferreds and bonds, but their purpose is to minimize risk. Examples: Financial Industrial Income Fund, Wellington Fund.

• *Specialized funds.* A relatively small but growing number of funds concentrate their investments in one or two fields or industries. They may invest largely in Canadian issues, stocks of utility companies, U.S. government securities, bank shares or stocks of South African gold mines. Examples: Dreyfus Gold Deposits, United Services Fund, Value Line Special Situation Fund.

• *Money-market funds.* High interest rates have made these funds the most popular of all in the past couple of years. They invest in U.S. Treasury bills, commercial paper (essentially the IOUs of corporations), certificates of deposit and other, more esoteric short-term debt instruments. They usually credit interest to your account daily; most allow you to draw checks on the balance in your fund. Money-market funds are discussed in detail later in this chapter.

• *Tax-free funds.* For investors interested in tax-free income, there are funds that invest in municipal bonds and pass along the interest. There are also funds that have come to be known as tax-free money-market funds because they keep maturities in their portfolios quite short. There's more on both of these kinds of funds in chapter 22.

You can get lists of funds and information about their investment objectives and performance from a number of sources. *Forbes* magazine publishes an annual survey of funds each year in its mid-August issue. Weisenberger Financial Services publishes an exhaustive compilation of information on investment companies and updates it annually. The book, called *Investment Companies,* is quite expensive, but brokerage offices and libraries have copies. *Johnson's Investment Company Charts,* also expensive but also available at brokers' offices and libraries, is another good source of comparative information about funds. You can get a list of the members of the No-Load Mutual Fund Association for a dollar by writing to that organization at Valley Forge, Pennsylvania 19481. A listing of load and no-load funds is available free from the Investment Company Institute, 1775 K Street, N.W., Washington, D.C. 20006. A number of magazines, including *Changing Times,* report regularly on developments in the mutual funds industry.

Once you have compiled a list of funds that seem to meet your investment objectives, write for their prospectuses and annual reports and compare the funds on past performance in good markets and bad. See which are members of families of funds, meaning you would have the flexibility of switching your money among different types of funds as market conditions changed. All other things being equal, choose a no-load fund over one that charges a commission. There is nothing about charging sales commissions that makes a fund perform better than one that doesn't.

Here are the addresses of the funds mentioned in this section:

D. L. Babson Investment Fund, Inc.
Three Crown Center
2440 Pershing Road
Kansas City, Mo. 64108

Dreyfus Gold Deposits, Inc.*
600 Madison Ave.
New York, N.Y. 10022

Fidelity Fund, Inc.
82 Devonshire St.
Boston, Mass. 02109

Financial Industrial Income Fund, Inc.
7503 Marin Drive
P.O. Box 2040
Denver, Colo. 80201

Northeast Investors Trust
50 Congress St.
Boston, Mass. 02109

Oppenheimer Special Fund*
Two Broadway
New York, N.Y. 10004

Penn Square Mutual Fund
101 N. Fifth St.
Reading, Pa. 19603

T. Rowe Price New Horizons Fund, Inc.
T. Rowe Price New Income Fund, Inc.
100 East Pratt St.
Baltimore, Md. 21202

*Load Fund

Twentieth Century Growth Investors
605 W. 47th St.
Kansas City, Mo. 64112

United Services Fund, Inc.
P.O. Box 29467
San Antonio, Tex. 78249

Value Line Special Situations Fund, Inc.*
711 Third Ave.
New York, N.Y. 10017

Wellington Fund, Inc.
Vanguard Group
1275 Drummers Lane
P.O. Box 2600
Valley Forge, Pa. 19482

CLOSED-END INVESTMENT COMPANIES

Mutual funds represent only one, albeit the largest, part of the investment company field. The other is composed of "closed-end" companies, which also pool shareholdes' capital for investment but rarely issue new shares. You buy the shares on a stock exchange or in the over-the-counter market and sell them the same way, paying a commission to a broker. The funds do not redeem their own shares.

Closed-end company shares often sell at substantial discounts from their net asset values. A few go at premiums from time to time. No one seems to have a completely satisfactory explanation for either phenomenon. The discounts don't automatically make the shares a bargain, since you usually have to accept a discounted price when you sell them. You could profit if for some reason the discount narrows, but you could lose if the discount widens.

The closed-end funds, like the mutuals, invest in diversified or specialized groups of securities. One type of closed-end company, called dual purpose funds, sells two kinds of shares—income and capital.

Those who buy income shares receive all the current income payable on both the income and the capital shares: If the fund is split between 1,000,000 income shares and 1,000,000 capital shares, the income share-owners are entitled to receive all the dividends earned by the entire 2,000,000 shares.

Any capital gains made on the 2,000,000 shares are credited solely to those who hold capital shares. The funds don't distribute realized capital gains; they are retained.

The funds will redeem their income shares at net asset value at a scheduled future date. Theoretically, the funds will also redeem the capital shares at their net asset values (not the market price). But in practice the capital shareowners will vote either to terminate their part of the fund or to continue it in some form.

Some of the funds are nearing their scheduled redemption dates. Since most of the capital shares are available at discounts from net asset values, and those shares will be redeemed at their net asset values if the funds terminate or convert to a mutual fund, the approaching deadlines offer profit potential for alert investors.

MONEY-MARKET FUNDS

In the last few years investors have flocked to the money-market funds because of their high yields. Early in 1981 the total net asset value of the money funds topped $100 billion, making them the phenomenal success story of the mutual fund industry.

The funds were originally designed as a place to park money temporarily between more permanent investments. Only by circumstance—the sharp rise in short-term interest rates in 1978, 1979 and again in late 1980—did they become a long-term haven. They should continue to be a useful money-management tool for investors who understand them.

Money-market funds invest the proceeds from the sale of their shares in securities known as money-market instruments. The money market is the collective name for transactions used by the government, banks, big corporations, securities dealers and others to borrow and lend money for short periods. The deals may be for overnight or a few days—never more than a year.

Each fund's prospectus spells out the types of instruments and investment techniques it may use, and its quarterly financial statements report current holdings. You can't judge a fund sensibly until you get the hang of what those instruments are. The makeup of the portfolio determines the yield and safety of your investment. These are the principal instruments you're likely to find in a fund portfolio.

• *Treasury bills and notes.* Bills are issued with three-month, six-month, and one-year maturities. Notes run longer, but they, like bills, are widely traded and can be bought when they are closer to maturity. Treasury issues constitute direct obligations of the federal government, so they rate tops in safety.

The funds may also buy short-term securities issued by individual government agencies. Some are backed by the full faith and credit of the federal government; others are guaranteed only by the agencies, but they rank just below Treasuries in safety because it's assumed that the government would not permit an agency to default.

• *Commercial paper.* Essentially, these are IOUs issued by corporations to raise funds for limited periods, usually 60 days or less. Paper is rated for quality by credit analysis firms according to the issuing company's financial strength. Standard & Poor's top rating is A-1; Moody's, Prime-1; and Fitch's, F-1.

• *Banker's acceptances.* These loans originate largely in import and export transactions in which a seller draws a draft payable by the buyer within a fixed period of time. The bank financing the transaction accepts the draft, guaranteeing payment at maturity and thereby making the draft salable in the open market. The money-market fund can buy the acceptance at a discount and get paid the full amount at maturity.

• *Certificates of deposit.* The money market deals in large-denomination, negotiable certificates not subject to government limits on interest rates. Domestic CDs are issued by U.S. bank offices here. Yankee CDs are issued by foreign bank branches in the United States; Eurodollar CDs are sold by U.S. bank branches in Europe and payable in U.S. dollars. Eurodollar issues are regarded as a shade riskier than the others because of the possibility that redemption of the CDs might be impeded by some unfavorable action, such as the imposition of exchange controls by the foreign government.

• *Repurchase agreements.* Repos, as they are known in the money-market trade, work along these lines:

A bank wishes to borrow money for a short while, maybe only one day. The bank sells Treasury bills it is holding to a money-market fund with the agreement to buy them back the next day at a higher price or a specified interest rate. In effect, the buy-back, or repurchase, constitutes a loan with Treasury securities as collateral.

In a reverse repurchase agreement the transaction goes the opposite way—the fund sells its bills to a bank and agrees to buy them back. Here it's the fund that is borrowing money from the bank. A fund may leave itself the option of executing reverse repos as a means of handling heavy shareholder redemptions—a policy that should be disclosed in its prospectus. The borrowed money can be used to pay shareholder withdrawals so portfolio securities that the fund wants to retain don't have to be sold.

How safe are they? Unfortunately, it isn't easy to assess the overall safety of a fund's portfolio because so many fine financial shadings are involved. A fund may be heavy in Eurodollar CDs, but limit the risk by buying only from the giant banks on the assumption that they would be better able to redeem the CDs if their foreign branches couldn't make good. And since most of the funds hold several kinds of securities, the risk often depends on the portfolio's distribution.

If you're worried about safety, look for a fund with a high proportion of U.S. government securities, CDs from well-known domestic banks and top-rated commercial paper. Some investors prefer the funds that invest only in U.S. and U.S.-guaranteed securities— Fund for Government Investors, Capital Preservation Fund, Merrill Lynch Government Fund, First Variable Rate Fund and a few others. Normally you sacrifice a percentage point or two of yield for the safety of U.S. government securities.

You can fine tune the risk to some extent by diversifying among two or more funds with different portfolios.

How they value their assets. This is one of the trickiest aspects of fund operations. If you follow yields, you will notice that occasionally one or more funds report surprisingly high or low yields. Some of the differences may result from fund managers' superior or inferior performance. But the big spreads often stem from the way the funds compute the value of their portfolios.

Most funds prefer to maintain a fixed net-asset value, either $1 or $10. Interest income and net gains on the sale and redemption of securities are paid out in the form of dividends. And the dividends buy additional fixed-price shares to add to your account.

However, a portfolio's value really fluctuates daily as short-term interest rate changes raise or lower the market price of the securities in the portfolio. A growing number of funds, in effect, ignore those gains and losses through what's called an *amortized cost* method. Others, called *mark-to-market* funds, revalue all or part of their portfolios daily as prices of the securities rise and fall. Ordinarily net-asset values would rise and fall along with portfolio prices, but to avoid having to adjust the net-asset value, the mark-to-market funds employ one of two methods:

• The *full-payout funds* pay out any rise in net-asset value in extra dividends. Thus, a drop in interest rates may lift the fund's yield above those reported by other funds that day. A rise in interest rates, on the other hand, will force the fund's yield down. If the portfolio's value drops by more than the interest earned that day, the fund will report a negative yield, and it will have to subtract shares from each person's account to compensate.

• Other mark-to-market funds use a *penny-rounding* procedure that masks the changes in the portfolio's value. The fund need not adjust for changes in the net-asset value until it falls below $.995 or rises above $1.005 per share.

Don't be overly alarmed or encouraged, therefore, by the extraordinary yields that crop up when interest rates are moving wildly. It is true that fund valuation differences can result in extra gains or losses if you withdraw from or buy into a fund at critical times. Still, the actual dollar difference may not be very large (unless you're dealing with big investments) because the distortion may last for only a few days.

Services and fees. Variations in services and fees may appear trivial, but they sometimes produce unnecessary costs and annoying delays.

• *Account and sales fees.* The overwhelming majority of money-market funds do not charge sales fees. Some funds, though, charge account maintenance fees of a couple of dollars a month. Those fees are in addition to the advisory fee paid to the fund's management company.

• *Checking privileges.* Virtually all the funds offer a checking service and most give it to you at no extra cost. By all means, sign up for the check plan because it's one of the money-market funds' most attractive features. Your money continues to earn dividends in the fund until your check clears. Minimum check, however, is usually $500.

• *Dealing with the fund.* Normally you deal with funds directly, although in a few cases you may have to go through the brokerage firm that sponsors the fund and perhaps open an account with the firm. If you buy shares through a bank or a broker—unless you buy them from the sponsoring broker—you might be charged a fee for services.

• *Expedited purchases.* The slowest way to buy shares is by sending a check through the mail. To expedite the process, your bank, for a fee, will wire money directly to the fund. Investors in a broker-sponsored fund should be able to make the purchase through the firm's local office. If you buy shares by mail and your check is drawn on a member bank of the Federal Reserve System, funds start paying dividends one or two business days after your check is received. But to guard against nonpayment, most of the funds won't allow you to redeem shares bought with a personal check until the check has been paid by your bank. The wait may be only a few days, but some funds fix arbitrary waiting periods that run much longer.

• *Expedited redemptions*. You can redeem shares by mail, as you would with other mutual funds. However, the money-market funds usually allow telephone and telegram redemptions and send the money directly to your bank. They will also usually wire payments above a certain amount (for free, in many cases), so you can have access to the money either the same business day or the next one. If you plan to use the telephone and wire services, you must register your bank account with the fund beforehand.

It's impractical to close out a fund account by writing a check against it because the account earns dividends daily and you can never be sure of the exact total. If you like, you can write a check for most of the total and then redeem the rest by mail, telephone or wire.

The Investment Company Institute (see address on page 287) will send you a list of money-market funds that belong to it. Another good central source of information—names, addresses, services offered, portfolio makeup, recent performance records—is *Donoghue's Money Fund Directory*, available for $12 from Box 540, Holliston, Mass. 01746.

Listed below are ten large money-market funds that

sell shares to the general public. Those marked with an asterisk are sold only through stockbrokers, meaning you must open an account with the brokerage firm in order to invest. All other funds sell directly to the public, although a few may also be sold by brokers. Comparing prospectuses and annual reports from the funds on this list will give you a good idea of the range of money market investments available.

fund	minimum initial invest- ment	minimum subsequent investment	mini- mum check	checking service charges
Capital Preservation Fund, Inc. 755 Page Mill Road Palo Alto, Calif. 94304 800-982-5844 (Calif. only) 800-227-8380	$1,000	none	$500	none
Daily Cash Accumulation Fund, Inc. 3600 S. Yosemite Denver, Colo. 80237 303-770-2345 800-525-9310	$2,500	$100	$500	$6 initial
Dreyfus Liquid Assets, Inc. P.O. Box 600 Middlesex, N.J. 08846 1-800-345-8501	$2,500	$100	$500	none
Fidelity Daily Income Trust 82 Devonshire St. Boston, Mass. 02109 617-523-1919 (collect, Mass. only) 800-225-6190	$10,000	$500	$500	none
InterCapital Liquid Asset Fund, Inc. One Battery Park Plaza New York, N.Y. 10004 212-422-6700 800-221-2685	$5,000	$1,000	$500	none
Merrill Lynch Ready Assets Trust* 165 Broadway New York, N.Y. 10080 212-637-6310 (collect, N.Y. only) 800-221-7210	$5,000	$1,000	$500	none

fund	minimum initial investment	minimum subsequent investment	minimum check	checking service charges
MoneyMart Assets, Inc. 100 Gold St. New York, N.Y. 10038 212-791-7123 (collect, N.Y. only) 800-221-7984	$3,000	$3,000	$500	$5 initial
Paine Webber Cashfund, Inc.* 140 Broadway New York, N.Y. 10005 212-437-2121	$5,000	$500	$500	none
Rowe Price Prime Reserve Fund, Inc. 100 E. Pratt St. Baltimore, Md. 21202 301-547-2308 (collect, Md. only) 800-638-5660	$1,000	$100	$500	none
Reserve Fund, Inc. 810 Seventh Ave. New York, N.Y. 10019 212-977-9880 800-223-5547	$1,000	$1,000	$500	none

UNIT INVESTMENT TRUSTS

If you buy into a unit trust, you get an interest, called a unit, in a fixed portfolio of securities. Unit trusts are an immensely popular way to buy tax-exempt bonds, and are also used by brokerage firms to package offerings of corporate bonds, utility stocks and pools of government-backed mortgages known as Ginnie Maes (a shortened form of Government National Mortgage Association).

For investors who want to put money into a particular type of security, unit trusts provide professionally selected, diversified portfolios that can usually be bought in multiples of about $1,000. Since the bond trusts hold onto their original securities instead of trading them, the investor gets a fixed dollar return that won't change materially for a long period. The trusts don't dissolve and return the remaining capital to investors until most of the bonds in the trust's portfolio have been redeemed or called.

The ability to lock in a certain rate is a prime concern to people who want a steady, assured income and to those who think interest rates will decline, thereby increasing bond prices. Of course, if interest rates increase, investors are stuck with a low-level return that produces price losses for everyone. Those are the risks faced by anyone who buys fixed-income securities.

Unfortunately, trust units are sold so casually that many investors mistakenly assume they are interchangeable pieces of the same product, differing only in yield and type of security. Actually, trusts are far more complex than they seem—as anyone who reads a prospectus quickly learns—and they can differ significantly.

Sketchy information. The sponsoring brokerage firms try to sell out the trusts within a matter of days after they are registered with the Securities and Exchange Commission. As a result, investors often have to place their orders before they receive a prospectus, relying on advance information from their brokers.

Usually, you can't get more than a few sketchy details in advance—the approximate yield, the sales charge, the distribution of the bonds according to quality rankings (AAA, AA, etc.) and a summary description of the issues in the portfolio. But there are a lot of other facts you should know. For instance, if you're trying to lock in a high yield for the long term, you want to know the call provisions of the bonds in the portfolio.

Bonds with short-term call dates give the issuers greater freedom to call the bonds for redemption if interest rates decline; the high-rate bonds can then be paid off with funds raised by selling new bonds at lower rates.

You have an opportunity to check those and other details when you receive the prospectus with your bill. If the information given to you earlier by the broker turns out to be incorrect, you can ask to have your order cancelled. Brokers may comply as a matter of good customer relations even when no mistake has been made. To avoid misunderstandings, make clear when you place the advance order that it's conditional on your being satisfied with the prospectus.

Commissions. Brokers' sales charges on newly issued trusts vary by firm and trust. You can expect to pay about 3% to 4½%. The percentages work out somewhat higher when the fees are computed on the net amount of the investment used to buy the underlying securities instead of the public offering price, which combines the net investment and the sales commission. Here's an illustration:

amount per unit invested in bonds	$ 970.57
sales charge	45.73
public offering price per unit	$1,016.30

The $45.73 commission represents 4.5% of the $1,016.30 but 4.712% of the $970.57.

A seemingly small difference of one percentage point in a sales charge becomes more impressive when you consider that some trusts require a $5,000 minimum purchase.

Some sponsors graduate fees downward for large purchases. For instance, John Nuveen & Company, a leading sponsor of tax-exempt trusts, cuts its fee from 4½% to 3½% if you invest $100,000 to $499,999, to 3% for $500,000 to $999,999, and to 2½% for $1,000,000 and more.

Repurchases. You can dispose of your units either by redeeming them through the trust or by selling them to or through the broker.

Trusts redeem units on the basis of the bid rather than the offering prices of the securities in the portfolio. The spread between bid and offering prices widens and narrows with market conditions. Municipal bond bid prices average 1% to 2% less than offering prices.

Although not obligated to do so, as prospectuses carefully point out, unit trust sponsors maintain a secondary market for their own units and are prepared to buy or sell them as they would other securities. The brokers don't charge a commission when they buy from you.

18

The basics of real estate investing

WHY REAL ESTATE IS SO ATTRACTIVE

Many people shy away from investing in real estate, and for good reasons. Unlike stocks and bonds, real estate can't be bought and sold with a quick telephone call to a broker. You can't keep track of a property's value simply by consulting a published price list. And it's just as easy to lose money on property as it is on any other investment. Nevertheless, real estate as an investment does have its attractions.

The lure of leverage. Normally, you buy property—whether it's a house or a commercial building—with some of your own funds plus a long-term mortgage loan. That use of borrowed money gives you leverage by enabling you to acquire a more expensive property than you could on your own.

The larger the loan, the greater your potential gain. Say you purchase a $60,000, one-family house with no loan and sell it for $75,000. The $15,000 gain represents a

25% return on your $60,000 outlay. Assume, instead, that you had invested only $12,000 of your own money and borrowed the other $48,000. Now you have made $15,000 on a $12,000 investment, a splendid 125% return (ignoring for the sake of simplicity both the cost of the loan and the tax angles). The lender does not share in your good fortune. He is entitled only to interest on the loan and repayment of the $48,000 principal.

Unfortunately, leverage also acts to deepen losses. For example, if you are forced to sell the $60,000 house for $45,000, the $15,000 loss wipes out all of your $12,000 investment *and* you might have to dig up another $3,000 to add to the $45,000 sale proceeds in order to pay off the mortgage. (The lender doesn't share in your bad fortune, either.)

Leverage, as you can see, is potentially a two-way street.

Tax breaks. Few, if any, other investments can match the tax benefits available in real estate.

• *Capital gains.* The profit made on the sale of a property held more than a year usually qualifies as a long-term capital gain. Therefore, only 40% of the gain need be included with the income subject to federal income taxes.

• *Deductibility.* While you own rental property, your operating costs, mortgage interest payments, real estate taxes and other expenses can be deducted from rental income just as you would offset income with expenses in other businesses. (Amortization payments, which reduce the principal balance of the mortgage loan, can't be deducted, of course, because they are not actually an expense. On the contrary, they increase your equity in the property.)

• *Depreciation*. The crowning tax break, the one that distinguishes real estate from such investments as stocks and bonds, is the right to deduct each year a certain amount of depreciation for the building and its equipment when they are used for business purposes.

Depreciation represents a noncash expense. You need not spend a cent for repairs or maintenance to claim it. Nor does the property have to be deteriorating physically at the same pace at which you are depreciating it, although the rate must stay within IRS limits. The fact that the building's market value is rising does not stop you from claiming a depreciation deduction.

If you buy the property from someone who has already depreciated it, you can start the depreciation cycle over again, as can the next buyer after you.

Depreciation helps create a tax shelter because the effect is to shield part of your income from taxes. As an illustration of how the shelter works, consider these two simplified accounting statements for a property producing $5,640 rental income a year:

GROSS INCOME		$5,640
minus: mortgage payment		
interest and principal	$4,194	
operating expenses	420	
real estate taxes	840	
		5,454
cash flow before tax		$ 186

That $186 is the property's approximate cash flow, the amount of spendable money left after paying all cash costs. Depreciation is left out at this point because it doesn't require a cash outlay. To compute the property's *taxable* income, depreciation is substituted for the principal payment on the mortgage, as follows:

CASH FLOW BEFORE TAX	$	186
add principal payment on mortgage		413
net	$	599
minus depreciation		1,680
taxable income or (loss)		$(1,081)

You now have $1,081 to declare as a loss on your income tax return. If you're in the 40% bracket, that saves you $432 in taxes, which, combined with your $186 cash flow before taxes, gives you a total of $618 spendable after-tax income from the property.

Refrigerators and other equipment can be depreciated separately on the basis of their shorter useful lives. Land is not depreciable.

The government eventually recaptures some of the taxes given up through depreciation when a property is sold. Then, the depreciation is deducted from the cost of the property, thereby increasing the amount of taxable gain realized on the sale. But a good part or all of that gain will be subject to the lower long-term capital gains tax rates.

Some real estate deals appeal to high-bracket investors because they produce a loss that can offset income from salaries and other investments. Real estate tax shelters are discussed in chapter 22.

Protection against inflation. House prices have generally kept up with or surpassed the rise in consumer prices over the years.

Naturally, averages do not necessarily reflect the results for individual pieces of property. Real estate prices are strongly influenced by local conditions. Two identical houses one block apart might sell for widely different prices.

Nevertheless, real estate prices have risen steadily in so many parts of the country that investors have come to depend on capital gains for part of their investment return. If their faith is to be justified, they must take care to select properties carefully.

SELECTING RENTAL PROPERTY

Select properties for investment in much the same way you would if buying your own home. A study of 1,000 investors over a 20-year period showed that those who did best bought what *they* liked, rather than what they thought others would like.

- Compare prices of similar homes to make certain the property isn't overpriced.
- Be skeptical of a seller's assurance that you can raise the rent once you take over. If it's so easy, why didn't he do it? Compare rents for similar units nearby.
- Put everything you and the seller agree upon in writing.
- Make sure the agreement requires the seller to turn over tenants' damage deposits on closing title.
- Examine existing leases before closing.
- Keep loan payments affordable so you won't get hurt by occasional vacancies.
- Be wary of investing in property on which maintenance has been put off. The seller's income and expense statements could show a handsome return because he hasn't spent enough for repairs.

REAL ESTATE INVESTMENT TRUSTS

A real estate investment trust is to real estate what a mutual fund is to stocks. A shareowner in a REIT participates in the pooled ownership of income-producing properties, such as apartment houses, shopping centers, office buildings, warehouses or a combination of these, or in the pooled ownership of mortgages secured by either construction and development loans or long-term "permanent" loans on real estate. The shares are traded every day and thus have a ready market.

During the late 60s and early 70s, buying shares in a real estate investment trust was regarded as an ideal way to participate in real estate if you didn't want to buy property or make a mortgage loan on your own. Consider the many advantages the REITs offer, said their salespeople:

- Buying a share gives you an immediate stake in a professionally managed trust that invests in such big commercial properties as apartment houses and shopping centers, or lends construction money to developers at high interest rates, or makes long-term mortgage loans.
- You can pull out any time you like by selling your shares on one of the exchanges or in the over-the-counter market. There's none of the delay you encounter in disposing of an individual property.
- If you buy shares in an equity trust—the kind that invests in property—the part of your dividends that reflects depreciation charges in excess of net income might be tax-free. The trust does not have to set aside cash to cover those charges. The passed-through depreciation must be deducted from the cost of your shares, thereby increasing the potential profit when

you sell. But if you hold the shares long enough, the profit you realize qualifies as a long-term capital gain.

It all looked so safe, so promising, that individual investors and institutions plowed billions of dollars into REITs before the commercial real estate market collapse of 1973–74. And what a fall it was. By the end of 1974 the REIT stock price index prepared by the National Association of Real Estate Investment Trusts had crashed to a low of 17 from its 1972 base of 100.

REITs that suffered the most were principally the short-term mortgage trusts, those that made construction and development loans to builders. They constituted a majority of REITs then; now they are a distinct minority. Equity trusts—those that own and collect rent on buildings, shopping centers and other developments, did not fare as badly in the big crunch. They are the principal focus of investor interest today.

REITs are sold through brokers. Since the days of their great decline they have been considered speculative investments, although a number of well-managed trusts have done quite well lately. If you're interested, talk it over with your broker, examine prospectuses and annual reports, and stick with high quality.

UNDEVELOPED PROPERTY

If you buy an undeveloped homesite, whether as an investment or a place to live, vacation or retire, you may be taking risks you didn't consider.

Tens of thousands of buyers in virtually every state have invested thousands of dollars in land that is worth much less than they have spent, and in a number of cases it is worth nothing at all on the resale market. They are stuck with property with no sewer, water or electric lines. It may not support a septic tank and a well, or the expense of those improvements could double the cost of the plot. The land might be subject to periodic flooding. Local ordinances might effectively prohibit building there at all.

There really isn't much to protect you from becoming a victim except your own awareness. Some laws at the federal level and in some states and localities are designed to protect buyers. Overall, however, crackdowns generally come only after buyers have been gulled.

One federal statute aims specifically at stemming consumer problems with land sales. This law, the Interstate Land Sales Full Disclosure Act, affects companies that sell or lease subdivision lots across state lines, with certain exemptions.

Affected companies are required to file with the Office of Interstate Land Sales Registration (OILSR) a statement of record, which is a detailed description of the lots for sale or lease, plus financial and legal information. The company must also file a shorter version, called a property report, which includes information on sewers, water lines, possible flooding conditions, legal problems and so forth. It should be required reading for any prospective buyer, and the law insists that you be given a copy of the property report before you sign a sales contract.

If you are seriously considering buying a piece of undeveloped property, take your time and follow this procedure.

• Write for and read two publications. One is *Before Buying Land ... Get the Facts,* available from OILSR, Room 4108, 451 Seventh St., S.W., Washington, D.C. 20411. It's free. The other is *The Insider's*

Guide to Owning Land in Subdivisions, available for $2.50 from a public interest group called INFORM, 25 Broad St., New York, N.Y. 10004.

- Ask one or more independent brokers in the area whether they would be willing to list the property and what its selling price would be. INFORM spent more than three years compiling over 1,000 pages of detailed and dispassionate reports on major subdivisions in the West, Southwest and Florida and found that buyers in many cases can't resell for what they paid and sometimes can't resell at all.

- Visit the property; don't buy anything sight unseen. If the developer is willing to give you a free trip to visit it later (usually only the cost of a motel room for three days), why shouldn't he give it to you now, before you buy?

- Make sure that any representations about property improvements and the services that will be provided are added to the sales contract and signed by the sales manager. If he won't sign it, you shouldn't either.

- Find out whether the land can actually be used as a homesite. Write, phone, or visit the appropriate offices of the local government. Ask what kinds of permits must be obtained before you can build on the property, and whether sewer and water hookups are available.

- Determine whether the developer's bonds for improvements—swimming pool, utility lines and the like—are the surety kind so that if he goes bankrupt the money will still be available. Escrow accounts can also be used for this purpose. A corporate bond for further improvements is only as good as the corporation itself.

- Understand clearly what will happen if you default on your payments. You could lose everything.

- Read the property report, the sales contract and all other papers thoroughly. Then take them to an attorney who deals in land transactions for his evaluation before you sign anything.

INVESTING IN FARMLAND

A number of analysts think that farmland will be one of the best investments of any kind over the next several years. But they are careful to point out that they are talking about producing land that can take advantage of the steady increase in food prices resulting from the competition for supplies on world markets. Land that fills the bill could easily triple in value by 1990, these analysts say. About two-thirds of that increase will probably be due to inflation alone.

Which land will do best? Its ability to produce high crop yields is important, of course, especially of corn and soybeans, which will have huge export markets. But even less-abundant farmland should increase in value if it is located near growing cities and thus has potential for development.

19

Stock options and futures contracts

If you're interested in shortening the wait for profits from your investments and don't mind stepping up the risks in exchange, then stock options or futures contracts may be to your liking. Options give you a *right* to buy or sell a certain stock at a specified price within a specified time. Futures contracts *commit* you to buy or sell a specified amount of a particular commodity—ranging from plywood to pork bellies to Treasury bills—at a specified price within a specified time. Both kinds of transactions have attracted growing numbers of investors over the past several years.

BUYING STOCK OPTIONS

Although options trading is best suited to the sophisticated investor, anyone who takes the time to learn the special techniques involved can do it.

There are essentially two kinds: A *call* gives its buyer the right to buy, and its seller the obligation to sell, a particular stock at a specified price while the option is in force. A *put* gives its buyer the right to sell at a specified price within a specified time, and obligates its seller to do the buying. As a rule, calls are bought and puts sold by traders who think the price of the underlying security will rise. Sellers of calls and buyers of puts think the price will fall, or at least remain the same.

Options didn't mature into a broad-scale investment medium until 1973 when the Chicago Board of Trade opened the Chicago Board Options Exchange, CBOE, for trading in calls. Puts were added later. The CBOE adopted an ingenious system, patterned on another type of option, commodity futures, that makes it easy for anyone to participate. The other exchanges use pretty much the same plan.

How it works. Each exchange specifies a list of stocks against which puts and calls can be sold and bought. For the most part, the stocks represent big, nationally known corporations, such as Alcoa, IBM, Sears, Abbott Laboratories, Disney, Texaco and so on.

The options are standardized contracts covering 100 shares of the particular underlying stock. The exchange opens trading in options to buy a stock at a set price, known as the exercise or striking price, within a certain period. The "strikes" are fixed near the current market price of the stock in $5 or $10 multiples. If the stock is selling for $48 per share, the exchange would place the striking price at $50 per share. If and when the stock's price changes substantially, the exchange launches another option with a new striking price closer to the new market value. Trading in the old option continues, so after a while brokers may be dealing in three, four or more options for the same stock at different striking prices.

Because of the different striking prices and time periods, it's possible to trade in different options for a single stock not only at several striking prices but also in several time periods. The CBOE could list, for example, options for a company's stock at $35, $40, $45 and $50 per share for exercise at the end of April, July and October.

In practice, some of the possible option combinations may not be offered or traded because of lack of interest among buyers and sellers.

Suppose you are the seller, or "writer," of an April 35 call. This means you pledge to sell 100 shares of a particular stock at $35 a share by the prescribed date in April if formally requested to do so through the exchange. For that right, you receive whatever price, called a premium, you can get on the exchange at the moment. The buyer is paying you for the right to buy 100 shares at $35 a share before a certain date in April no matter what the price of the stock happens to be at the time he buys.

Keep in mind that what you are selling is not the stock itself. The premium pays only for the option. If a buyer exercises his call—that is, says he wants the stock—he has to put up $3,500 for those 100 shares, in addition to the premium he previously paid for the option. You as the call seller receive that $3,500, in addition to the premium obtained earlier.

The buyer and seller do not negotiate with each other when a call is exercised. Once an option is sold, the link between the two is broken by the Options Clearing Corporation, an organization set up by the exchanges.

This clearing arrangement makes it possible for buyers and sellers to move in and out of the options market as they like by closing out their original transaction with an offsetting one. For example, if you *sell* an

April 35 call you can cancel your obligation to deliver 100 shares at $35 a share by *buying* an April 35 call for the same stock. If you originally bought an option, you'd cancel it by selling one. Most transactions are consummated this way and not through the delivery of the underlying stock.

Brokers charge lower commissions for option transactions than for stock trades. But when an option is exercised, the buyer and the seller are each charged regular stock commissions for the sale of the underlying securities.

How you win—or lose. Most options contracts are for calls. Premiums for calls rise and fall with the price of the stock, although not necessarily by the same amount. Rising stock prices tend to increase premiums; declining prices depress them.

A call with a striking price under the stock's current price maintains an intrinsic value equal to the difference between the two. For example, when a stock is selling at $55 a share, an option to buy it at $50 a share should sell for at least $5 a share, or $500 for the 100-share option. Normally the option will sell for somewhat more than the difference right up to the expiration date because there's always a chance of a stock price increase. The option becomes worthless after the exercise deadline. Calls that have an intrinsic value because the striking price is under the stock price are known as "in the money" options; calls that exceed the stock price are "out of the money."

Options with more distant expiration dates should command a higher premium than those with closer dates, all other things being equal. The longer the period, the longer the option holder can afford to wait for a rewarding rise in the stock's price.

For an idea of how a seller can win or lose trading in

options, start with a basic, nonspeculative transaction. You buy 100 shares of one of the stocks on the options list at $40 a share, or $4,000 for the lot. (To keep things simple, omit commission costs, although on small amounts they could become an important consideration.) You then sell an April 40 call on the exchange at a premium of, say, $2 a share, or $200 for the option. That gives you an immediate 5% income on the $4,000 investment. Also, you continue to receive whatever dividends the stock pays.

Furthermore, the option provides a hedge against a drop in the stock's price. For example, assume that the stock falls to $38 some time after you sell the option. You have lost $2 a share, or $200 on the 100 shares originally purchased. But you received $200 for the call, so you remain even. You don't lose, therefore, until the stock falls below $38. In market parlance, the call produced "downside protection to 38."

If the stock remains under $40, it's unlikely that someone will exercise the call and compel you to sell the stock at that price. You could merely wait for the option to expire at the prescribed date in April and keep the $200 premium. If you don't want to risk the possibility that the price will rise to over $40, which would put the April 40 in the money and make the option more likely to be exercised, you could buy an April 40 call to cancel out the April 40 sale.

As you might expect, the April 40 premium would fall as the stock declined to $38. By the middle of April the option could be selling for as little as 1/2 (50 cents), or $50 for the 100 shares. By buying the call at that point, you net $150 on the deal ($200 received for the original sale of the call minus $50 paid for the closing call).

What happens, though, if the stock jumps to $42? The 100 shares you own are now worth $4,200. But if the call you sold is exercised, you will have to sell the shares at the $40 striking price, or $4,000. The loss of that $200 gain is offset by the $200 received for the option.

The $42 price represents the upside break-even point. Not until the price rises above that level will the potential gain on the exercise exceed the premium received. If the stock rises to $43 and the option to 3, you will have to pay at least $300 to buy an April 40 option to cancel out the one you sold for $200. If you do, you lose $100. If you don't, the stock could be called at the 40 striking price (which is what you paid for it) and you miss out on the price rise. You still have the $200 for the option you sold, but commissions could cut deeply into that.

The key: leverage. Given the proper circumstances, a call option seller can obtain immediate income on his stock plus some downside protection. But what's in it for the buyer?

What usually attracts buyers is leverage. It makes a little money do the work of a lot. In stock options it operates this way:

Say you are interested in buying a stock now selling at $40 because you think it could soon go up to $45. If you buy 100 shares outright for $4,000 and stock does hit $45, the investment produces $500, or a 12½% gain.

Assume that instead of buying the stock, you purchase an April 40 call option at 3 that costs $300 in all. In order for you to make back your premium, the stock must rise to $43. A seller is prepared to write the call because *he* thinks the stock won't go up, at least not above $43. But if the stock does increase to $45, the April 40 call becomes worth at least $500, or $5 a share, its intrinsic value. You close out the transaction by selling your April 40 call at $500 and make a net of $200.

That $200 represents a 66⅔% return on your $300 investment. Actually, you would probably make more than that because the April 40 call probably would rise to more than $5 a share on the possibility of even further gains in the stock.

You come out ahead on your April 40 call any time the stock goes over $43. At $44, for instance, the option should be worth at least its $400 intrinsic value and you can close out with a $100 or 33⅓% profit. Had you bought the shares, they would have appreciated to $4,400, a 10% return on the $4,000 investment.

However, the leverage that produces those exciting returns can also result in painful losses. If the stock tops out at $42, the intrinsic value of the option would be only $2 a share, or $200. If you close out the transaction at that point by selling the April 40 call, you lose $100 ($300 minus $200), or 33⅓% of the amount put into the option. If you had simply bought the shares at $40 and sold them when the price rose to $42, you would have made a *profit* of $200, or 5%, before commissions.

The option, though, has one advantage: You can't lose more than the $300 it cost, and that assumes you hang on to it until it expires, worthless. Losses or gains could be much heavier than those shown in the example if, instead of spending $4,000 on stock, you buy not one but several options totaling that amount in order to boost the potential return and reduce commission charges on each option.

You can play this same game in a declining market by trading puts instead of calls. Relatively few investors buy and sell puts, however, possibly because they are more difficult to understand. What's more, puts were available on only a handful of stocks until recently.

Puts can be used by conservative investors to protect capital gains on stocks they don't wish to sell. If you fear a drop in the price, you can buy a put and sell it when the price when the price of the underlying stock goes down. That permits you to hedge against the decline without actually selling your stock and incurring capital gains taxes.

Playing the spread. The options market lends itself to many sophisticated investment strategies. One that particularly delights experienced traders is "spreading." For a quick grasp of the underlying principle, consider this example.

Say a stock selling at $40 is represented on the exchange with two April calls, an April 40 and an April 45. The April 40 is offered at 4½, the April 45 at 1¾. The 2¾ difference between the two premiums constitutes the spread.

You buy the April 40 call (4½) and sell the April 45 (1¾). Actually, the precise premiums for each option aren't important as long as you manage to keep the 2¾ spread.

Assume the stock rises to $48, the April 40 premium to 9½ and the April 45 to 4½. The spread has widened to 5, which is what you hoped would happen. You now close out the spread with these results:

APRIL 40	APRIL 45
bought $450	sold $175
sold $950	bought $450
gain $500	loss $275
Net gain: $500 − $275 = $225	

In trading parlance, you bought a 2¾ spread and sold it for 5.

That particular operation is known as a bull price spread because it anticipates the widening of the gap between the two options, which typically accompanies a rise in the underlying stock. By reversing the original buy/sell—that is, by selling the April 40 and buying the April 45—you would have created a bear spread, which succeeds when the gap narrows in response to a decline in prices.

In another variation, called a calendar spread, you can create bull and bear positions by straddling two calls with the same striking price but different expiration dates.

For various technical reasons, the profit or loss on a spread is limited to the value of the original spread position. In the example, you could not make more or lose more than the $275 difference in the costs of the two options.

Obviously, options are not long-term investments, the kind you salt away in a safe-deposit box. They have to be watched closely and turned over frequently. As with many other investments, the rewards depend on your daring, skill and luck.

TRADING IN FUTURES

The futures exchanges make it possible to trade in a remarkable array of products—from basic farm crops, such as corn, wheat, soybeans and oats, to financial instruments, such as U.S. Treasury bills and foreign currencies.

As a futures trader you won't be bothered with corporate annual reports or voting proxies because you are not investing in companies. Nor will you have to keep track of dividends or interest checks because futures don't pay any. Whether you win or lose depends completely on whether the price of your futures contract moves in the direction, up or down, you think it will.

Actually, what you trade in the futures markets is not

a product but a standard agreement to buy or sell a product at some later date at the price set when the contract is negotiated for you on the floor of the exchange by open bids and offers.

All the contract terms other than price are fixed by each exchange for each of the products in its jurisdiction. For instance, the live cattle contract of the Chicago Mercantile Exchange specifies that you deal in 40,000 pounds of steers. The CME prescribes the minimum amount of earnest money, or the margin, that you must deposit with a broker when you buy or sell the contract.

You may choose a CME live cattle contract that expires in February, April, June, August, October or December. Those trading months, often called the delivery months, vary according to the seasonal or marketing patterns associated with the product and its storability. Fresh shell eggs, unlike most other products, are traded in all months because they are perishable. Like other futures, though, not all the egg deliveries are traded at one time.

The trading months revolve. As one delivery month expires or nears expiration, a corresponding position is added to the end of the roster.

22,500 dozen eggs. As an illustration of how the futures business operates, suppose you decide to take a flyer in shell eggs. The first step is to open an account with a commodities broker. You think prices are likely to rise, so you instruct the broker to buy one June contract calling for delivery of 22,500 dozen eggs at 50 cents a dozen before the contract expires on June 21. You give the broker a margin deposit of, say, $700 and sit back to wait for the price to go up.

At this point, you may be wondering what you will do with the 22,500 dozen eggs that the seller of the June contract is obligated to deliver. How will you pay the $11,250 for the entire lot? For that matter, how will the seller, who may be another outside speculator like you, get together 22,500 dozen eggs for delivery?

Only in extraordinary circumstances will either the buyer or the seller be forced to make good on a delivery. More than 95% of the futures contracts are settled by an offsetting transaction. When the buyer wants to get out of his purchase, he sells an equal number of contracts for the same delivery period. To liquidate your June shell egg contract, you sell a June contract. If the price has gone up by more than the brokerage commission plus the interest lost by keeping the margin deposit with the broker, you have made a profit. If the price rises by less or if the price drops, you have lost.

But what about the seller? Any time up to the cessation of trading in June contracts he can "cover" his short position by buying a June contract. That he reverses the customary sequence by selling first and buying second makes no difference. If he can buy back a June contract for less than he sold one, he makes money. If he is forced to buy at a higher price, he loses.

Because trades are normally offset and must be wound up by a fixed expiration date, brokers base their commissions on a "round turn"—a buy and sell in either order.

Spreads and hedges. Straight speculative purchases and sales constitute only part of the activity on the exchanges. As an alert trader, you must know something about spreading, which people like yourself can do, and hedging, which is done by businessmen or farmers who deal with the actual commodity and who might be the seller when you buy or the buyer when you sell.

• *Spreads*. In the usual spread you simultaneously buy a contract for delivery in one month and sell a contract for delivery of the same commodity in another month. They do not offset because they are not in the same position. Why anyone should do that becomes clear with this illustration:

The May delivery of a commodity is selling for $2.50 a pound, the December for $2.95. Normally for this commodity, December is priced only 35 cents a pound over May instead of 45 cents, and you expect that relationship to be reestablished. You sell December at $2.95 and buy May at $2.50. Sure enough, the two positions close up to a 35-cent spread—the December declines to $2.82 and the May to $2.47. You then un-wind your spread by selling a May contract and buying a December, offsetting both positions.

Now look at the results: You lost 3 cents a pound in the May contract, but you gained 13 cents on the short sale of the December delivery. That's a gross profit of 10 cents a pound.

Of course, that spread might have worked against you. If the May had held firm at $2.50 and the December had gone up to $3, you would have lost 5 cents a pound. Still, spreads in storable commodities are considered a relatively conservative operation and usually require less margin because of the possibility that losses in one position will be offset to some extent by gains in the other.

• *Hedges*. Hedging is designed to protect commodity producers, dealers and users from price losses. The grain dealer who is storing wheat bought at $2.70 a bushel wants some insurance against a price decline. He protects his inventory by selling futures contracts at corresponding prices, taking into account storage and other costs. If prices decline, he can offset his short position by buying back lower-priced contracts. That gain should compensate for some of the loss he suffers by having to sell the grain itself at a lower price.

The big attractions of futures markets are leverage and the promise of a fast turnaround. You can buy into a contract for about 5% to 10% of its dollar value, giving your profits—and losses—a boost hard to obtain anywhere else. As for speed, the overwhelming majority of futures contracts are liquidated within 60 days. Many last less than a week.

20

Gold, silver and other "hard" assets

Among the investment success stories of the past decade, none has been quite as spectacular as that of those who placed their faith in gold, silver, diamonds or some other so-called hard asset. While stock investors counted themselves fortunate to emerge from the 1970s with their capital intact, hard asset investors with a good sense of timing and a little bit of luck were rolling up stunning profits.

• *Gold.* Had you bought bullion in 1975, shortly after Americans could once again legally own it, and held it until early 1981—passing up the chance to sell when the priced roared past $850 per ounce in 1980—you still would have achieved a gain of better than 300%. Had you purchased gold coins in 1971, your gain for the decade would have surpassed 1,000%.

• *Silver.* Over the past ten years its price has increased at an annual compounded rate of more than 20%. For its early devotees, a buy-and-hold strategy paid off handsomely.

• *Diamonds*. Knowledgeable investors who dealt carefully in this sometimes treacherous market reaped substantial rewards. Salomon Brothers, a major investment firm, reports that diamonds appreciated at a compounded rate of about 15% per year between 1970 and 1980.

• *Collectibles*. Stamps, antiques, paintings, rare coins, Chinese ceramics, oriental carpets—these are some of the hobbies-cum-investments that have turned tidy profits for successful collectors in the 1970s. The markets for such items are relatively small, but Salomon Brothers has managed to keep tabs on some of them. The firm reports that the value of a selected portfolio of rare U.S. stamps increased by more than 20% per year during the last ten years. The price of Chinese ceramics rose nearly as much on an annual basis, and paintings by the Old Masters appreciated at a rate of about 13% per year. Each of those rates easily outpaced inflation over the same period.

Can this sort of success continue? Probably not in such a spectacular fashion. Big dips in gold and silver prices in mid 1981 actually wiped out a large part of the gains just described. Market forces in the years ahead won't be the same as those in the past. But hard assets will continue to offer profit potential to investors who take the time to be informed and have the ability to wait out the inevitable dips in price that affect investment markets.

INVESTING IN GOLD

Contrary to what many people believe, gold has not been a reliable long-term hedge against inflation. Its price movements have been erratic. It can be costly to buy, sell, assay, insure and store. It pays no interest or dividends while you're waiting for the price to rise.

On the other hand, gold has exceptional qualities in addition to its beauty, virtual indestructibility and suitability for various industrial requirements. As an investment it generally performs well when stocks, bonds and other widely owned vehicles are doing poorly. It is one of the few mediums of exchange that have endured through the centuries; governments and currencies have come and gone, but gold has survived wars, famine, pestilence and economic upheavals.

Gold has traditionally thrived on adversity. Its price has been an anxiety index. When inflation, economic chaos, violence or other troubles erupt—or even threaten—some people turn to gold.

Conversely, when peace and prosperity prevail, gold loses favor and the price falls. This is the opposite of what usually happens to securities and other investments that benefit from human productivity. Additional factors affect the price of gold, including the output from mines, new discoveries, industrial demand and government monetary policies.

Should you invest? A number of professional financial advisers agree that investment portfolios should include about 10% to 15% gold as insurance against an economic Armageddon. Many, perhaps most, independent analysts look for an upward trend in prices over the years.

That does not mean that gold is a protection against inflation. An historical study of gold's performance in that respect was conducted by Roy W. Jastram, a University of California business professor. From an analysis of 13 inflations and seven deflations in the United States and England over 400 years, Jastram found that gold was consistently a poor hedge against inflation but did very well during deflations.

The price has ben "remarkably similar for centuries," he declares, adding: "Anyone who fears the collapse of his country's currency is acting rationally when he shelters his assets in gold. It is when these judicious measures are translated into a strategy for protection against recurring price inflations that the reasoning breaks down."

These and other conclusions are detailed in Jastram's book, *The Golden Constant: The English and American Experience, 1560–1976* (New York: John Wiley & Sons, 1977).

Ways to invest. There are several ways to invest in gold.

• *Bullion*. It comes in everything from tiny wafers to 400-ounce bars and is sold by refiners, fabricators, currency dealers, so-called private mints and some securities brokers and banks. The metal should be certified at least 99% pure and bear the stamp of a recognized refiner, such as Englehardt Minerals & Chemicals Corporation or Handy & Harman. The weight should be expressed in troy ounces.

Keeping gold around the house is foolhardy, and you'll normally need special insurance even in a safe-deposit box (few banks insure customers against losses from boxes). Some dealers provide storage facilities and insurance. You may have to have bullion assayed when sold to confirm its authenticity, at a cost of $50 to $100 or more.

• *Coins*. Bullion coins, which contain a high percentage of gold, provide the safest, simplest and most convenient investment medium for most individuals. The South African Krugerrand is the most widely sold. Other popular coins include the Austrian 100 Corona, the Mexican 50 Peso and the Canadian Maple Leaf.

Gold coins are widely exchanged and easy to handle and can be authenticated by gold dealers without an assay. Most sell at a premium of 5% to 8% above the value of their gold content. Standard Krugerrands contain exactly one troy ounce of the metal, which simplifies trading. Rarer gold coins, such as those that were once used as money, usually have numismatic value, which complicates matters for nonexperts. Their prices may move independently of the price of gold itself.

• *Stocks*. By investing in U.S., Canadian or South African mining companies, you could play the gold market and collect dividends, too. Yields of some issues have sometimes reached over 20%. The risk is that government policies, political disruptions and labor troubles can affect profits even if company management is good. A few mutual funds invest all or part of their assets in precious-metal securities. (See chapter 18).

• *Depository certificates*. You can buy an interest in bullion stored in a vault and receive a nonnegotiable certificate as proof of ownership. A major provider of these is the Deak-Perera Group, an international dealer in currencies and precious metals. The gold is kept in Switzerland and is insured. You pay 1/2 of 1% of the asset value annually for storage and insurance, plus a 3% sales charge. A similar plan is offered by Dreyfus Gold Deposits, whose clients can have their gold stored in Delaware or sent to them. New York's Citibank sells $1,000 certificates and accepts follow-up orders for as little as $100.

• *Gold jewelry*. It's an investment you can flaunt while hoping for a price rise. Selectivity is all-important, however. Quality varies over a wide spectrum, and prices are, as a rule, substantially higher than the intrinsic value of the gold. Buy only from reputable, established dealers.

Before you invest. Don't be swayed by scare talk or wild predictions. Doomsaying is quite profitable for certain authors and publishers. Much publicity about gold is generated by dealers and producers.

Add up the costs before you make a commitment—sales commissions, storage and insurance charges, taxes and assay fees. Figure how much the price would have to rise before you'd start making money. (Note: The more you buy, the lower the transaction costs are likely to be.)

Never deal with strangers over the phone. Con artists who once sold Florida swampland and worthless stock by phone have been selling gold, diamonds and other trendy speculations. One operative recently pleaded guilty to defrauding more than 1,200 people in 45 states of about $6,000,000 through phone solicitations. Report suspicious or objectionable calls to the Commodity Futures Trading Commission.

INVESTING IN SILVER

Investors who find gold attractive may also be drawn to silver. Like gold, its price seems to thrive on bad news. However, although gold and silver are often mentioned in the same breath, as investments they are quite different in several important respects. For one thing, the silver market is considerably smaller. It is so small, in fact, that the buying and selling of a relatively few very wealthy individuals can greatly influence the price—something that has happened in the past and could well happen again.

Industrial usage plays a far more important part in the market demand for silver than it does for gold. And when prices rise, industrial users, such as manufacturers of film, electronic parts, batteries and other products, have a strong incentive to find substitutes for silver or recycle what they use. Either action is eventually reflected in the market demand for silver, which softens. Meanwhile, high prices also serve to spur faster production from the world's silver mines, thus adding to supplies. The combination of less demand and more supply is ultimately reflected in the price—it goes down. This is exactly what happened late in 1980 and early in 1981. The growth in industrial demand for silver was leveling off while production was increasing. The result was a decline in silver prices of more than 30% in a four-month period.

Undeterred silver investors base their hopes on the belief that the world is running out of the metal. However, while it is true that the demand for silver has exceeded supplies for most of the past decade, forcing countries to dip into stockpiles to satisfy the market, there are strong indications that supply and demand may have reached equilibrium in the past year or so. U.S. industry stocks of silver were higher at the end of 1980 than they were in either 1979 or 1978. If this trend continues, the major demand for silver will be created by speculators, and there is some question about whether their activity can sustain price rises in the future anything like those of the past.

The historic supply deficit could recur, of course, and if it does the price of silver would no doubt take off again. For the short term, however, many analysts question silver's potential for major gains.

Ways to invest. There are a number of ways to invest in silver if you are so inclined. The most obvious is to buy bullion, which you can do through major dealers such as Deak-Perera or smaller ones that have set up shop in the past few years. Possibly the most popular method is to purchase bags of pre-1965 U.S. silver coins. Dimes, quarters and half dollars were minted with 90% silver in those days, giving them a current value far above their original spending power. Bags usually contain $1,000 in face value but sell at prices determined by the market value of the silver in them at the time of the transaction. Half bags are also available.

As you can imagine, coins with a face value of $1,000 take up considerable space and weigh quite a bit. (A bag weighs about 55 pounds.) People holding bags of silver coins need a place to store them safely and should insure them against theft. Like gold, they produce no income until you sell.

There are other ways to invest in silver. Numismatic coins—those that increase in value because they are in demand by collectors, rather than strictly because of their silver content—tend to be more resistant to dips in silver prices, but they require an expert's eye or the advice of an expert for successful speculating.

If you'd rather not bother with actually holding onto silver or coins, you could still hook into silver's future by buying securities issued by mining companies. One of the largest silver mines in the United States is owned by Sunshine Mining Company of Dallas. In addition to common stock, Sunshine has issued silver-indexed bonds in $1,000-denominations that holders can redeem in the future for a specified number of ounces of silver. If silver prices fall, holders can elect to get their $1,000 back instead. Sunshine reserves the right to call in all the bonds starting March 15, 1985, if the price of silver makes them worth $2,000 or more for 30 consecutive days. Otherwise, at that time the company will start calling in 7% of the bonds each year until the issue matures in 1995. If you're interested, see a broker for information.

In addition, major brokerage firms have responded to the demand for silver in recent years by setting up accumulation plans for their customers that allow them to make relatively small investments and relieve them of the problem of storage. A broker can supply details.

INVESTING IN DIAMONDS AND COLORED GEMSTONES

By some accounts more than 200 organizations, mostly of recent vintage, are aggressively hawking so-called investment-grade diamonds as a key to riches or, at the very least, insurance against inflation. Razzle-dazzle sales pitches are delivered by phone, at "diamond seminars" held in plush hotels and in glossy brochures that come by mail.

You may even hear diamonds extolled by an insurance agent or mutual fund salesperson. A number of gem companies are urging sellers of financial products to include diamonds among their offerings.

But a lot of gem investors will end up poorer. An officer of the Gemological Institute of America, an educational and research arm of the jewelry industry, flatly rates gems as very poor investments for the average layman. (Such warnings do not necessarily spring from an altruistic desire to protect the public. Jewelers and their suppliers worry that speculation will drive prices beyond the reach of their customers.)

Diamond basics. You should know that diamonds suitable for investment are not necessarily the kind you find in the average jewelry store. Diamonds vary greatly by color, clarity, cut and carat weight—referred to in the business as the four C's. Although there is no real agreement on what constitutes an investment-grade diamond, the most readily acceptable ones weigh at least a carat, rank very near the top of the scale in color and clarity, and have been expertly cut for maximum brilliance. A certificate from a recognized gemological laboratory attesting to a stone's four C's should be part of every investment diamond deal. The Gemological Institute of America is a recognized lab, as is the European Gemological Laboratory.

Something like 80% of the world's rough diamond sales are controlled by DeBeers Consolidated Mines through its Central Selling Organization. The cartel attempts to maintain an orderly market by controlling supplies. In 1981, confronting a market in which the price of top-quality diamonds had tumbled by some 30% in the previous year, DeBeers cut back sharply on the amount of uncut stones it released. This ability of DeBeers to control supplies and thus manipulate prices is what gives many investors their faith in diamonds. And indeed, DeBeers can be counted on to act in its best interest and, by extension, the interest of diamond investors.

All of this doesn't make diamond profits a sure thing. To begin with, most investors have no choice but to buy at retail prices and sell at wholesale. Since markups can range from 30% to even 100% or more, that builds in the necessity for considerable price appreciation just to break even. This makes diamond investing a long-term proposition. Furthermore, gems, like gold and silver, pay no current income. Instead, you pay to store and insure them.

When it comes time to sell, you must be willing to wait. Whether you sell the stones yourself, consign them to an auction house or peddle them to a local jeweler or through a broker, it takes time to find a buyer, time to ascertain certification and time to get reliable appraisals. In all, arranging and carrying out a sale can easily take a month or two.

If you are interested in investing in diamonds, don't do it without investigating thoroughly. Know your dealer and insist on certifications from an impartial lab. Don't buy anything over the phone.

Colored gemstones. The special difficulties confronting diamond investors are multiplied for colored gems. Standards for grading aren't as well developed. The market isn't as organized. Records of historical price movements are hard to find. Investors can't even agree on what sorts of colored stones make good investments. For now, rubies and emeralds are most popular, but that could change. In short, colored gemstones are a highly specialized investment best left to those who know the markets. Ordinary investors should probably stay away.

INVESTING IN COLLECTIBLES

Collecting can combine the exhilaration of a treasure hunt with the joy of acquiring things you like. And the folklore of collecting is filled with tales of fabulous finds. A few years ago somebody discovered that the shade of an old lamp that had hung for years in a church rectory in New York City was a genuine Tiffany worth thousands of dollars. A baseball-player card picturing Honus Wagner, star shortstop for the Pittsburgh Pirates of old, was found to be worth more than $3,000. (Wagner forced a cigarette company to stop using his picture in its advertising, and only 19 of the cards are known to exist.)

Unfortunately, everyone doesn't come out a winner.

• Prices of collectibles can skid as well as climb. The value of some timepieces and stringed instruments fell by about 30% in 1975. Paintings and furniture dropped, too. A man who sold the Gutenberg Bible for $1,800,000 in 1978 got no more than he had paid for it in 1970.

• The market has always been heavily salted with fakes and flawed merchandise. Whenever something becomes popular, forgers grind out reproductions in massive quantities. There is also an abundance of schlock, such as certain commemorative medals and limited-edition offerings.

• Collectibles pay no interest or dividends. They often entail costs for insurance and storage. They may be hard to sell. And profits are often illusory. Say you pay $1,000 for a Victorian clock and sell it at an auction five years later for $1,500, less $300 for the auctioneer (commissions typically run between 10% and 25%). Your net gain is $200, or 4% a year.

Do it right. Yet none of the above should be cause for despair if collecting interests you. It can pay off—in enjoyment and satisfaction as well as in financial rewards—if you learn the ropes. What you collect should be something you like and can use, perhaps period furniture, paintings, decorative objects or classic cars.

Whatever you choose, learn all you can about it. The best way to make money collecting is to know more about your collectible than others know.

There is extensive literature to guide collectors—books and book clubs, magazines, newsletters, price guides, show and flea market directories and more. There are countless organizations of people with similar interests who meet, correspond, buy and sell, exchange information and get together socially. The *Encyclopedia of Associations*, available in most libraries, lists over 100 such groups, including the Society of Caddy-Spoon Collectors, the International Chinese Snuff Bottle Society and the Beer Can Collectors of America.

Taking courses, attending auctions, shopping at shows and flea markets, visiting museums and talking with other devotees will increase your knowledge. Collectors and dealers tend to be gregarious types who love to swap yarns and give advice. Try to find—and cultivate—a reputable dealer. Buying from him can have advantages over other methods of building a collection. A dealer can offer you a better selection of pieces and will generally stand behind them.

When you start collecting, buy the best you can afford. The higher the quality, the less risk you take assuming the price is fair. Articles you can use in your home—lamps, furniture, rugs, paintings, chandliers, musical instruments and such conversation pieces as wind-up phonographs—are especially good bets.

Be sure to get signed receipts, plus any other papers that attest to the value and include such information as the price, lot number and description of the object. A provenance, or historical fact sheet, comes with more expensive pieces.

Auctions are probably the best places to find bargains. In most other places you can probably beat the asking price by haggling, which nearly everyone tries. Prices of comparable items vary widely and tend to be lower in small towns.

Obtain an expert's appraisal before making a major outlay. Experienced personal-property appraisers are scarce—only about 350 are tested and certified by the American Society of Appraisers (P.O. Box 17265, Dulles International Airport, Washington, D.C. 20041) —but some others are doubtlessly qualified. The ASA roster includes specialists in antiques, gems, coins and stamps.

PART FIVE

PROVEN WAYS
TO CUT TAXES

21

Get all the tax breaks you have coming

The tax cut package passed by Congress in the summer of 1981 should be good news indeed for harrassed taxpayers who have watched their purchasing power suffer over the past several years, not only because of inflation but also because of their steady march up through the tax brackets.

But there's a funny thing about taxes: Most people approach them backwards. They sit down sometime between January 1 and April 15 and start sifting through the records of things they've already done, looking for ways to save.

The problem is, by then it's too late to take advantage of many of the opportunities that do exist to save. A smarter way to approach the task would be to look ahead, not behind. You can chart a tax strategy that will take you through the year in a manner calculated to yield the lowest possible tax bill come the following April 15. Sitting down and filling out your return is only the last step in such a strategy. Run through this checklist of ten tax-saving techniques to make sure you're paying attention to the steps leading up to your return.

CHECKLIST OF TAX-SAVING IDEAS

1. Seek tax-free income. No federal tax at all is due on interest from municipal bonds issued by states, cities and towns, though your state might tax it. This federal subsidy of state and local borrowing is especially attractive to people in higher tax brackets. At the beginning of 1981, a tax-free yield of 10%, for example, was the equivalent of about a 14.7% taxable yield for someone in the 32% bracket (taxable income of $24,600 to $29,900 on a joint return). But for someone in the 59% bracket ($85,600 to $109,400 taxable income) a 10% tax-free payoff equaled a taxable yield of 24.4%. Municipal bonds and other sources of tax-sheltered income are explained in chapter 22.

2. Keep close track of interest and dividends. In the past all "unearned" income—such as interest from savings accounts, money-market mutual funds and corporate bonds—was taxed at the top marginal rate, which could be as high as 70% in some cases. For 1981, however, Congress has decided to ignore the first $200 of interest on individual returns and $400 on joint returns. This is actually an expansion of the old dividend exclusion that has permitted owners of stock to escape tax on the first $100 ($200 on joint returns) of the dividends they received. In 1982 the exclusion reverts to the $100/$200 limit for dividends only.

3. Seek long-term capital gains. Only 40% of the profit from the sale of property and securities you own for more than one year is taxable.

4. Defer taxes. Certain kinds of investments allow you to postpone paying taxes from the year in which income is earned to a later year, when perhaps you'll be in a lower tax bracket. A sure advantage of tax deferral is that money that otherwise would go to the government continues earning for you. Series EE U.S. savings bonds offer this feature, as do deferred annuity contracts. Interest on savings bonds isn't taxed until they are cashed. With an annuity you postpone taxes on the interest until the income is actually paid out. Taxes are also delayed on income that builds up in Individual Retirement Accounts and Keogh plans. You can deduct from taxable income the amount you contribute to your plan each year (see chapter 24).

Another way to put off paying taxes is by delaying receipt of capital gains income with an installment sale. Not only could an installment sale keep this year's tax tab down—you pay only on the share of the profit you receive during the year—but it might also let you avoid a big bulge in income that could force you into a higher tax bracket. Congress recently simplified the installment sales tax rules. IRS publication number 537, *Installment and Deferred Payment Sales,* has details.

5. Take advantage of the new tax law. The new law offers numerous chances to save.

• All-Savers certificates can yield up to $1,000 in tax-free income, $2,000 on a joint return. See page 278.

• Tax rates are scheduled to be cut by 25%: 5% in 1981, 10% in 1982 and again in 1983. Keep this in mind when making decisions about the timing of income you receive in those years. Starting in 1985, tax brackets will be indexed to reflect inflation. Other things being equal, you now have more incentive to defer taxable income to a later year.

• If you are in an extremely high tax bracket, delay receiving taxable dividends and interest until 1982 or later, when the top tax on such "unearned" income falls to 50% from 70%.

• If both you and your spouse work for pay, take advantage of the marriage penalty deduction. It allows you to deduct 5% of the first $30,000 of the lower-paid spouse's income in 1982, 10% thereafter.

• If you pay to have a child or children cared for while you work, investigate the liberalized child-care credit in the new law. Even though you didn't qualify before, you may qualify now.

6. Look for tax shelters. The goal in the early years of many of these big-time deals and intricate schemes isn't to make money at all but to create losses that can be used to reduce the taxes on other income. Tax shelters are the subject of the next chapter.

7. Watch the small stuff. If you own a vacation home, you have a chance for some tax-free income. If you rent out the house for 14 or fewer days during the year, you don't have to report to IRS any of the income you receive. Go beyond that 14-day limit, though, and all rental income is taxable.

There are only a few other ways that you can receive money without the IRS stretching out its hand. Life insurance proceeds and gifts you receive aren't subject to income taxes. If you drive for a car pool, you can pocket the money from riders without paying extra taxes.

8. Use gifts and trusts. The theory is simple enough. Income from property you own—stock dividends or rent, for example—has to be reported by you and is taxed in your top bracket. If the assets were owned by another family member in a lower tax bracket, however, the income would be treated more gently by the IRS. By using gifts, trusts, or interest-free loans, you may be able to shift the tax burden to a lower bracket.

Assume, for example, that to save for your daughter's college education, you deposit in a special account the dividends from a group of securities. In 1981 the dividends come to $800, but you have to pay tax on the income. In the 32% bracket, that costs $128 (after you claim your $400 dividend exclusion), so you have only $672 to put aside for the future college costs. Had your daughter owned the securities, the entire $800 could probably have been saved. Even if part of the income was taxable, your daughter no doubt is in a much lower tax bracket.

You could give the securities to your daughter outright, or if she is a minor, you could set up a uniform-gifts-to-minors account that would permit you to name a custodian to control the assets until she reaches the age of majority. This tax break has its cost, of course: The gift is irrevocable, as discussed in chapter 5.

Under the federal gift tax law, beginning in 1982 you can give any number of people up to $10,000 each without incurring any gift tax liability. If you are married and your spouse agrees, the tax-free limit is $20,000. Bigger gifts may be subject to the gift tax, but your unified estate and gift tax credit would probably cover it. See chapter 25.

You could also shift income-producing property for a while by using a short-term trust. Although more expensive and difficult to use than a gift, a trust gives you the right to regain ownership to the property after as little as ten years and one day. For more details on gifts and trusts as tax savers. See chapter 5.

9. Make interest-free loans to dependents. Interest-free loans are a tax-saving device the IRS doesn't like but so far has been unable to block in court. These loans must be payable to the lender on demand.

Assume that you give your dependent parents $2,000 a year for their support. In the 49% bracket you have to earn $3,922 in pretax income to wind up with $2,000 after taxes. However, if you could lend your parents enough money—at no interest—so that by investing it they could earn $2,000, you could keep helping them while cutting back on what you pay Uncle Sam. The income would be taxable to your parents, presumably in a much lower tax bracket. You could regain control of your assets at any time by recalling the loan.

Should you do this, keep in mind that income the borrower receives could cause you to lose him as a dependent. Among the criteria for claiming dependents are that you provide more than 50% of their support and that they receive less than $1,000 in taxable income during the year. The $1,000 limit doesn't apply to a child who is under 19 or a full-time student.

10. Keep good records. As you're pulling together information to do your tax return, flaws in the year's record keeping will become apparent. Haphazard record keeping can cost you money in the form of lost deductions and credits.

Don't let that happen. Get your files in order and commit yourself to keeping them up to date. Here are some of the categories in which good records can yield tax savings.

• *Sales taxes*. It's fairly simple to keep track of what you pay for local property and state income taxes because these deductible expenses are usually paid in big chunks. But general sales taxes are forked over in dimes, nickels and even pennies at a time. Keeping track of all those little receipts can be maddening. It's not too tough, though, once you get in the habit of depositing them in a file.

For those who don't keep receipts, the IRS has drawn up tables that estimate sales tax deductions based on income and family size. That's the easy way—just look up a number. But it can be a costly shortcut.

Ronald Reagan's 1979 tax return shows, for example, that he deducted actual sales tax expenditures rather than using the IRS estimate of how much he paid out. Though the tables would have allowed Reagan a paltry $727 write-off, he claimed $2,148. The president's 1979 income was more than half a million dollars, but even the less well-to-do individual can benefit from good record keeping. Saving receipts is essential for people who live in a few states that don't impose a general sales tax. Keep records of tax paid on out-of-state purchases to substantiate any sales tax deduction.

• *Your car.* Here again, for those who don't bother with receipts, the IRS lends a hand with the standard mileage rate. For unreimbursed business use of your car you can deduct 20 cents a mile; for auto use connected with charitable and medical purposes you get 9 cents a mile. In addition to the standard rate, you can also deduct the cost of tolls and parking. You need records of such expenses.

But running your car might be costing you far more than 20 cents a mile. If you want to try to beat the standard business rate, you need to keep track of what you spend for gas, oil, repairs, maintenance, insurance, licenses and garage rent and how much depreciation costs you each year. However, the IRS says that when you're figuring your actual per-mile cost for medical and charitable driving, you can count only out-of-pocket costs, such as oil and gas.

• *Medical expenses.* Into this file go receipts and cancelled checks for health insurance premiums and for doctor and hospital bills. Remember, too, to keep track of what it costs to get to and from physicians and dentists, what you pay for medicine and drugs (right down to the aspirin and cold remedies) and expenses for such items as eyeglasses, hearing aids, false teeth and crutches. Save records of any expense connected with, as the IRS says, "the diagnosis, cure, relief, treatment, or prevention of disease." Since you can generally deduct only the share of medical costs that exceeds 3% of your adjusted gross income, it's important to keep track of all expenses that move you toward that threshold.

You can deduct medical expenses you pay for yourself, your spouse and anyone who qualifies as your dependent. You can also write off medical bills you pay for someone who receives more than $1,000 in taxable income but would otherwise qualify as your dependent.

Suppose that you and your brother support your elderly mother but neither of you can claim her as a dependent because her independent income exceeds $1,000. You could arrange for whichever of you is in the higher tax bracket to pay your mother's medical bills while the other directs his support to nondeductible items. That way Uncle Sam will pick up the biggest possible share of the medical expenses.

• *Charity.* Set up a file for records or charitable contributions to your church, the community chest, your college and so forth. When you don't get a receipt, write a note showing the date, amount and recipient. Your contribution doesn't have to be in cash to earn a tax deduction. Old clothes, a car or furniture given to a charitable organization generates a deduction based on the item's fair market value. If you drive your car in connection with church or synagogue work, to get to the Red Cross to donate blood or for other charitable purposes, you can deduct the actual cost or 9 cents per mile plus the cost of tolls and parking. In 1982 and after, you can deduct part of your charitable contributions even if you don't itemize.

• *Energy.* This file is for receipts for things that qualify for the energy tax credit: storm doors and windows, automatic setback thermostats, insulation, caulking. You can take a credit for 15% of the first $2,000 you spend on such items if your home was built before April 20, 1977. If you install solar, wind-powered or geothermal equipment to produce energy for your home, you can take a credit for 40% of the first $10,000 you spend.

• *Your house.* If you want to cut your tax bill, buy a house. Consider the case of the young couple who bought their first home recently. Their $110,000 mortgage carries a 12¾% interest rate, making the monthly payments almost $1,100. Add $100 a month for property taxes and they're paying over $1,200 a month—$40 a day—for the roof over their heads. They both work and are in the 50% bracket. Almost the entire mortgage payment is deductible interest, and they can write off the property taxes, too. The government is paying almost 50 cents of every dollar.

Other tax angles of homeownership deserve attention, too.

What you spend to maintain the place isn't deductible, but improvements will affect your tax bill sooner or later. The cost of a fence or a new driveway where none existed before, for example, increases your cost basis for the house, and that's the figure you subtract from the sales price to determine the taxable profit when you sell. Whenever a household bill might qualify as an addition to the cost basis, keep the receipt. For more on this, see chapter 6.

• *Expenses of Working.* Whenever you spend money for a job-related expense, ask yourself: "Is this deductible?" Union dues are, for example, as are the costs of special work uniforms, subscriptions to professional journals and certain unreimbursed business travel expenses, including food and lodging if you're away from home overnight.

In some cases educational expenses can be deducted as a business-related expense. The key test is whether they prepare you for a better job or are necessary to keep your performance up to snuff in your present job. The latter expenses are deductible; the former aren't. And when you hunt for a new job, many of the expenses you incur are deductible.

If you have to hire someone to care for your children or another dependent so you can work or look for work, you may be able to take advantage of the child care credit. It permits a direct deduction from taxes for 20% of actual expenditures, within limits. In 1981, the top credit allowed is $400 for the care of one child, $800 for two or more. In 1982 those limits jump to $720 and $1,440. When your income exceeds $30,000, the credit is reduced in stages.

YEAR-END TAX TACTICS

If you keep suggestions like the above in mind throughout the year, you should see results the following April. But remember that December 31, not April 15, is the deadline for most tax-saving moves. That makes the last couple of months of the year an important time for reviewing where you stand and taking steps to protect your position.

Shifting income. Sometimes there are good reasons for packing as much income as possible into either the current year or the next one. Suppose you expect a big infusion of income next year—from the sale of property, perhaps, or from moving to a much higher-paying job. In such cases it may make sense to concentrate as much of your income as possible into the current year, to protect it from next year's higher tax bracket.

Before you take such a step, however, note this: If your income is unusually high this year compared with prior years, or if you expect it to be unusually high next year, you may do better by income averaging in one of the years. You can average if your income for the year in question is more than 20% over your average income during the prior four years, plus $3,000. Income averaging can save substantial sums in taxes in the upper brackets. Computations are made on Schedule G of form 1040, and it might pay you to work through the form before deciding which year would be the better one in which to concentrate income.

On the other hand, suppose you expect to retire next year or take some other action that will cut your income considerably. Then you might want to shift as much income as possible into next year, when your tax rates will be lower.

Unfortunately, most people don't have a great deal of control over the timing of their income. Salaries and wages are usually paid on a fixed schedule and there's not much you can do to change it. But if your employer pays an unexpected year-end bonus, for example, you may be able to arrange to receive it in the more advantageous tax year. If you're self-employed and a cash-basis taxpayer, you could speed up or slow down sending bills to customers near the end of the year in hopes of having the desired effect on income flow.

Investors can exercise some control over their income by deciding when to take capital gains or losses. Tax considerations aren't always uppermost in these decisions, but they can sometimes be important.

Timing capital gains and losses. As the end of the year approaches, the important distinction to make is between long-term and short-term gains and losses. A long-term gain or loss is one that results from the sale of property or securities held for more than a year. A short-term gain or loss results from a sale of property or securities held a year or less. The tax law makes important distinctions based on the holding period:

Short-term gains are fully taxable; short-term losses are fully deductible up to the $3,000 annual limit for capital loss deductions. (Excess losses may be deducted in future years.)

Only 40% of net long-term gains is taxed and only 50% of net long-term losses can be used to offset ordinary income. It takes $6,000 in long-term losses to offset $3,000 in ordinary income.

When you have net long-term and net short-term gains, you report both and each gets its specialized tax treatment. The same goes if you have both net long-term and net short-term losses. But if you have a mix, a net long-term gain and a net short-term loss or vice versa, you use one to offset the other—without worrying about their differing tax values—to find your net gain or loss for the year. This is important to keep in mind as you consider year-end transactions.

Assume that transactions so far have resulted in $3,000 in short-term gains that will be taxed as ordinary income in your top marginal bracket. Check your list of stocks with their paper profits and losses. Any sale that produces a $3,000 loss would wipe out the gain and its added taxes, but a long-term loss would be best, since using it to offset a short-term gain effectively doubles the tax value of the long-term loss.

When used to offset ordinary income, a long-term loss is worth only 50 cents on the dollar, whereas a short-term loss can offset ordinary income dollar for dollar.

When it comes to offsetting a gain, though, long- and short-term losses are treated equally, offsetting the profit dollar for dollar. (If you have a long-term as well as a short-term gain, the long-term loss would first be used to offset the long-term gain and only the excess could be used to balance the short-term gain.)

Similarly, if your tally sheet for the year shows a net short-term loss, you may want to postpone until after the first of the year a sale that would produce a long-term gain. Taking the gain this year would mean offsetting the loss dollar for dollar. Postponing it, though, gives you a chance to take advantage of the tax law's differing treatment of long- and short-term transactions.

A $3,000 net short-term loss, for example, can reduce taxable income by $3,000. Taking a $3,000 long-term gain to cancel the loss would mean giving up that saving. Of course, waiting until next year to realize the long-term gain means you can't use this year's loss to offset it. But even though you have to pay tax on the gain, you come out ahead. Only 40% of the gain, or $1,200 in this case, would be taxed.

Guarding dependents' exemptions. These are worth $1,000 apiece and are by no means guaranteed from one year to the next. Five dependency tests must be met each time: Generally, you must provide more than half your dependents' support; their gross income must be under $1,000 each for the year, unless they are your children under age 19 or full-time students for at least five months of the year; in most cases they must live with you, unless they are your children, parents, close relatives or in-laws; they generally must be United States citizens or residents of the United States, Canada or Mexico; and they must not file a joint return with someone else. Unusual circumstances can sometimes imperil dependency exemptions:

- If it appears that a potential dependent may end the year supplying more than half of his own support, consider whether to step up your payments between now and the end of the year. Would it save you money in the long run? To a couple filing a joint return with $30,000 of taxable income, a $1,000 dependency exemption is worth about $370 in the pocket. You can also suggest that the dependent put a larger portion of his own earnings in savings rather than spending it for self-support.
- If you share the cost of supporting a dependent with others but none of you contributes enough alone to claim the exemption, any one of the contributors paying more than 10% of the cost of support can claim the dependent, assuming all the other dependency tests are met. The other contributors of more than 10% must declare to IRS in writing that they won't claim the exemption that year. You accomplish this with form 2120, called the "Multiple Support Declaration," available from IRS.

Assessing medical expenses. Unless your medical expenses amount to more than 3% of your adjusted gross income, they are worthless to you as tax reducers. Late in the year you can look back on expenses you've paid so far and anticipate the nonemergency care that lies ahead. If it is apparent that the bills won't amount to more than 3% of income this year, consider delaying optional treatment and putting off payment of some bills until the following year. Your medical expenses may be higher then, and maybe the government will absorb some of the cost.

Timing other transactions. As the end of the year draws closer, your timing of transactions with tax consequences becomes crucial. Look for deductions to shift from one year to the next by speeding up or slowing down payment. In addition to payments for medical care, good candidates are charitable contributions, subscriptions to professional or job-related publications, union or professional association dues, rent on a safe-deposit box (if the box is used to store taxable income-producing papers) and certain state and local taxes.

GETTING HELP
WITH YOUR TAX RETURN

Every year about half of all Americans hire someone else to do their tax returns. Counting those who get someone to do their taxes for them free, the proportion of taxpayers needing help filing returns rises to about three-fourths. Fortunately, there is plenty of assistance available.

The IRS. With offices scattered throughout the nation and toll-free telephone lines, the Internal Revenue Service itself is the busiest of the taxpayer helpers. Besides providing instructions and forms and answering your questions, IRS employees will actually prepare returns under some circumstances. The phone number of the nearest IRS office is in your local phone book.

IRS also runs the Volunteer Income Tax Assistance program, through which it trains volunteers to provide free tax help in their communities, primarily for low-income, elderly and non-English-speaking taxpayers. Check with a local IRS office to see whether there's a VITA program in your area.

To some people, going to the IRS for tax help may seem like asking for trouble. It's true that many tax rules are open to different interpretations and IRS may take a stingier view of your tax liability than other authorities —such as the courts—may allow. Looking beyond IRS for assistance usually means having to pay for it, but remember that the cost is deductible on your tax return.

Commercial preparers. H&R Block, Inc., prepares more tax returns by far than any other firm in the country—about 10,000,000 or more a year. The convenience of Block's offices (the firm has almost nine times as many offices as the IRS, many of which are open nights and on weekends during the filing season) and the company's extensive advertising are part of the reason so many taxpayer's are willing to pay about $30 apiece to buy H&R Block treatment for their returns. That fee includes changes for the 1040 long form plus Schedules A and B. State and local income tax returns are extra.

How good is the help provided by Block and other national firms such as Beneficial Income Tax Service and the Tax Corporation of America? Most preparers employed by national firms receive a substantial amount of training to learn the basics and keep up with changes in the tax law. And most returns are double-checked for accuracy. At Block offices, for example, another preparer goes over returns done by his colleagues; at Tax Corporation of America a computer does the review.

There are no federal standards for commercial preparers. In fact, the IRS staunchly opposes any kind of testing or licensing program. However, all taxpayers are covered by rules imposed by the Tax Reform Act of 1976. A preparer can be fined for deliberately or negligently understating a taxpayer's liability, for failing to give the taxpayer a copy of the completed return or for failing to sign the return himself. These regulations are aimed at rooting out unscrupulous and incompetent preparers.

By exercising care, you can eliminate much of the risk. Be wary of local tax-preparation operations that pop up in the spring and are likely to disappear just as quickly in mid-April.

Here are some tips to help you choose a commercial preparer that will give you the most for your money.

• *Go early*. One criticism of commercial firms is that they rush taxpayers in and out to build a high-volume operation. If you're part of the last-minute crunch, you might be shortchanged.

• *Find out in advance how much you'll be charged*. The more complex your return, the higher the fee is likely to be. Ask whether the fee includes preparation of any necessary state and local forms.

• *Ask the preparer about his qualifications and experience*. Also ask how completed returns are checked for accuracy.

Be suspicious of a preparer who doesn't ask you a lot of questions. The preparer's job is to probe into your financial affairs and apply what he learns to get you all the tax breaks you deserve.

• *When you get your completed tax return, check it over carefully*. Remember, you are the one who suffers if your tax liability is overstated, and you are ultimately responsible for errors. Be certain all forms and schedules the preparer discussed with you are included. If, for example, you are eligible for a credit for child-care expenses and the preparer filled out the proper form, be sure it's attached to the return.

Professional help. The more complex your return, the wiser it might be to turn to a professional tax practitioner, such as an enrolled agent or an accountant. Many charge by the hour, since what they're selling is their knowledge of how to use the tax laws to your advantage.

Public accountants' fees for preparing itemized 1040s generally run to over $50. Enrolled agents and certified public accountants are usually more expensive. Fees vary widely, so the only way to find out what they charge in your area is to ask them. You need to know what it will cost to have your return prepared, whether the person doing the job will represent you in case of an audit and, if so, the estimated cost of that service.

• *Public accountants* needn't be licensed in most states, and their competence and experience can vary a great deal. Before hiring an accountant, ask about his education and experience and find out whether he's a member of his state accounting society and the National Society of Public Accountants. The NSPA has relaxed its prohibition against advertising, so you may see more accountants out looking for your business.

• *Enrolled agents* are the only tax practitioners who have to meet IRS standards. Whether or not they're accountants, enrolled agents earn their status by having worked as IRS auditors for at least five years or by passing an IRS exam on technical tax matters and accounting. Enrolled agents can argue their clients' cases at IRS audits and appeals. (Though commercial preparers can attend an audit with a taxpayer, they appear as witnesses to explain how the return was prepared, not as representatives of the taxpayer.)

Enrolled agents may be hard to locate, since there are fewer than 20,000 in the country and until comparatively recently they were prohibited by IRS from advertising their special status. Check the yellow pages.

• *Certified public accountants* must pass an examination and have a certain amount of experience to earn their title. If yours is a highly complicated financial situation, it might be wise to choose a CPA to help you with your tax return and also to offer tax-planning advice. Check with your banker or lawyer for recommendations. Some CPAs specialize in corporate accounting and have neither the time nor the inclination to do individual tax returns.

In some cases attorneys who specialize in tax law will help their clients with tax returns, although their primary activity is advising clients on knotty areas of the law. Lawyers and CPAs, like enrolled agents, can represent clients at IRS audits and appeals.

WHAT IF YOU'RE AUDITED?

The first step signaling an official disagreement between you and the IRS is the audit. There are three types: *Correspondence* audits, as their name suggests, are handled entirely through the mail and generally involve only minor matters requiring documentation.

Office audits, which are held at district IRS offices, are used to examine returns that raise questions too complicated to be settled by mail. *Field* audits, in which an auditor or agent comes to your home or place of business to inspect your tax records, are reserved for those people or businesses filing very complex returns that require voluminous records for verification.

If your return is selected for an office audit, the IRS notifies you by mail of the questions being raised and asks you to appear with your records at a nearby IRS office on a specified day. If the problem was caused by an error or misunderstanding on your part, you may decide to agree with the auditor's findings and sign a form stating that you do. You'll have to pay whatever additional tax has been assessed, plus the interest on it that has accumulated since the date the audited return was due. (The interest rate has been 12% recently.) The paper you sign will cut off any additional interest 30 days later provided you pay up with a reasonable time after that. Of course, if you pay immediately, the interest stops then.

You needn't decide right away whether to agree with the auditor. You can go home and think it over. Meanwhile, the IRS will send you a copy of the auditor's report on your return, along with literature that spells out your alternatives, which are to sign the agreement form and pay up, to set the administrative appeals process in motion by requesting a conference with higher-ups, or to sit tight until the IRS issues a formal notice of deficiency, permitting you to take your case to the Tax Court.

If you decide during the course of the audit that you disagree with the auditor's position, you can ask to meet right away with his supervisor. If you can't get a more favorable ruling that way, you can go home and wait for the letter of deficiency and then take your case directly to the U.S. Tax Court, or you can pursue your appeal within the IRS. Most people try the IRS route first.

At the initial conference, IRS supervisors can weigh the hazards to IRS of litigation for cases in which the disputed amount of tax doesn't exceed $2,500 in a single year. This authority has made compromises possible at the district level, and most disputes are settled there. Taxpayers still dissatisfied can take their cases to court or go to the next step in the administrative appeals process.

Appeals conference. This is as far as you can go within the IRS. Most taxpayers hire an accountant or a lawyer to do their negotiating at this level.

The court system. You can wait until you've exhausted the administrative procedures available, or you can abandon the IRS appeals route any time after the audit and take your case to court. There are three courts empowered to hear tax cases.

• *U.S. Tax Court.* This one is the most commonly used, and it hears cases in which the IRS is attempting to collect more tax than a taxpayer thinks is due. Unlike a criminal trial, where the government has the burden of proof, in a Tax Court trial the law presumes that the IRS is correct, except in fraud cases. In other words, the burden of proof is on you. However, you need prove only that the original assessment is wrong; you don't have to show what the correct one should be. Verdicts are often compromises in whch the judge decides partly in favor of the taxpayer and partly in favor of the government.

If the taxes in dispute amount to $5,000 or less in a single year, you can ask to have your case heard by the

Tax Court's small-case division. Decisions here can't be appealed to a higher court, but it's easier to represent yourself and most people do. Proceedings are informal and written briefs aren't required. Small cases can be heard in any of more than 100 cities. For information about filing a case and the necessary forms, write to Clerk of the Court, U.S. Tax Court, 400 Second St., N.W., Washington, D.C. 20217.

• *U.S. District Courts*. Most cases not tried in the Tax Court are brought in U.S. District Courts, which are located in most principal cities. District Courts differ from the Tax Court in several ways. Most important, they hear only suits for refunds. Some taxpayers consider District Courts more lenient than the Tax Court and shift their cases there by paying the disputed taxes and then filing for a refund. If the refund is denied, the taxpayer can then bring suit in District Court.

• *U.S. Court of Claims*. This court has the same jurisdiction over refund suits as the District Court, but it is not used nearly as much. One reason is that all cases must be tried in Washington, D.C.

If you lose in any of these courts (except the small-case division of the Tax Court), you can appeal to a

---

HOW DO YOUR DEDUCTIONS COMPARE?

Knowing how much people with similar incomes deduct on their tax returns can be helpful as you work on your own. The table at right lists the average itemized deductions claimed on 1978 returns by taxpayers at various income levels who took those deductions. The figures shouldn't be considered guides to how much you can deduct; only your records of qualifying expenses can determine that. But if your totals fall far short of the averages, you may be overlooking several valuable deductions.

adjusted gross income	medical expenses	taxes	donations	interest	other
$ 10,000-$ 11,999	$1,071	$1,141	$ 522	$1,864	$ 406
$ 12,000-$ 13,999	1,004	1,255	557	1,868	447
$ 14,000-$ 15,999	1,000	1,380	513	1,993	460
$ 16,000-$ 17,999	657	1,531	508	2,164	468
$ 18,000-$ 19,999	657	1,646	568	2,149	441
$ 20,000-$ 24,999	561	1,876	570	2,280	455
$ 25,000-$ 29,999	498	2,245	644	2,456	480
$ 30,000-$ 49,999	503	3,007	869	2,880	613
$ 50,000-$ 99,999	668	5,309	1,825	4,585	1,136
$100,000-$199,999	963	10,001	4,676	7,933	2,123
$200,000 and over	1,510	26,699	25,913	19,633	7,269

higher one. From Tax Court and District Court, you go to the U.S. Court of Appeals, then the U.S. Supreme Court. From the Court of Claims, appeals go directly to the Supreme Court.

How to improve your chances. Preparation for your battle should begin before the initial audit. The letter you receive from IRS will generally indicate the areas being questioned, but the auditor doesn't have to limit the examination to those items. You should review your entire return.

During the audit, don't volunteer more information than you're asked for. If the auditor raises a point you didn't anticipate, you needn't fumble for an explanation on the spot. Remember, you don't have to decide whether you agree or disagree with the auditor at the meeting. If you're not sure of what you should do, wait for the auditor's report and study it in a more relaxed atmosphere at home. Then you can plan your approach.

At every step of the appeals process, you'll have to decide whether you want to continue to the next. Time and money will always be major considerations. If you stick with it and your case involves a question of law that a court must arbitrate, the dispute could stretch on for years. That helps explain why so many taxpayers decide to settle for a compromise somewhere along the way.

22

Tax shelters you can use

Thanks to inflation and the progressive federal income tax, a lot of people who once thought of tax shelters as havens only for the rich are busy looking for shelters of their own. And no wonder. You'd need $44,000 to live as well in 1981 as you could on $20,000 of income in 1971, inflation having pushed up the cost of things some 120% in the ten-year period. Actually, you're even worse off than that comparison suggests. Consider: A $20,000 taxable income in 1971 put you in the relatively humble 28% tax bracket on a joint return. But if your taxable income has kept up with inflation, you're now in the considerably loftier 43% bracket. A single person on the same income ladder would have climbed from the 36% bracket in 1971 to the 49% bracket in 1981.

So the lure of tax shelters is not difficult to understand. Actually, just about any use of your money that legally allows you to escape, reduce or defer taxes could be called a shelter. You already have one if you own your own home, have life insurance, buy U.S. savings bonds or receive certain benefits from your employer, such as a qualified pension plan. Corporate securities offer a form of shelter: Gains in value aren't taxed until realized, the tax treatment is favorable, losses may be deductible, and a portion of the dividends escapes taxation. Professional people can often shelter income through self-incorporation. The list of possibilities goes on and on.

Other chapters in this book deal with the tax advantages of various kinds of investments. This chapter will discuss in detail three of those that are expressly designed to be tax shelters: municipal bonds, real estate limited partnerships and oil and gas drilling deals. Each has growing appeal in an era of inflation.

WAYS TO BUY MUNICIPAL BONDS

The investment packagers of Wall Street have responded imaginatively to the public's demands for tax-free income from municipal bonds. Years ago they figured there was a market for a product that would help guide investors through the sprawling marketplace of municipal debt, where some 35,000 different governmental units compete for dollars. The result was the appearance in 1961 of the first municipal bond unit trusts. They made available, for a small sales fee, portions of a fixed portfolio selected by the fund's professional underwriters. The minimum investment in most cases was $5,000.

Then, in 1976, the mutual fund idea came to municipals. Minimum investment dropped to only $1,000 in most cases, for which you got a slice of a portfolio of bonds that the fund's managers would buy and sell to take advantage of market conditions.

There's a third way to acquire a portfolio of municipal bonds—the old fashion way, by buying your own instead of letting someone else choose them for you. If you are in the market for municipals, you'd do well to compare the different ways of acquiring them. You could discover that some prominent features of particular methods fade in importance while others you might have overlooked begin to loom large.

But before you take the plunge, you'd be wise to learn as much as you can about what municipal bonds are and where they come from.

What is a municipal bond? It's a catchall name that describes the debt issues of cities and towns, states and territories, counties, local public housing authorities, water districts, school districts and similar governmental or quasigovernmental units. Because interest paid to buyers of the bonds is exempt from federal income taxes and, usually, income taxes of the state in which the bond is issued, municipals can pay less interest than corporate bonds of comparable quality and still deliver the same after-tax yield.

The higher your tax bracket, the more valuable this tax-exempt feature becomes. The table on page 369 shows how tax-free yields compare with taxable yields at various income levels.

Municipal bonds come in two principal varieties.

- *General obligation bonds* pledge the faith and credit of the government that issues them, meaning that the taxing authority of the issuer stands behind the bond to insure payment of interest and principal.
- *Revenue bonds* carry a more limited backing. Their repayment is generally tied to particular sources of revenue, such as bridge or highway tolls, or to specific taxes, such as those on alcohol or cigarettes. Uses of revenue bonds include financing of construc-

tion projects, such as waterworks, airports, rapid transit systems and sports complexes.

Municipal bonds, just like corporate issues, vary in quality according to the financial soundness of their issuers. To serve as quality guides for investors, Standard & Poor's Corporation and Moody's Investors Services, Inc., study available financial data and determine credit ratings for municipal bond issues. Bonds considered least risky get rated AAA by S&P and Aaa by Moody's. These triple-A's are considered prime or gilt-edge investments. Next in quality comes S&P's AA, the equivalent of Moody's Aa, followed by the A rating used by both services, then BBB (Baa by Moody's), BB (Ba) and so on down the line. Bonds rated below BBB or Baa are considered speculative issues that might make them risky investments over the long run.

It stands to reason that the higher a bond's rating—in other words, the safer an investment it appears to be—the lower the interest it needs to pay to attract investors. Thus, the riskiest bonds tend to yield the most. That's an obvious fact, perhaps, but an important one.

HOW MUCH TAX-FREE
INCOME IS WORTH

This table shows the approximate equivalent taxable yields for tax-free yields ranging from 8% to 12% in tax brackets ranging from 28% to 70%. Your tax bracket is the highest rate at which your income is taxed. To use the table, find the tax-free yield at the left, then read across to where that line intersects the column headed by your tax bracket. For example, a 9% tax-free yield is the approximate equivalent of a 15.79% taxable yield for someone in the 43% bracket. The table does not reflect the effect of state income taxes.

(Note: These were the brackets in effect for 1981.)

FEDERAL INCOME TAX BRACKET

TAXABLE EQUIVALENT YIELD

TAX-FREE YIELD	28%	30%	32%	34%	37%	39%	43%	44%	49%	54%	55%	59%	63%	64%	68%	70%
8.00	11.11	11.43	11.76	12.12	12.70	13.11	14.04	14.29	15.69	17.39	17.78	19.51	21.62	22.22	25.00	26.67
8.25	11.46	11.79	12.13	12.50	13.10	13.52	14.47	14.73	16.18	17.93	18.33	20.12	22.30	22.92	25.78	27.50
8.50	11.81	12.14	12.50	12.88	13.49	13.93	14.91	15.18	16.67	18.48	18.89	20.73	22.97	23.61	26.56	28.33
8.75	12.15	12.50	12.87	13.26	13.89	14.34	15.35	15.62	17.16	19.02	19.44	21.34	23.65	24.31	27.34	29.17
9.00	12.50	12.86	13.24	13.64	14.29	14.75	15.79	16.07	17.65	19.57	20.00	21.95	24.32	25.00	28.13	30.00
9.25	12.85	13.21	13.60	14.02	14.68	15.16	16.23	16.52	18.14	20.11	20.56	22.56	25.00	25.69	28.91	30.83
9.50	13.19	13.57	13.97	14.39	15.08	15.57	16.67	16.96	18.63	20.65	21.11	23.17	25.68	26.39	29.69	31.67
9.75	13.54	13.93	14.34	14.77	15.48	15.98	17.11	17.41	19.12	21.20	21.67	23.78	26.35	27.08	30.47	32.50
10.00	13.89	14.29	14.71	15.15	15.87	16.39	17.54	17.86	19.61	21.74	22.22	24.39	27.03	27.78	31.25	33.33
10.25	14.24	14.64	15.07	15.53	16.27	16.80	17.98	18.30	20.10	22.28	22.78	25.00	27.70	28.47	32.03	34.17
10.50	14.58	15.00	15.44	15.91	16.67	17.21	18.42	18.75	20.59	22.83	23.33	25.61	28.38	29.17	32.81	35.00
10.75	14.93	15.36	15.81	16.29	17.06	17.62	18.86	19.20	21.08	23.37	23.89	26.22	29.05	29.86	33.59	35.83
11.00	15.28	15.71	16.18	16.67	17.46	18.03	19.30	19.64	21.57	23.91	24.44	26.83	29.73	30.56	34.38	36.67
11.25	15.62	16.07	16.54	17.05	17.86	18.44	19.74	20.09	22.06	24.46	25.00	27.44	30.41	31.25	35.16	37.50
11.50	15.97	16.43	16.91	17.42	18.25	18.85	20.18	20.54	22.55	25.00	25.56	28.05	31.08	31.94	35.94	38.33
11.75	16.32	16.79	17.28	17.80	18.65	19.26	20.61	20.98	23.04	25.54	26.11	28.66	31.76	32.64	36.71	39.17
12.00	16.67	17.14	17.65	18.18	19.05	19.67	21.05	21.43	23.53	26.09	26.66	29.27	32.43	33.33	37.50	40.00

How costs affect yields. You should, of course, shop for the highest yield consistent with the risks you're willing to take. Let's assume for a moment that each of the three options mentioned earlier—unit trusts, mutual funds and individual bonds—offers precisely the same yield. Will your earnings be the same, whichever you buy?

The answer is no, and the reasons lie in the costs associated with the different forms of ownership. First comes the sales fee. If you buy the bonds directly from a broker, it is included in the cost. Brokerage houses normally sell bonds from their own accounts, and when they raise the price to add in their sales charge, they usually recalculate the yield to reflect the additional cost to the investor. This means that when you buy, for example, a bond issued to yield 8.25%, you might get a return on your investment of only 8%. Part of that missing 0.25% would be lost not just to the dealer's commission but also to market demand that is driving the cost of the bond up and thus driving its yield down. But from your point of view, what you are purchasing is a bond yielding 8%.

Unit trusts and mutual funds don't work that way. Trusts, and funds sold by brokers, carry fees that reduce your actual return. The front-end load, or sales charge, is deducted from your gross investment. If you buy $10,000 worth of a unit trust charging a 4.5% sales commission, what you get is $9,550 worth of bonds earning interest for you. The same thing happens with a mutual fund sold by a broker. Sales fees are typically 3% to 4.5% for unit trusts and 4% to 4.75% for mutual funds. No-load funds, of course, don't charge a sales fee.

There are other costs involved as well. Mutual funds, including the no-loads, require the services of investment advisers to manage portfolios. For this the managers generally take 0.5% or more of the fund's average net-asset value as a fee. This reduces your return by the same amount. A mutual fund earning 8% on its portfolio and keeping 0.5% for management can pay out only 7.5% to its investors.

Because unit trusts normally don't trade in the market once the portfolio is set, they don't need managers. But they do require trustees and administrators, who don't work for free. Their fees generally amount to about 0.1% of net-asset value. Thus, a trust earning 8% on its portfolio will return 7.9% to its investors.

The question of risk. All municipal bond investments entail some degree of risk. The bonds are rated on the same scales used for judging the quality of corporate bonds, but issuers aren't required to reveal as much about their financial affairs as corporations are. Nevertheless, municipal bonds have had an excellent safety record over the years, and defaults are extremely rare. Some unit trusts offer insured portfolios to ease investors' fears on that count. Unit trusts and mutual funds in general tend to stick to the higher-rated issues.

A bigger risk for most investors is getting locked into a return that looked fine at the beginning but turns out to be inadequate in the face of increased inflation and rising interest rates. If you have to sell the bond under those circumstances, you'll suffer a capital loss.

You can ease the pain somewhat by performing what is known as a "tax swap". Tax swapping is especially suited to municipal bonds and can be a valuable year-end tax-saving move. You merely sell your devalued bonds and reinvest the proceeds in issues paying the higher, current rate. This gives you a capital loss for your tax return and, ignoring commissions and delays, keeps your bond income at the same level.

Example: Say you are holding $5,000 in municipal

bonds purchased in January and yielding 8%. That gives you an annual income of $400. By December, rates have climbed to 10%. You are still earning $400 from your bonds, but their market value is now down to $4,000. You sell the bonds, take a short-term $1,000 loss and reinvest the proceeds in 10% bonds. Since 10% of $4,000 is $400, you've maintained your level of income while achieving a capital loss that can be used to shelter taxable income from other sources.

Mutual funds offer the opportunity to ride along with rising interest rates if their managers are alert enough to spot the signals in time to make the necessary portfolio changes. The risk with mutual funds lies in the possibility that the funds' managers will make the wrong decisions or wait too long to make the right ones, thus depressing the fund's net-asset value and handing you a capital loss if you have to sell your shares.

When interest rates are volatile, sticking to short maturities is a sensible way to hedge the risks of the market. That's the approach taken by a group of mutuals that have come to be known as the tax-free money-market funds. These funds put their money into short-term notes issued by state and local governments and their agencies. The notes are considered temporary financing that will be paid off with revenues from taxes, bond issues and other sources. That's why you will find such securities as these in fund portfolios: bond anticipation notes (BANs), tax anticipation notes (TANs), revenue anticipation notes (RANs), grant anticipation notes (GANs), tax and revenue anticipation notes (TRANs), temporary loan notes (TLNs), and project notes (PNs). PNs are sold by the Department of Housing and Urban Development to help local authorities finance urban renewal and housing developments. There is a list of tax-free money-market funds on page 375.

Of course, if interest rates fall after you've bought your bonds, your return will look pretty good regardless of how you bought them, and you'll have a capital gain if you sell.

In a unit trust or a mutual fund you get another measure of protection that is difficult to obtain on your own: diversity. Consider a unit trust consisting of 16 different issues. You can buy a piece of some trusts for as little as $1,000. Since the great majority of individual bonds sell in $5,000 minimums, you'd need a portfolio worth at least $80,000 to buy that much diversity on your own.

Tax Treatment. All municipals pay interest that is exempt from federal income taxes, but you still owe state and local taxes in most cases unless the bond is issued by a unit of your state or local government. This can be an important distinction, depending on where you live.

You can control the taxability of bonds you purchase on your own by restricting your portfolio to state and local issues that carry the overall exemption. And there are unit trusts available that invest only in issues of a certain state. For example, underwriters have put together trusts that specialize in the issues of California, Massachusetts, Minnesota, New York and Pennsylvania. With mutual funds and most unit trusts, though, you have no control over the proportion of out-of-state issues in the portfolio.

Liquidity. Mutual funds redeem their shares on demand, and unit trusts generally maintain a secondary market for their units. There's also an active market for individually held bonds, but you usually have to pay a premium if you want to sell only one or two. An investor with a single bond to sell should count on getting $10 to $15 under the going market price for a larger batch of the same issue.

Convenience. To calculate what this is worth to you, consider what is involved in maintaining your own portfolio of municipals. Most are issued in "bearer" form, so you'll need a place to safeguard them, probably a safe-deposit box. You have to watch the papers and other sources if you own any "callable" bonds, and you need to watch dates for sending in coupons to claim your interest. Interest is nearly always paid semi-annually, whereas most unit trusts and mutual funds let you choose monthly or quarterly distributions instead. In addition to professional selection and management, that's the sort of service they are selling you.

Unit trusts are put together by brokerage houses and you have to purchase them there. Following are some examples of mutual funds that invest in municipal bonds. Before deciding to invest in any of them, write for their prospectuses and compare their portfolios, management staffs and shareholder services. No-load funds are indicated by an asterisk.

Dreyfus Tax Exempt
  Fund, Inc.*
600 Madison Avenue
New York, N.Y. 10022

Federated Tax-Free
  Income Fund, Inc.*
421 Seventh Avenue
Pittsburgh, Pa. 15219

Fidelity Municipal Bond
  Fund*
82 Devonshire Street
Boston, Mass. 02109

IDS Tax-Exempt Bond
  Fund, Inc.
1000 Roanoke Bldg.
Minneapolis, Minn.
  55402

Kemper Municipal Bond
  Fund
120 S. LaSalle St.
Chicago, Ill. 60603

Oppenheimer Tax-Free
  Bond Fund, Inc.*
Two Broadway
New York, N.Y. 10004

T. Rowe Price Tax Free
   Income Fund, Inc.*
100 E. Pratt Street
Baltimore, Md. 21202

Scudder Managed
   Municipal Bonds*
175 Federal Street
Boston, Mass. 02110

The following funds stick to short-term municipal notes and permit shareholders to write checks on their accounts. All are no-load funds.

Chancellor Tax-Exempt
   Daily Income Fund,
   Inc.
100 Gold Street
New York, N.Y. 10038

Scudder Tax-Free Money
   Fund
175 Federal Street
Boston, Mass. 02110

Fidelity Tax-Exempt
   Money Market Trust
82 Devonshire Street
Boston, Mass. 02109

Vanguard Municipal
   Bond Fund
Money Market Portfolio
Drummer's Lane
Valley Forge, Pa. 19482

REAL ESTATE TAX SHELTERS

Investor interest in real estate limited partnerships has run so high in the past few years that many brokerage firms have set up special departments to handle the sales. The result is that today you can invest in a real estate partnership as easily and quickly as you can buy stocks and bonds. And if you express an interest in doing so, you are likely to be swamped with more information than you ever received about a stock or a bond: a ponderous prospectus or comparable document, a sales brochure, pictures of buildings and sometimes even a booklet explaining the principles of tax shelter investing.

The pictures are usually attractive and the booklets can be informative, but the prospectus—the key document—makes difficult and perplexing reading for those who are not experts. It's doubtful whether anyone except the people who draft them ever reads an entire prospectus.

You will need a lot of information, however, to evaluate a real estate tax shelter and avoid the many pitfalls. The first thing to check is whether you truly belong in this kind of shelter. The prospectus will spell out income and net worth criteria for prospective investors. Shelters that are not registered with the U.S. Securities and Exchange Commission, called private placements, may impose additional criteria.

You probably should not go into this kind of tax shelter until you're in a 49% or higher tax bracket. Based on federal income tax rates in effect at the beginning of 1981, that meant a taxable income—after deductions and exemptions—of at least $45,800 on a joint return, or at least $34,100 if you're single. Below that level, you might be better to stick with investments such as municipal bonds, which produce tax-exempt income instead of generating losses you can use to apply against income from other sources.

It takes some effort to comprehend the bizarre economics of tax shelters. You may have heard the old joke about an investor whose accountant calls to tell him, "We're in trouble. This deal is starting to make money." Whatever your income and financial resources, you can't tell whether it's worth buying into a real estate shelter until you examine its risks and rewards.

How they are set up. In a typical arrangement the tax shelter syndicator sells interests in a new partnership that will construct or buy apartment houses, shopping centers, theaters, mobile home parks, or other commercial real estate. Buying an interest makes you a limited partner. Customarily, as a limited partner, you would be responsible only for the amount of capital you have contributed. For instance, your salary or other assets couldn't be attached by the partnership's creditors if it couldn't pay its debts.

The partnership business is run by a general partner. In certain circumstances limited partners might be able to vote on a general partner, but otherwise they usually can't participate in management.

You can buy partnership interests from several sources. Your attorney and accountant might have regular contact with syndicators who put together private offerings. Securities firms market both private offerings and shelters registered with the Securities and Exchange Commission.

• *Size of investment.* Public offerings are commonly issued in $1,000 units with a $5,000 minimum purchase. You need considerably more to get into a private placement. One recent private offering for an apartment development required $95,000 payable in six installments geared to the construction schedule.

• *Cash flow.* A partnership functions as a conduit, passing through both income and losses to you. You report your share of the loss or income on your tax return.

As a member of the partnership you are taxed on your share of its taxable income, if any, even if it is not distributed to you. Before the partnership reaches the taxable income stage (some never get there), your financial return will probably consist largely of tax losses and cash distributions that are considered a return of capital. Capital gains may come into the picture later when the partnership sells its properties.

• *Liquidity*. Each partnership sets a termination date, but the partnership is likely to dispose of its properties well before then—say in seven to 12 years—and distribute the proceeds. By that time the partnership may have used up much of its deductions, and investors may be impatient for their money.

Assume, though, that you want to sell your interest before the windup. Getting out of a tax shelter is much more difficult than getting in, for at least four reasons:

1. Although the general partner or the securities dealer who originally sold the plan might try to help find a buyer, there is no organized secondary market for partnership interests.

2. Since a partnership characteristically produces the biggest tax losses in early years, there's less incentive for investors to buy into it later on.

3. The value of your share in the partnership cannot be accurately determined until the properties have been sold.

4. The general partner must restrict transfers because the partnership can lose certain tax benefits if 50% or more of the interests are sold in a 12-month period.

How they work. As a partner in a syndicate, you're entitled to the same tax benefits you would receive if you owned property directly, plus some additional write-offs that come from investing in commercial property.

• *Depreciation*. Each $1 of ordinary depreciation neatly offsets $1 of income. More important for the tax shelter is that depreciation may exceed the taxable income left after other deductions are taken. With $1 in taxable income and $1.25 in depreciation, the partnership can pay you $1 that is considered a return of capital and is thus not taxable. It also allocates to you an ordinary income tax loss of 25 cents that you can use to wipe out taxable income from other sources.

Keep in mind that tax losses are not necessarily real losses. You incurred no out-of-pocket cost to earn that 25-cent loss. Depreciation losses may catch up to you later, however, because they reduce the basis on which you compute the gain or loss on the sale of the property, thereby increasing the potential gain and the tax on that gain.

• *Mortgage interest*. Typically, shelters have large interest deductions because they employ large amounts of borrowed money. That leverage considerably increases the amount of property they can buy and customarily the allowable tax deductions. With 75% mortgage financing, $1,000,000 of equity money makes it possible to buy a $4,000,000 property; with 80% financing, the partnership has $5,000,000 to work with. Mortgage payments consist largely of interest in early years, thereby building up the front-end deductions.

• *Nonrecourse loans*. Real estate, by congressional exemption, remains the one field where investors can get the tax deduction benefits of nonrecourse loans—a tremendously important advantage.

In other fields you can't deduct more than you invested plus your share of partnership *recourse loans*. Those are debts you are personally obligated to pay if the partnership can't and if a forced sale of the property pledged as collateral wouldn't produce enough to cover the loan balance. (Your home mortgage is a recourse loan.)

With a nonrecourse loan, a common type of financing in commercial real estate, the lender has no call on your assets other than your interest in the partnership itself.

Nonrecourse financing multiplies each partner's tax deductibility. If you invest $10,000 and your share of the partnership's mortgage loans is $30,000, you have a tax deduction base of $40,000 even though you are not liable for the $30,000 debt.

• *Expenses*. Operating expenses can be offset against rental income.

• *Investment tax credit*. The partnership may also be able to take a tax credit for certain types of equipment and building rehabilitation expenses.

Role of the general partner. The prospectus will quickly make it clear that the general partner may not be one person or one company but a constellation of affiliated people and companies that run the partnership from start to finish. They put the shelter deal together; they buy, build, or contract for the construction of properties for the partnership; they rent the buildings; they manage the property; they may sell insurance to the partnership; they handle the partnership's relations with limited partners; and they act as agents for refinancing or selling the properties.

The partnership's success depends to a great extent on the general partner's honesty and competence, so carefully check the prospectus material on the general partner's previous projects and the leading officials involved. Naturally, you want administrators with substantive experience in real estate (not just in organizing and selling shelters) and with demonstrable records of having performed well for their investors.

The newcomer to tax shelter deals may well be dismayed by the heavy fees that are drained from the partners' investment and the partnership income. At the top of page 381 are the estimated initial charges for one recent syndication stated as a percentage of the proceeds from sales of interests in the limited partnership.

organization expenses	1.1%
brokerage firm commission	8.0
property acquisition fees to unaffiliated firms	1.6
working-capital fund	2.0
real estate commissions to general partner and others	9.0
total	21.7%

In this case, only 78.3% of the limited partners' investments would be available for down payments on the properties.

Moreover, the 21.7% represents only front-end costs. The general partner and its affiliates will cut into the deal at many other places: rental fees, property management fees, refinancing charges, a share in the partnership's cash flow, a commission on the sale of the properties, and a part of the profit made on the sale.

Of course, you might have to pay many of those fees if you bought commercial property on your own. As a limited partner, though, you have no choice because the fees are laid out in the partnership agreement. You can guard against unreasonable fee arrangements to some extent by testing the shelter on the following points.

• *How much of your initial contribution will be left for investment?* The prospectus should contain detailed figures, but you may need help in interpreting them because of vague or overlapping expense categories. In the example just given, the prospectus seemed to indicate that the front-end charges would be 13%. They were far from the 21.7% computed, on request, by an executive of the brokerage firm selling partnership units.

- *Are there percentage or dollar limits on the general partner's fees?*
- *Does the partnership agreement prohibit dealing with affiliated companies that serve only to increase the general partner's revenues?* For example, are independent appraisals required for properties bought for the partnership from an allied company? Is the general partner's insurance brokerage firm required to get competitive bids from a few insurance companies?
- *Are you entitled to a prescribed minimum return before the general partner takes part of the cash flow?*
- *Are some of the fees contingent on successful performance?* For instance, will proceeds from the sale of properties first be applied toward repaying your investment before the general partner takes a share?

How to assess the risks. Partnerships differ so much that it's unwise to rely on generalizations. But the following guidelines may help you screen offerings for investigation.

• *Types of property.* Subsidized housing projects are regarded as high-risk (and high-fee) enterprises. Partnerships set up to construct other kinds of buildings rank lower. Investments in existing buildings are considered safest.

• *Tax vulnerability.* You may feel more comfortable with a shelter that has obtained an advance IRS ruling on its partnership qualification than one that depends solely on an attorney's opinion. However, a ruling does not bar the IRS from later disallowing certain deductions or losses or the allocation of profits and losses among the partners. Also, the general partner's conduct of partnership affairs may adversely affect your tax position. And there's always a risk that the IRS or

Congress may change the rules. The closer the partnership hews to accepted practices, the less risk of an upset.

• *Leverage*. Risk rises with leverage and can assume many forms: A big debt may strain the partnership's cash flow; the lenders may foreclose if the partnership can't meet the mortgage payments; the limited partners may be asked for additional contributions to keep the business going; a mortgage with a balloon payment (a large lump sum payable usually at the expiration of the mortgage) might force the partnership to refinance when loan rates are temporarily high.

• *Write-offs*. Understandably, investors are drawn to deals with big tax losses. But those losses may be achieved at the expense of creating a viable real estate business. Projects with the biggest and fastest tax benefits generally have the fewest long-term business benefits.

Cutting the risks. Investing in two or more shelters may make more sense than putting everything in one, no matter how attractive. Someone with, say, $20,000 to invest might put half in a real estate shelter and half in an oil and gas partnership, or spread the money between two real estate partnerships with different types of properties.

Since shelters normally produce their biggest tax losses early on, you can maintain a higher level of deductible losses by staggering your investments.

Should you get professional advice? Yes. An experienced lawyer should be able to review a prospectus in two to four hours because much of it consists of standard provisions. Many accountants also analyze tax shelters for clients. However, lawyers and accountants can be expected only to identify the risks for you.

Checking out all the financial details might raise their fees prohibitively.

Also, an attorney or accountant may not be very helpful if the partnership involves an unfamiliar business. Real estate and gas and oil tax shelters are probably the most popular, but many other types of enterprises are being turned into tax deals—equipment leasing, cattle feeding, mining, producing plays or movies, or even such fancy things as lithographic plates and master recordings.

Hot new businesses inevitably attract some unethical promoters. Government officials report, for example, that many of the most flagrant abuses over the past few years have been in coal mining, where big increases in demand were expected because of oil conservation programs. Brokers who sell shelter programs are supposed to exercise "due diligence" by checking out the facts. But one way you can protect yourself is to learn something about the business in which the partnership invests.

OIL AND GAS TAX SHELTERS

When you hear about the billions being poured into explorations for oil and gas, keep in mind that a lot of that money comes from investors like you.

For as little as $5,000 you can buy from securities dealers an interest in a limited partnership that is supposed to give you fat tax deductions in the first year and tax-sheltered income in later years. The combination has proved irresistible to many small and big investors seeking tax relief.

Companies that run and sponsor the partnerships raised over a billion dollars through such deals in 1980, and that figure covers only the public offerings, those registered with the Securities and Exchange Commission. Still more capital was drawn into the business through private offerings sold to limited numbers of investors willing to lay down $50,000 or more for a partnership interest. But oil and gas shelters can be quite risky. They require careful investigation.

Controlling the risks. Though chance plays a large role in all oil and gas drilling, you can to some extent tailor the financial risks—as well as the potential rewards—by selecting appropriate programs.

The sponsor's prospectus for a publicly registered partnership or the offering circular for a private deal will tell you the kind of drilling operation for which your investment will be used. Exploratory drilling ventures, which include wells in new fields and extensions of old fields, present the greatest risks and the largest potential returns. Less risky are development programs, which drill in areas close to proven sites, and balanced programs, which combine exploratory and developmental operations.

Each partnership tempers the risks by drilling a number of wells. The prospectus broadly identifies the areas where the partnership intends to drill or owns land leases. But you usually can't pinpoint drilling sites because most programs are set up as blind pools, an arrangement that gives the company acting as general or managing partner the flexibility to select whatever site it considers most promising.

Ultimately, you have to put your faith in the skill of the general partner and the company's geological advisers in locating and negotiating rights to land with oil and gas prospects.

The prospectus should spell out in detail the drilling

and financial results of previous programs run by the manager. Even that information might not be enough for an effective evaluation. The manager's record may be based on properties far from the ones the current partnership will drill, and the prospectus does not directly disclose the oil and gas reserves on which the previously developed wells' future revenues depend.

Costs and revenues. The partnership's provisions for sharing costs and revenues between the limited partners (the investors) and the general partner also influence the financial results.

Typically, the investors pay virtually all or most of the partnership expenses in one way or another. Right from the start about 15% of your investment is likely to be taken off for a management fee to the general partner, certain overhead expenses, and sales commissions to the organization marketing the limited partnership interests.

After that, expenses and revenues are usually apportioned according to one of four systems.

• *Functional allocation.* The limited partners pay for labor and supplies and other items categorized as "intangible drilling costs," which can be quickly written off for tax purposes. The general partner pays the costs that have to be capitalized—that is, amortized over the equipment's useful lifetime. In return the general partner receives a share, say 40% to 50%, of the revenues. Much of the capitalized equipment may not be needed until the presence of oil or gas is confirmed, so the general partner gets a free look, or a "peek in the hole," as it's characterized in the business.

• *Reversionary interest.* The limited partners pay almost all the costs and get first claim on the revenues from each well or group of wells until they recover 100% or a specified higher proportion of their money. Then the general partner cuts in for a share of the further revenues and expenses.

• *Carried interest*. The general partner pays a small part of the cost, say 1%, but usually takes 15% of all revenues. The investors, therefore, bear nearly all the costs and receive 85% of the returns.

• *Promoted interest*. The general partner contributes about 10% of all expenses (both capital and intangible) and receives a larger share of the revenues, perhaps 25%. With this plan the general partner assumes a significant financial responsibility for failures—for the dry hole costs. Relatively few programs use the promoted-interest pattern.

Tax advantages and tax traps. Oil- and gas-drilling programs throw off quick tax deductions for many of the partners' drilling expenses. If the well produces, part of the revenues will be sheltered by depletion allowances. And you may be able to take as a long-term capital gain part of any profit that results from the sale of your interest or from the partnership's sales of the wells.

The investor gets his biggest deductions during the first year, when the partnership is paying the intangible drilling costs and not receiving any offsetting income. Those first-year write-offs can run over 90% on a functional allocation plan and 65% to 80% on other programs.

Oil and gas deals, though, contain a lot of potential tax traps, so read the tax section in the prospectus with particular care and consult an accountant if you have any doubts. Some of the intangible drilling costs and percentage depletion allowances are considered "preference items" that may increase taxes for people in high tax brackets. You might become liable for taxes on the partnership's earnings without any corresponding cash payout from the partnership when it uses income to pay back loans. Also, deductions for losses are limited to the amount the investor has at risk in the partnership.

Privately offered partnerships known as leveraged programs stretch their operating funds and the basis for investor's tax deductions with standby loans from the limited partners. In addition to their initial investments, investors give the partnership promissory notes that fall due in, say, three to five years. The notes are guaranteed by letters of credit purchased from a bank at an annual cost of ½ of 1% to 2%. The partnership can borrow against the letters of credit for operating money. If all goes well, the partnership will earn enough money to pay the debt and take the limited partners off the hook. If not, they can be held responsible for the amount due on the notes.

That leverage can multiply the limited partner's write-offs to 200% to 400% of their initial investment. If the investor, for instance, puts up $50,000 in cash and $100,000 in notes and all of that sum is spent on deductible items, he could get deductions of $150,000.

Even in a nonleveraged deal, the partnership agreement may permit the general partner to assess investors for additional funds, usually up to a fixed percentage of their original participation. If they refuse to contribute the extra money, they give up the rights to some of the partnership income.

The problem of liquidity. Getting into an oil and gas deal is much easier than getting out. Limited partnership interests can't be sold as you would sell stocks and bonds.

The general partner may undertake to buy a certain percentage of the limited interests after the organization has been operating for a couple of years. Instead of cash, you may be offered stock in the general partner's company.

In either case, however, the general partner will heavily discount the value of oil and gas reserves discovered by the partnership. As a result, you will get back far less than you invested, particularly if you cash in your interest during the first few years, when it's difficult to estimate reserves accurately.

What to look for. Despite all the information in the voluminous prospectuses, the attractive brochures that often accompany them and the broker's verbal explanations, you're likely to feel somewhat lost when you search for a suitable oil and gas program. For guidance, try these suggestions from tax shelter experts:

- First, review your tax situation to make certain you can benefit enough from the tax savings to warrant assuming all the risks inherent in oil and gas deals. You might find that less risky tax-favored investments would be more appropriate.
- Look for a program that matches your risk preference. The development programs, which tend to be the least risky, generally produce the best results.
- All other factors being equal, you're better off with a promoted-interest partnership. It cuts the tax deductions somewhat, but it increases the general partner's incentive to find productive wells because it shares in all the costs, including the expenses of drilling dry holes. Be careful, though, that the general partner doesn't grab too much of the revenues in return. If it

contributes 10% of the costs and raises its share of the revenues by 15 percentage points to 25%, it's within the bounds considered reasonable in the business.

- Watch out for excessive up-front expenses. They should not take appreciably more than 15% of your investment.

- When you evaluate the general partner's past programs, check out both the total revenues and the cash distributed to the limited partners. Those two sets of figures are not the same.

- Don't limit yourself to the large public programs. You are likely to hear about them first because they are sold by the national brokerage firms. Smaller programs are usually handled by smaller securities dealers.

- Keep in mind that limited partnership interests are sold on a commission basis. It is to be expected that a broker will stress the benefits of the program he has available for sale. Give yourself time to investigate a few programs and, if you like, hold out for something better. There's no shortage of oil and gas deals.

PART SIX

YOUR JOB, YOUR RETIREMENT, YOUR ESTATE

23

Making the most of your job

ARE YOU KEEPING UP WITH INFLATION?

Unless you happen to be independently wealthy, you are probably counting on a steadily increasing paycheck to protect you against inflation and provide the wherewithal you'll need to achieve financial security in the years ahead.

In many ways your job is your most important asset of all, since it demands so much of your time and energy. You should know whether the pay you're getting is keeping up with inflation, whether your fringe benefits compare favorably with other people in the same line of work, and whether there are opportunities for growth and advancement ahead. If your job is seriously deficient on any of those points, you must be prepared to act.

Start your analysis with a look at your salary increases over the past several years. Inflation has damaged almost everyone's standard of living, but most groups of workers have managed to come close to matching the year-by-year increases in the cost of living. Here's what those increases have amounted to for each year since 1973, when things really started to get bad: 1973—8.8%; 1974—12.2%; 1975—7.0%; 1976—4.8%; 1977—6.8%; 1978—9.0%; 1979—13.3%; 1980—12.4%. With compounding that comes to a 103% increase in the consumer price index for the eight-year period.

To find the comparable percentage change in your earnings, simply subtract the amount of your salary in a starting year from your salary figure this year. Divide the difference by the salary figure from the earlier year, then multiply the answer by 100 and you'll have the percentage that your earnings changed in that period. Match that figure with the inflation total for the same period to see how you fared. Here's an example of the math involved:

$$
\begin{aligned}
&\text{1980 salary: } \$35,000 \\
minus \ &\text{1973 salary: } \underline{\$18,000} \\
&\text{difference} \quad 17,000 \\
&17,000 \div 18,000 = .94 \times 100 = 94\%
\end{aligned}
$$

Since the cost of living increase for the corresponding period was 103%, this person suffered an 9% loss in purchasing power.

That's a quick way to figure out where you stand, but it tends to overstate the actual gain or loss. A better way is to use this slightly more complicated formula:

$$
\frac{\% \text{ change in wages} - \% \text{ change in prices}}{100 + \% \text{ change in prices}} \times 100
$$

In the case of the example above, then:

$$
\frac{(94) - (103)}{100 + 103} =
$$

$$
\frac{-9}{203} \times 100 = -4.4\%. \text{ Not as bad as it looked.}
$$

The next step in your assessment of where you stand is to figure out, with the help of your old tax returns, how big a bite taxes take out of your income now compared with the starting year. As your income has increased, you have been climbing the tax-bracket ladder. That dictates careful attention to the kinds of tax planning and sheltering techniques described in chapters 21 and 22.

The value of fringe benefits. Fortunately, your paycheck isn't all you get from your job. Your fringe benefits most likely include some items that can be worth a big chunk of money. And an especially appealing aspect of fringe benefits is that normally they don't increase your tax bill the way cash income does. Thus they can boost what you get from your work without setting you up for the tax-plus-inflation double whammy.

The total dollar value of your combined fringe benefits probably ranges from 18% to 65% of your regular salary, depending on how generous, enlightened, and prosperous your employer is. If you receive a normal amount—nothing to really brag about, but certainly enough to be appreciated—your fringes should be worth at least a third of your annual salary.

Your employer considers as fringe benefits everything he pays out for you in addition to your salary. Fringes include your vacation time and sick leave, lunch and coffee breaks, and what the company pays for you into government-required unemployment and workers' compensation funds.

You would be perfectly justified in noting that these kinds of fringe benefits don't help put food on the table now. But there are other fringes that do.

If you were a heavy user of medical services—for example, if you have children of the age at which trips to the doctor's office for everything from sore throat to plantar warts are frequent—and your company-paid health insurance covered most of the bills, that fringe benefit has shielded you from one of inflation's harshest blows. As medical costs continue to increase, the insurance will become all the more valuable.

Some fringes help in another way, too, by easing the need for cash in certain categories of spending, thus making more money available for use in other inflation-sensitive categories. Fringes that clearly free up cash include low-priced meals (in a company cafeteria, for instance), free parking, use of a company car, van pool rides, free job training or funds for extracurricular education, payment of your dues in clubs and associations, free legal services, and recreation facilities and equipment.

You can use the fringe benefits checklist and work sheet on page 398 to evaluate the elements of your fringe benefits package. Put down only what your employer pays for your fringes, not any share you contribute. You may have to ask your personnel office for some figures—for instance, how much your employer pays for your medical and hospitalization insurance coverage, how much the company puts into your pension fund each year, and so on—but you can figure out the value of many benefits yourself. If you have a free parking spot, value it at the going rate for commercial space in the same neighborhood. If you eat lunch in the company cafeteria, its value to you is the difference between the cost of meals there and what you'd pay for comparable ones in a restaurant. If you've called in sick, multiply the number of days by your daily pay.

When you consider the dollar value of your total compensation from the job—cash income plus fringes—you may conclude that even though your salary increases have barely kept even with rising prices, you are better off than you thought because fringe benefits are cushioning you against certain kinds of price increases.

HOW TO IMPROVE YOUR SITUATION

If your analysis shows you've done all right so far in this inflationary economy, congratulations. But if you conclude that inflation has been siphoning off your purchasing power faster than you've been able to increase your compensation from the job, corrective action is in order. Here are your options.

Ask for a raise. If your analysis of what you're getting convinces you that you are falling behind in the inflation race, and you believe that your job performance entitles you to more pay, ask for a raise. Your chances of getting a raise are best if you can make your case in terms of your own demonstrably increased productivity.

Earn a promotion. Don't expect a promotion just because you want and need the increased income. Build a solid case for promotion by demonstrating your value to your employer on the basis of efficiency, productivity, initiative, dedication and ability to deal effectively with others—all the attributes that go to making a person promotable.

A critical factor, of course, will be your relationship with your boss. He will probably have the biggest, if not the sole, say on your promotion. The decision could turn on any number of considerations. These might range from how consistently you've brought work in on time and under budget to how conscientiously you've attended to whatever degree of apple polishing is expected in your shop to how much support you've given your boss in compiling a record that makes *him* promotable. It's a route around the inflation impasse that's worth exploring.

Get a transfer. Say your work is excellent. You deserve a promotion. Your boss says so. Unfortunately, there just aren't any openings on the next rung of the ladder.

If that's the case, maybe you'd be wise to get into another part of the company where there's more chance of moving up. In many companies the career path in various divisions is different and so is the pace of promotion.

For example, a department like purchasing may offer limited opportunities for advancement, particularly if the people in jobs to which you aspire are solidly entrenched and sitting tight.

Over in sales or systems analysis, on the other hand, things may move at a breakneck pace. Business growth has an immediate impact there and the number of jobs is expanding, so more supervisors are needed. Employees who are on the ball move to higher-paying positions with regularity.

In short, the situation is made to order for outrunning inflation.

Getting the transfer may not be difficult if you have a good work record and the company wants to hold onto you. Many companies encourage internal transfers by routinely posting openings in every department and offering any training needed for a new spot to qualified employees who want to make a switch.

Improve your fringe benefits. Some employers now offer fringe benefits on the cafeteria plan. Each employee is given a benefits allowance, and within it he can select from a variety of fringes the combination that is most valuable to him.

For instance, young employees with no dependents might pass up a pension plan and opt for more time off and as much job training and education as they can get at company expense. Senior employees might prefer to increase their medical coverage and put more money into thrift plans in which their contributions are matched by the employer and taxes on earnings are deferred.

In a typical cafeteria plan there are a few basic or "core" benefits to which you can add to suit your current needs, with the option of altering the package as your circumstances change. And you might earn additional benefit credits as you gain seniority with the company.

Since fringes can help counteract inflation, the possibility of obtaining more advantageous benefits is worth looking into. If your employer doesn't take the cafeteria approach to benefits or doesn't provide some fringes that most employers do, maybe you can start the company thinking about making improvements that will help mitigate the effects of inflation. In some circumstances a company might be more agreeable to boosting benefits than raising salaries.

Add another income. If the lid is firmly on at work, you can use your off-duty time to produce the extra inflation-hedging income you need. You could take on a moonlight job or start a side-line business.

A word of caution about this approach: Extra jobs bring extra costs in dollars and personal energy. Analyze your situation and goals carefully before taking such a step. You don't want to jeopardize your primary source of income or any savings you've socked away in your effort to boost your earnings on the side.

COMPARE YOUR FRINGE BENEFITS

Figures are from a survey of 922 firms conducted by the Chamber of Commerce of the United States.

fringe benefit	% of companies that provide it	average annual amount paid by employer	what your employer pays for you
life, hospital, surgical, medical, major-medical insurance	100%	$ 861	$
paid holidays	95	482	
paid vacation time	96	710	
pension plan	86	825	
paid lunch and rest periods	79	539	
paid sick leave	78	187	
Christmas or other bonus, service awards, etc.	45	64	
long-term disability insurance	49	46	
education (tuition refunds, etc.)	48	25	
meals furnished by employer	18	23	
employer's contribution to thrift plan account	20	43	
profit-sharing payments	21	216	
dental insurance	33	40	
discounts on goods and services bought from the company	15	14	
legally required benefits*	100	1,368	

*Employer's payment for social security, unemployment compensation, workers' compensation, etc.

Get a better job. A last resort, obviously, but it's a valid one, not to be overlooked in the campaign to work your way around inflation. A job change should bring a pay increase of 15% to 20%—on the low side for sales and administrative jobs, on the high side for engineering and technical positions.

But don't be too quick to jump. Better be sure you won't land in the same sort of trap you are in now, even if you would be starting out at a higher salary. Inflation isn't a short-lived phenomenon. Figure on it as a permanent part of your career planning.

24

Money enough to retire on

The distant glitter of what are supposed to be your golden years can fade fast if you don't take steps to enhance it before you get there. Most people don't spend much time worrying about retirement in their early adult years, but someone in his 30s or early 40s really isn't starting too early. If you wait until retirement is near at hand to take stock of what awaits you, it could be too late to do anything about it.

Actually, the dream of a comfortable life in your later years is probably behind a lot of the decisions you make about saving, investing, tax planning and other financial matters. Still, there are a number of considerations that have to do directly with retirement.

HOW MUCH INCOME WILL YOU NEED?

Fortunately, retirees can usually get along on a lower income than people working full time. They tend to spend less on clothing, transportation, food and other daily expenses, and they generally pay out less in taxes due to their lower income and the special tax breaks available to people 65 and over.

Actuarial experts estimate that a retired couple ordinarily needs anywhere from 60% to 70% of preretirement income to maintain the same standard of living. But it's difficult to state a rule because there are so many variables—where you live, whether you rent or buy a place, the level of income you had prior to retirement. On that last point, it stands to reason that the lower your preretirement income, the greater the proportion of it you will need after retirement.

The table at right bears this out. It estimates the equivalent retirement incomes for singles and couples retiring in 1980. The table was prepared by Preston C. Bassett, an actuary associated with the consulting firm of Towers, Perrin, Forster & Crosby and an actuary for the President's Commission on Pension Policy.

This key will guide you through the calculations:

- Gross preretirement income *minus* preretirement taxes *equals* disposable income.
- Disposable income *minus* work-related expenses and outlays for savings and investments *equals* net preretirement income.
- Net preretirement income *plus* postretirement taxes *equals* equivalent retirement income (the amount needed to replace gross preretirement income).
- The final column shows the ratio of the equivalent net retirement income to the gross preretirement income. For example, a single person who earned $50,000 before retirement would need 51% of that income after retirement to maintain the same standard of living, or the same relative income level. A married couple would need 55% to maintain their level.

gross pre-retirement income	preretirement taxes		disposable income	preretirement outlays		net pre-retirement income	postretirement taxes§		equivalent re-tirement income	
	federal*	state & local†		work-related expenses‡	savings & investments		federal income	state & local†	dollars	ratio
married couples retiring in 1980										
$10,000	$ 1,785	$ 223	$ 7,992	$ 480	$ 240	$ 7,272	$ 0	$ 0	$ 7,272	.73
15,000	3,259	444	11,297	678	678	9,941	0	0	9,941	.66
20,000	5,055	728	14,217	853	1,280	12,084	166	32	12,282	.61
30,000	8,926	1,429	19,645	1,179	2,357	16,109	1,077	205	17,391	.58
50,000	18,921	3,328	27,751	1,665	4,163	21,923	3,153	599	25,675	.51
single people retiring in 1980										
$10,000	$ 1,311	$ 133	$ 8,556	$ 513	$ 257	$ 7,786	$ 0	$ 0	$ 7,786	.78
15,000	2,550	310	12,140	728	728	10,684	0	0	10,684	.71
20,000	3,968	520	15,512	931	1,396	13,185	0	0	13,185	.66
30,000	6,986	1,061	21,953	1,317	2,634	18,002	53	10	18,065	.60
50,000	15,202	2,622	32,176	1,931	4,826	25,419	1,651	314	27,384	.55

* Federal income and social security (OASDHI) taxes.

† Based on state and local 1978 income tax receipts, which were 19% of federal income tax receipts. Does not include property tax.

‡ Estimated as 6% of disposable income.

§ Postretirement taxes are on income in excess of social security benefits, which are nontaxable. Retirees without social security benefits would need higher replacement ratios.

Where will you get the money you need for retirement? The kinds of investments that help produce it are described in earlier chapters of this book. But chances are you will be relying heavily on the traditional sources of retirement income—social security and pension plans, whether the plans be those of your employer or ones that you devise yourself.

SIZING UP A PENSION PLAN

About half the people working for private companies are covered by pension plans. But working for a company with a pension program does not necessarily mean you are a member, or that you will actually receive a pension, or that the pension will be adequate.

Ideally, you should check a company's pension plan before you take a job; it could influence your decision. Knowing the plan's provisions beforehand could prove helpful for another reason. Usually you must wait a year or more to become a full-fledged member of a pension plan. During that time you might be able to save for retirement on a tax-deductible basis through an IRA—an Individual Retirement Account. Starting in 1982, anyone with earned income can set up an IRA. They are discussed beginning on page 419.

A one-time examination of a pension plan isn't enough. The company may amend the provisions from time to time, and your benefits will change with your salary and service. In effect, you have to keep track of pension rights just as you do your other fringe benefits.

Most of the required information should be clearly presented in the annual statements to members and in the plan description, which the company must provide employees under terms of the 1974 Employee Retirement Income Security Act, known as ERISA.

Though it doesn't oblige employers to offer pension benefits, ERISA sets minimum-disclosure and administrative standards for those that do.

If the summary of the plan leaves unanswered questions, you may be able to get some clarification from the company's pension office or your union. The ultimate authority is the plan's formal agreement, a document that, unfortunately, is likely to be weighted down with dense legal wordage. To penetrate those complexities, concentrate on ten crucial features.

1. What kind of plan is it? Essentially, there are two types.

• *A defined contribution plan*. In this arrangement the company contributes a fixed amount each year to a fund that's invested in securities or some sort of insurance contract. When you retire, the money credited to your account will be used to purchase an annuity. You get only as much annuity income as your fund will buy. Defined contribution plans include deferred profit-sharing and stock bonus programs. You may hear those and similar plans referred to as "money purchase" plans.

• *A defined benefit plan*. This plan prescribes a formula for determining your pension, and it's up to the employer to contribute enough into the pension fund to buy an annuity that will provide that much income at retirement. The pension is usually tied to both years of credited service and salary. All other factors being equal, you stand to come out best when the plan bases the pension on a few top earning years or your salary in the final few years of service, when you're likely to be earning most. Least favorable is a plan that gears the pension to the average earnings for all years.

Both types of plans may require or allow contributions by employees.

Notice that with a defined contribution plan you take two risks: First, that annuity purchase rates will rise, thereby reducing the monthly income that the amount in your fund will buy; second, that the fund will earn a subpar return or take a loss. With a defined benefit plan the employer bears those risks.

2. When do you become a member? Ordinarily, you can't join the plan until you've met certain age and service requirements. ERISA sanctions four age-service eligibility standards, depending on other characteristics of the plan: age 25 and one year of service; age 25 and three years of service; age 30 and one year of service; and three years of service but no age requirement. The last requirement applies to Keogh plans, those used by self-employed people for themselves and their employees.

Those combined limits constitute the maximum restrictions. An employer can make you a member sooner.

There is one special ERISA provision you should be aware of, particularly if you're in your fifties and considering a job change. The law permits a defined benefit plan to exclude from membership a person who begins work within five years of the plan's normal retirement age.

3. How fast do you accrue benefits? Once you become a member, you start building up pension benefits year by year. In a defined contribution plan your accrued benefit at any point equals the amount credited to your account. If the plan puts the money into a cash value life insurance policy, the amount for which the policy could be surrendered represents your accrued benefit.

The accrual process works differently for defined benefit plans because your pension isn't a special sum set aside for you in the pension fund but a fixed monthly income that will be paid on retirement. One accrual formula employs a ratio of actual service to the time you could spend in the plan. As an example, say you join the plan at age 35 and, therefore, could work another 30 years until normal retirement at 65. If you leave the company after 20 years of covered service, you have participated for two-thirds of the potential period and are entitled to a two-thirds of the estimated pension at 65.

Other arrangements for defined benefit plans schedule accruals at a fixed percentage each year. The law permits a plan to use a flat rate of not less than 3% a year so that an employee accrues 100% of the projected pension after no more than $33\frac{1}{3}$ years of covered service. ERISA also allows plans to apply different percentages for early and later years, subject to certain limits. The practice of accruing at a faster rate in later years of service, which favors employees who stay with the company, is called back loading. The opposite practice, front loading, helps shorter-term employees. ERISA prescribes that the percentage applied to a later year can't be more than one and one-third times the current year's rate.

4. How fast will you be vested? The fact that you've accrued part of your ultimate pension does not mean you actually own that accrued portion in the sense that if you left the company, the plan would set aside a sum or buy a deferred annuity to pay you a monthly income when you reach retirement age.

You own the money you may have contributed to the plan, but you don't completely own the accrued benefit created by the employer's contributions until you're 100% vested. If you are only 30% vested, then you own 30% of the accrued benefit. If you have not been vested at all when you go, you have no assured pension rights.

ERISA's enactment was motivated largely by the desire of Congress to set minimum vesting standards to make sure more people earn pension rights. But even now it's possible to work a lifetime for companies with plans and not earn a pension if you change jobs frequently.

ERISA permits a variety of vesting systems. The most generous, mandatory for Keogh plans, immediately vests all benefits 100%. One of the least favorable and most common arrangements, called cliff vesting, defers all vesting until after ten years and then vests 100%. The "rule of 45" vests 50% when your age and service add up to 45 and you have a minimum of five years of service. You get an additional 10% each year thereafter. Graduated plans vest on a gradual schedule over 15 years. Profit-sharing and similar plans that vest each year's contribution into the pension fund separately are covered by another set of rules.

Vesting schedules may actually progress somewhat faster than is apparent because a plan must (with some exceptions) credit years of service you completed before you became a pension plan member. By contrast, accrual schedules ordinarily credit you only for those years in which you participate in the plan.

5. What do you lose for interrupted employment?
Each plan lays down rules defining your pension status when you have interrupted employment or fail to work what the plan considers a full year. ERISA's minimum standards reduce the chances that you will lose all rights because of a layoff or other break in service, but companies retain a lot of leeway. For example, the plan need not use a calendar year. It can base service on hours completed during any 12 consecutive months, provided it applies the same limits in all cases. Such a provision might help or hurt you, depending on when

you happen to lose time. Look for the sections defining plan year, hours of service, years of service and break in service.

6. What will your plan pay if you retire early? You will be entitled to a smaller monthly income than at the usual retirement age of 65, but the question is, how much smaller? The accrual period will be shorter. And normally the pension is reduced by an actuarial formula that takes into account the likelihood that you will receive the pension for more years. However, some companies encourage early retirement by paying more than the actuarial equivalent or by other incentives.

7. Will you earn benefits for work after 65? Companies can't in most cases force employees to retire before age 70. Most plans, though, have designed benefits for normal retirement at 65. The legal bars against age discrimination don't require a company to increase pensions for post-65 service. Your plan might nevertheless recognize that service in some way—by increasing the age-65 pension by an annual interest increment or by including the additional years of service or post-65 earnings in the pension computation.

8. How much will you receive if you are disabled? The company may have a long-term disability program that pays a monthly income until you become eligible for retirement. An alternative is to put employees on a retirement pension if they become disabled after they work for the company a prescribed number of years. The plan will specify any disability benefit to which you're entitled.

9. Are there any death payments? When you retire, you can choose one of the various types of annuities that will pay an income or lump sum to your spouse or other heirs on your death. Under ERISA, employers must give you the opportunity when you reach early retirement age—or ten years before normal retirement, whichever is later—to elect a joint and survivor annuity, which would give your spouse a pension income if you die while still on the job. The joint and survivor annuity form will automatically be used at retirement if you make no choice before then. That is one of the law's most important safeguards, but keep in mind that if you select the joint and survivor option, your pension might be reduced to offset the potential increase in cost to the plan from paying survivor pensions.

If you die before you've reached early retirement age, your beneficiaries are entitled to a refund of money you might have contributed to the plan or your fully vested credit in a defined contribution plan. The company might also pay a death benefit consisting of part of your accrued pension, which reflects its contributions as well as yours. The plan may have no death benefit; the company may cover that with group insurance instead.

10. Do you have any inflation protection? You're lucky if your plan adjusts pensions after retirement to compensate for cost-of-living increases. The few private plans that do usually limit the annual rise to a relatively small amount, say 3%. Some companies, though, have made voluntary increases for retirees.

PROFIT-SHARING PLANS

It's more difficult in some ways to evaluate a profit-sharing plan than a straight pension program.

Employers' contributions to profit-sharing plans are linked to company profits, which vary from year to year, so you can't depend on a fixed minimum amount. Also, according to a survey prepared for the Profit

Sharing Council of America, a trade organization, smaller companies tend to reserve the right to contribute as much or as little as they like instead of using fixed percentages. And the amount you eventually receive depends to a large extent on how successfully the money is invested.

If the contributed profits, or part of them, are paid out to employees each year, it's up to each person to invest the cash. Most plans though, defer payouts until you leave. Meanwhile, that money is usually invested by banks and professional investment counselors under the supervision of the trustees of the plan or an investment committee. A small percentage of profit-sharing plans give employees a voice in the selection of investments.

The Profit Sharing Council's survey indicates that about a quarter of the plans invest part of their funds (usually less than 50%) in the company's own stock. That can prove an advantage or disadvantage for the employee, depending on the company's dividend payment policy (since the stock held by the plan earns dividends, too) and whether the stock appreciates or declines.

Though they lack the guarantees of regular pension plans, profit-sharing programs make it possible to accumulate sizable retirement funds when you work for a successful company. The ideal arrangement—offered by about 30% of the companies in the council's survey—would probably be a pension program split between fixed-benefit and deferred-profit plans.

ESOPs & TRASOPs

The latest innovation in fringe benefits is the ESOP, a plan that provides free stock for employees and tax deductions plus new business funds for employers.

ESOP stands for Employee Stock Ownership Plan and it works along these lines:

The employer establishes an employee trust to administer the program. The company may merely contribute its stock instead of cash to the trust each year, according to a set formula, such as a percentage of total payroll. The contribution is tax deductible.

If the ESOP is also intended to raise capital, the trust purchases the company stock with money borrowed from the bank. The loan is backed by the stock and the company's repayment guarantee.

The trust uses the company's annual tax-deductible contributions to the plan to make payments on the loan. As the loan is paid down, the trust assigns some of the stock to member employees, usually in proportion to their earnings.

With a TRASOP, a Tax Reduction Act Stock Ownership Plan, the company gets additional tax credits for investments in new plant and equipment if it gives those tax savings to the trust to purchase shares. In effect, the company contributes money that would otherwise be paid in taxes.

Employees build up ownership rights in the ESOPs or TRASOPs stock according to the plan's vesting rules. ESOPs are subject to the same vesting regulations as other employee benefit programs covered by ERISA, the basic pension law. Thus, the employee may have to wait years until he has partial or full nonforfeitable rights to the shares allocated to his account. TRASOPs, however, must give plan members an immediate 100% interest in their shares. The stock, or its cash equivalent, is ultimately paid out when the member leaves, retires or dies.

ESOPs and TRASOPs have been advocated as a means of spurring productivity by giving workers a direct stake in the company's financial success, at no cost to them. As retirement programs, though, the plans have some potential drawbacks. Because all or most of your stake is invested in one company, you lose the protection of a diversified investment portfolio. And you can never be sure how much the stock will be worth when you pull out of the plan.

KEOGH PLANS FOR THE SELF-EMPLOYED

If you work for yourself, the government has provided you with big tax incentives for setting aside retirement money. Keogh plans have been available since 1963, but major liberalizations of the law since then have made them more attractive than ever. A Keogh plan lets you set aside up to $7,500 of self-employment income each year ($15,000 in 1982 and after) and deduct it from your income in that year. You usually needn't pay any tax on the money until you start withdrawing it years later. The law contains special provisions designed to make sure that the money is used for the contributor's retirement.

Who is eligible. Anyone who is in business for himself and contributes personal services to that business can set up a Keogh plan.

And the business need not be full time. A plumber who moonlights nights and weekends, for instance, can set up a Keogh plan for that extra money even though he is already covered by a pension plan on his regular job. Similarly, a housewife who spends a few days a week selling cosmetics or typing manuscripts can also take advantage of the Keogh tax benefits.

Limits to deductions. Normally on your federal tax return you can deduct up to 15% of your earned income or $7,500 ($15,000 in 1982 and after), whichever is less, for contributions to an approved Keogh plan. (Earned income does not include investment returns, such as dividends and interest). A self-employed person who earns $100,000 or more can deduct up to the entire $15,000; someone with less income would have to stop contributions at 15% of that income.

However, the law does provide an exception to this general rule. Suppose you are in a part-time business that makes only $1,000 in a year. That would rate a measely $150 deduction. But for small income like that, the law lets you ignore the 15% rule and deduct 100% of your self-employment income up to a maximum of $750. Such mini-Keoghs, though, are available only to people whose adjusted gross income from all sources is $15,000 or less.

Another special kind of Keogh plan permits you to exceed the normal limit. Under a so-called "defined benefit" Keogh, the annual allowance can sometimes be greater.

With a regular Keogh plan you decide, within the prescribed limits, how much you want to contribute each year. With a defined-benefit plan you decide, within broader limits, how much you would like to receive in annual retirement income, and then an actuary designs a savings program to attain that "defined benefit." In most cases you pay the actuarial fee—$100 to $600 a year or more—but the expense is tax-deductible.

How big a pension can you create? Figuring this is complicated. The actuary must take into consideration such factors as your age when you start the plan, your income, the number of years until your retirement, the maximum percentages of your earned income that can be used to calculate your benefit and the payout arrangement you choose.

As a simplified example, take the case of John Smith, 50, who is self-employed and will earn $50,000 this year. He plans to retire at 65. The starting point for figuring the yearly maximum he may place in a defined-benefit plan for someone his age to provide a lifetime annuity benefit starting at age 65 is 3% of his income, $1,500. (The percentage allowed varies by the age of the person when he begins the plan.)

Say that Smith's annual income remains at $50,000 until he retires, and that he contributes the maximum each year. That would entitle him to an annual retirement benefit of $22,500 (15 years times $1,500). Assume that a lifetime annuity that will pay $22,500 a year can be purchased for about $200,000. Accumulating $200,000 in 15 years would require annual payments of about $8,800 if the money earned 5¼% interest (with daily compounding), less if the return were higher.

By contrast, Smith could make contributions of only $7,500 a year to a regular Keogh account.

If a defined benefit Keogh appeals to you and you think you might qualify, proceed with caution. Such plans have their limits, too, and should be designed only with professional help to be sure of satisfying complicated IRS requirements.

Whatever kind of Keogh plan you set up, it must be handled by qualified trustees or custodians. Many savings institutions, insurance companies, mutual funds and other organizations can serve in this capacity, usually with prototype plans that are easily adapted to individual needs.

Not only do the qualified annual contributions go into the retirement fund tax-free, but any interest, dividends or capital gains earned by the contributions remain nontaxable until they are withdrawn. In effect, the fund compounds tax-free because income earned by the accumulated earnings is also sheltered from federal income taxes until withdrawal.

Employee coverage. If you establish a Keogh plan for yourself, you must also include all eligible full-time employees who have worked for you three or more years.

In a defined contribution Keogh, you are required to contribute to their Keogh accounts at least the same percentage of their salaries that you use for yourself. Contributions are deductible as a business expense on your tax return. Also, the law allows you under some conditions to reduce contributions to all accounts—theirs and yours—by the respective amounts paid for social security taxes.

In any plan, the assets in an employee's account belong to him. If he dies while employed, the fund passes to his beneficiary, not back to the employer.

Inclusion of an employee in a Keogh plan has two incidental advantages:

First, both you and the employees are then eligible to make additional contributions, called "voluntary contributions," to your respective funds. These voluntary contributions have been limited to $2,500 or 10% of income earned from the business, whichever is less. Voluntary contributions are not deductible, but the earnings accumulate tax-free until they are withdrawn.

Second, you can establish a retirement fund for a relative who works for you and deduct the contributions as a business expense.

As an employee you can't establish a Keogh plan unless your boss does. But you can set up a tax-free fund on your own under the Individual Retirement Arrangement program, explained later in this chapter.

Excess contributions. Contributions above your permissible limit are not deductible. In addition, they are subject to a 6% excise tax. An exception is made for excess contributions made to pay premiums for annuity, endowment or life insurance policies. They aren't taxed.

How funds can be invested. Subject to a few restrictions, Keogh contributions may be invested as you see fit. The money can be put into such things as securities, mutual funds, annuities, government bonds, gold, diamonds and other assets.

Generally, investments have to be made through a trustee or custodial arrangement with the institutions that invest the funds. An attorney can draw up an agreement specifically for you and submit it to the IRS for approval. However, the legal arrangements are often handled through standard "master" and "prototype" plans already approved by the IRS. What usually happens is that you sign a printed agreement sent to you by, say, a mutual fund, savings institution or bank.

No legal formality is required for buying annuities or government retirement bonds, but they can also be handled through a trust arrangement if that's more convenient.

You can diversify your Keogh fund either by splitting it among different investments or by using a single trustee or custodian who will allocate the money at your direction. You can also switch money from one investment to another, so you are not locked into your first choice. For example, you could cash in mutual fund shares and put the proceeds into certificates of deposit or an annuity. Make sure, though, to pay attention to the timing and procedures for transferring the assets.

Withdrawing retirement funds. To prevent the use of Keogh funds as an emergency savings account or as a means of accumulating an estate to be left to heirs, the law regulates withdrawals.

Money taken from a Keogh account before you reach 59½ is subject to a penalty tax except in case of death or disability. That restriction on withdrawals before 59½ does not apply to voluntary contributions, which may be taken out whenever the employer or the employee likes. However, the income earned by those contributions must be left in the account until it qualifies for withdrawal.

An owner-employee must begin withdrawing Keogh assets the year he reaches 70½, even if he does not retire. Employees can hold off until they retire.

Keogh funds may be paid out in a lump sum, installments or annuity payments and are taxed accordingly. The payouts, though, can't be scheduled to exceed the person's life expectancy or the life expectancies of the Keogh participant and his spouse. Again, the intent is to restrict the Keogh plan to its retirement objective.

The law does not require you to purchase an annuity in order to arrange for annuity-type payments. The proper installments can be calculated from IRS tables prepared for that purpose.

Taxes on retirement income. Keogh funds drawn out in installments running more than one year come under the federal income tax rules for annuities. The regulations are discouragingly complex in spots, but the underlying principle is that you do not pay income tax on that portion of the payments based on contributions you made out of taxable income.

To illustrate, assume you expect to draw out an $80,000 Keogh fund in $8,000 installments over ten years, and that your voluntary contributions—the ones you did not deduct—come to $30,000. Three-eighths of each annual installment, or $3,000 a year, would then be tax-free. That's because you are withdrawing $3,000 on which you have already paid income tax in some past year. Conversely, the $5,000 a year that is taxable represents contributions and earnings on which you did not previously pay income taxes.

When annuity payments during the first three years are scheduled to equal or exceed your nondeductible contributions, you are not taxed until your nondeductible contributions are recovered. This is the so-called three-year rule.

In some cases it might be better to draw out all the Keogh money in a lump sum instead of as an annuity. The voluntary-contributions part of the lump sum is not taxable, and the taxable part can be averaged out as if it were being received over ten years. The proceeds from cashed-in government retirement bonds, however, aren't eligible for ten-year averaging.

INDIVIDUAL RETIREMENT ACCOUNTS

Thanks to the 1981 tax law, beginning in 1982 anyone with earned income to report on a tax return is eligible to set up a tax-sheltered Individual Retirement Account. You can put aside up to $2,000 of your earnings each year and deduct it from your income. You owe no taxes on the money until it is withdrawn. A working couple can set up two separate IRAs, assuming both are eligible, raising potential contributions to $4,000 a year. If a worker is eligible for an IRA but his or her spouse doesn't work, they can still set up two separate IRAs, but the combined annual limit on contributions is $2,250.

As with Keogh plans, money withdrawn from an IRA before the owner reaches age 59½ is subject to a penalty tax. The owner *must* begin withdrawing the money in the year in which he or she reaches age 70½. (Unlike Keoghs, however, IRA distributions are always taxed as ordinary income. They do not qualify for the special ten-year averaging rule available to lump-sum Keogh distributions.)

Contribution schedules. Each year's contribution can be made in one lump sum or in installments. Since dividends and other earnings that accumulate in IRA accounts do not have to be declared immediately for tax purposes, it is normally to your advantage to make contributions early in the year.

If you intend to make periodic contributions, either for tax reasons or for budgeting purposes, you need an investment plan that accepts small amounts.

IRAs can be opened any time before the deadline for filing your federal tax return and the contributions deducted for the prior year. For ongoing plans, this gives you time to make sure that contributions do not exceed the legal limits. There's a 6% penalty for overages, and the excess is included in taxable income when withdrawn. You can absorb excess contributions by contributing less in a subsequent year and taking your deduction for the amount absorbed.

Custodial or trustee arrangements. Many IRA investments must be made through a custodian or trustee—in practice, a company that supervises the account and reports to you and the government each year. Banks, savings and loan associations, mutual funds and others who provide IRA plans have standard custodial or trustee arrangements that you join by completing a simple form.

You are permitted to maintain more than one IRA account with the same or different companies, and you can transfer IRA funds from one trustee directly to another at any time.

Rollovers. This refers to two unique types of IRA transactions.

In the first, under IRA law you may move your money from one IRA to another once a year without incurring the premature-withdrawal penalty. That gives you an opportunity to revise investment strategy from time to time. You have 60 days after withdrawal to reinvest.

The second rollover refers to lump-sum payments you might receive from a company pension, profit-sharing or similar plan when you leave a job or the employer terminates the plan. All or part of the lump sum can be put into an IRA within 60 days, without regard to the limit on annual contributions. This type of rollover must be treated differently from the first, so check the rules carefully. Lump-sum rollovers generally should be segregated in a separate IRA because these funds can later be rolled over into a regular company pension program tax-free if that opportunity ever arises.

Ineligibility. Prior to 1982, no contributions can be made to an IRA account in any year in which you participate in another pension program that qualifies for tax advantages. Furthermore, the contribution limit is $1,500 or 15% of income, whichever is smaller.

Employer's contributions to IRAs. The Revenue Act of 1978 allows employers to contribute to IRAs of their workers and take the appropriate tax deductions. If an employer puts in less than the maximum deduction, the employee may add funds of his own to bring it up. Such arrangements are called Simplified Employee Pension plans, and they provide for an employer's contributions to go straight to IRAs that employees have set up themselves with qualified sponsors.

If an employer does make IRA contributions, he must do so for all employees age 25 or older who have worked for him for any part of three of the previous five years. Contributions to an employee's IRA are deductible by both employer and employee. However, the employee is required to include in his gross income the employer's contribution to his IRA, then deduct it as an adjustment to income.

WHAT'S SOCIAL SECURITY GOT FOR YOU?

Social security benefits have a couple of distinct advantages over most other forms of retirement income. They are completely tax-free, for one thing. Efforts to tax part of the benefit received by retirees enjoying a certain income level have so far been unsuccessful. The other advantage of social security benefits has also received a lot of publicity in the past year or so: They increase automatically along with inflation. This indexing of payments had pushed the maximum monthly social security benefit up to about $680 by the summer of 1981.

How can you find out whether the program has something for you? Or how much you can expect to receive? Or how to apply?

First write to, call or visit one of the approximately 1,300 social security offices scattered around the country. They are listed in telephone directories under "U.S. Government, Social Security Administration."

If you're unable to travel because of ill health, call the nearest office and request that someone visit you. The administration regularly sends out representatives to assist people in their homes.

It's especially important to contact a social security office if someone in your family dies, if you're unable to work because of an illness or injury that's expected to incapacitate you for a year or longer or if you're 62 or older and plan to retire soon.

If you're nearing retirement and wonder how large your payments will be, you can make a rough estimate with the help of a pamphlet, *Estimating Your Social Security Retirement Check,* available from all social security offices. Or if you make a request on Form 7004, the office will obtain an estimate for you.

Even if you intend to keep working after 65, you should check in with the social security people three months before your 65th birthday to enroll in medicare, which will become available to you at 65 whether or not you retire.

Whatever your situation, be sure to obtain a set of explanatory pamphlets that the Social Security Administration gives free to anyone who requests them. They're concise, informative and easy to read. The basic publication has a blue cover and is entitled *Your Social Security.* Others include *Applying for a Social Security Number; Social Security Credits—How You Earn Them; SSI for the Aged, Blind, and Disabled; Medicare Coverage of Kidney Dialysis and Kidney Transplant Services; Your Claim for Supplemental Social Security Income; If You're Self-Employed . . . Reporting Your Income for Social Security;* and *You Can Work and Still Get Social Security Checks.* Another publication, *Your Right to Question the Decision Made on Your Claim,* tells how to go about applying for reconsideration of an adverse decision.

As the names of some of those pamphlets suggest, social security is far more than just a retirement program. There are actually seven different kinds of help available if you're covered.

• *Retirement checks.* You'll get them if you have worked a certain length of time under social security. Benefits automatically increase in any year in which the cost of living rises by 3% or more during the first three months of the year compared with the first three months of the prior year.

You can retire at 62, but your payments will be reduced. Your spouse can receive benefits even if he or she never paid social security taxes. If you retire at 65, your spouse, if 65, will receive an amount equal to half of your benefits—or a reduced amount as early as age 62. And a spouse entitled to benefits from his or her work record receives whichever is larger, his or her entitlement or an amount equal to half of the spouse's. A divorced wife of 62 or older can receive benefits if her marriage lasted at least ten years and her former husband was covered.

• *Disability income.* People who are blind or disabled in other ways that prevent them from working may receive assistance based on their average earnings under social security.

Disability is defined as an inability to work because of a physical or mental impairment that has lasted or is expected to last at least 12 months or to result in death. Blindness means either central visual acuity of 20/200 or less in the better eye with the use of corrective lenses or visual field reduction to 20 degrees or less. A person who was disabled before age 22 may qualify for benefits when a parent, or sometimes a grandparent, begins receiving retirement or disability payments or dies, even if the claimant has never worked.

• *Supplemental security income.* SSI is a separate program that provides a basic cash income for people in financial need who are 65 or older and for the needy of any age who are blind or disabled. The maximums are about $240 a month for individuals, about $360 a month for married couples.

It's possible to receive SSI even though you have other financial assets. Single people are allowed to own personal assets worth up to $1,500, not counting the value of a home. For married couples the asset limitation is $2,250.

• *Survivors' benefits*. The spouse, children, parents and, in some cases, grandchildren of a deceased worker may be entitled to cash benefits. Specifically eligible are:

1. A widow or widower 60 or older.
2. A widow, widower, or surviving divorced mother if caring for the worker's child who is under 18 (or disabled) and who is receiving benefits based on the deceased worker's earnings.
3. A widow or widower 50 or older who becomes disabled within seven years after the worker's death, or in the case of a widow, within seven years after she stops getting checks for caring for the worker's children.
4. Unmarried children under 18, or under 22 if full-time students, although these are phasing out.
5. Unmarried children 18 or older who were severely disabled before 22 and who remain disabled.
6. Dependent parents 62 or older.

Additionally, checks can go to a surviving divorced wife of 60 or a disabled surviving divorced wife of 50 if the marriage lasted ten years or more.

In general, a marriage must have lasted one year or more for dependents of retired or disabled workers to be eligible for social security payments, and survivors can receive checks if the marriage lasted at least nine months.

• *Medicare aid*. Medicare coverage now extends to people under 65 who have been entitled to social security disability payments for 24 consecutive months or more, and to people requiring kidney transplants or dialysis treatment. To receive kidney disease benefits, you must have worked sufficiently long in a job under social security or the railroad retirement system, or be the wife, husband or dependent child of an eligible worker. If you think you qualify, apply at any social security office.

• *Students' benefits*. A student between 18 and 22 may qualify for monthly social security checks because of the death, disability or retirement of a parent or, in some cases, a grandparent who worked long enough under social security. Students or their parents or guardians can apply at any social security office. (Note: Starting in 1981, student benefits were being phased out. Check with your social security office.)

• *Widowers' benefits*. A father can receive monthly payments if his wife died while insured under social security and he has not remarried and he cares for an unmarried child under 18 (or older if disabled before 22) who is entitled to benefits.

Earnings limitations while retired. You can do some work after retirement and still collect social security, and from age 72 on (70 starting in 1983) you can earn any amount and still receive your full benefits. If you're between 65 and 72, you can earn up to $5,500 in 1981 and no benefits will be withheld. If you make more than $5,500, $1 in benefits will be withheld for every $2 you earn above $5,500. The earnings limit for people between 65 and 72 will rise to $6,000 in 1982.

Those who retire before 65 can earn $4,080 in 1981 without losing benefits. That ceiling will go up to an estimated $4,440 in 1982.

An old rule that allowed retirees to collect full benefits for the months in which their earnings were low has been eliminated except for the year in which they retire.

WHAT TO DO WITH ASSETS
AT RETIREMENT

How can you turn lump sums of money into a guaranteed lifetime income without incurring any more tax than absolutely necessary? It's a problem faced by many people when they retire. One thing you could do with the money, if it is a lump sum distribution from a retirement plan, is roll it over into one or more annuities. In some cases that would let you postpone any tax until you started taking the money out. A couple of things you must take into account are your life expectancy (see the table on page 433) and how much of the money you can afford to take out each year (see the table on page 430-431).

In any case, you should also consider carefully the potential tax advantages of taking the money right away and using the ten-year averaging rule discussed earlier, or rolling it over into an IRA. If you don't need all or part of the income from the money right away, an IRA could shield it from taxes until you are ready to take it out. However, distributions would be taxed as ordinary income then and you will have forfeited the opportunity to use the ten-year averaging rule.

Annuities. Under an annuity contract you pay money to an insurance company and receive in return a guaranteed income or a lump-sum settlement at some later date. There are basically two types of annuity contracts: immediate and deferred.

With an immediate annuity the payout begins as soon as you put up your money; with a deferred annuity it begins some time later. Deferred annuities can be paid for with a single payment or with installment payments in fixed or flexible amounts.

A type widely sold today is called a *single-premium deferred annuity* contract. This is something of a misnomer, since one or more premium payments can be made (actually, each new premium creates a new contract) and (as is true with other plans), there is actually no obligation to convert the accumulated savings into an annuity—you can simply close the account and use the money for any purpose.

Deferred annuity contracts guarantee a minimum yield, or rate of interest, on premium payments during the accumulation period and a minimum income if you take an annuity. Yields are currently well above historic levels because interest rates in general have been pushed up by economic conditions.

By contracting for a deferred annuity, you can assure yourself of a specified income for life (or a shorter period if you so choose) at annuity prices in effect at the time of the purchase.

You can usually choose from several ways to receive the annuity—as a lump sum you can reinvest, for example, or as a guaranteed income for ten years, or as a guaranteed income for as long as you live or for as long as you and your spouse life. Naturally, the size of the payments will vary accordingly.

Annuity contracts have a tax advantage—no federal or state income taxes are owed on the interest or other investment earnings until the money is withdrawn. Also, no income tax is payable on isolated partial withdrawals of the principal during the deferral period.

There are other benefits, too. In some cases you can borrow against the savings or use them as collateral for a bank loan. Should you die, the contract value would pass directly to your designated heirs without probate. Annuity contracts can, with certain exceptions, be used to fund Individual Retirement Accounts and Keogh retirement plans.

But there are drawbacks. When both you and your designated survivor have died, the purchase money usually stays with the company. Also, income can be relatively low in proportion to the amount invested. Some contracts pay less than insured, long-term savings certificates. And if price inflation continues, which is all but certain, any kind of fixed income will buy less and less as years go by.

Here's a look at four types of annuities.

• *Life annuity*. It guarantees a stipulated monthly income for life. There are no death benefits or surrender values.

• *Life with ten years certain*. This type also provides a lifetime income but also guarantees that should you die during the first ten years, the payments would continue through the tenth year, going to your designated beneficiary.

• *Installment-refund annuity*. It guarantees you a lifetime income and also provides that should you die before the total of the payments equals the purchase price, payments would be made to your beneficiary until the payout equalled the purchase price.

• *Wraparound annuity*. A comparatively recent development, it permits you to choose from among a number of mutual funds in which the insurance company will invest your money. The funds can be primarily invested in bonds, stocks or the money market. If you pick a family of funds (see chapter 17), you can direct the company to move your money around as you see fit. It's this measure of control over how your money is invested that distinguishes the wraparound from other deferred annuities.

Buying tips. When comparing contracts, watch closely for disclaimers, qualifiers and ambiguities. Be sure the net income you would receive—after payment of any commissions or service charges—is clearly stated in the contract. Special taxes could lower your net income, too: Some states collect premium taxes on annuity purchases. The levies run as high as 4% of whatever sum of money you have paid in.

When you buy an immediate annuity, you're betting that you'll live long enough to come out ahead, or at least break even. Suppose that kind of gamble doesn't appeal to you. Well, you could set up a retirement fund yourself by putting the money into income-producing investments such as those described in chapter 16. You wouldn't get the same kind of ironclad guarantees, but neither would you surrender your capital. And the assets would not be lost at your death—they could be willed to members of your family or anyone else. Of course, you'll be liable for taxes on whatever your investments earn.

Another thing: Part of the principal could be used in an emergency, an option you don't get with an immediate annuity. In fact, you could provide yourself with a

---

HOW LONG WILL YOUR MONEY LAST?

The table, prepared by the U.S. League of Savings Associations, shows how long it would take to deplete an account at various interest rates and withdrawal amounts. It is assumed that withdrawals are made at the end of each month, that there are no premature withdrawals or penalties (such as there could be in the case of certificates of deposit) and that interest is compounded continuously under a formula called 365/360. In the case of daily compounding, funds would be exhausted slightly faster.

percent of principal withdrawn

interest rate paid	5%		6½%		7%		8%		9%		10%		11%		12%		13%		14%		15%	
	yrs.	mos.	yrs.	mos.	yrs.	mos.	yrs.	mos.	yrs.	mos.	yrs.	mos.	yrs.	mos.	yrs.	mos.	yrs.	mos.	yrs.	mos.	yrs.	mos.
5%	∞		37	0	25	6	19	11	16	5	14	0	12	3	10	10	9	9	8	11	8	2
6%			∞		33	8	23	7	18	7	15	6	13	3	11	8	10	5	9	5	8	7
7%					∞		31	1	22	1	17	6	14	8	12	8	11	2	10	0	9	1
8%							∞		28	11	20	9	16	7	14	0	12	2	10	9	9	8
9%									∞		27	2	19	7	15	9	13	4	11	8	10	4
10%											∞		25	7	18	7	15	1	12	10	11	2
10%													∞		24	4	17	9	14	5	12	4
11%															∞		23	2	17	0	13	11
12%																	∞		22	3	16	4
13%																			∞		21	4
14%																					∞	
15%																						

∞ *Infinity.*

bigger income by drawing out small parts of the principal along with the interest in accordance with a schedule that would preserve the nest egg for as long as you expect to live. The table on page 431 shows how long your money would hold out.

To illustrate, let's say you're a 65-year-old woman with $10,000 to invest. If your life span is average, you could be around for another 18 years or so.

Now assume you invest the money in a way that yields 9% for the foreseeable future. Reading along the 9% line, you'll see that the money would last 19 years and seven months if you withdrew 11% of the principal each year. That would give you monthly increments of $91.69.

Whatever type of plan you choose, be sure to factor in the tax consequences in calculating the monthly return. If you invest the money and withdraw interest only, leaving the principal intact, all of the income may be subject to federal income taxes. By contrast, part of the proceeds from annuities and self-liquidating funds is excluded, since it is a return of your own money. Whether this would make a significant difference depends on your tax situation, but it definitely should be taken into account in making income comparisons.

To determine how the proceeds from annuity contracts would be taxed, ask any Internal Revenue Service office for a free copy of Publication 575, *Pension and Annuity Income*. Publication 590, *Tax Information on Individual Retirement Arrangements*, tells about the tax treatment of employee-benefit rollovers.

WHAT'S YOUR LIFE EXPECTANCY?

This table shows the average life expectancy for men and women at various popular retirement ages. *Source:* U.S. Department of Health and Human Services.

Age	Average remaining life (years)	
	Men	Women
55	20.6	26.2
56	19.9	25.3
57	19.1	24.5
58	18.4	23.7
59	17.7	22.9
60	17.0	22.1
61	16.4	21.3
62	15.7	20.6
63	15.1	19.8
64	14.5	19.1
65	13.9	18.3

25

Make a will, plan your estate

THE IMPORTANCE OF A WILL

Making a will is a sobering act that's easy to put off, which is probably why so many people don't have one. But it's also sobering to realize what can happen if you don't leave a valid document describing how your property should be distributed.

When someone dies without a valid will, the state supplies a ready-made one devised by the legislature. Like a ready-made suit, it may fit and it may not. Abraham Lincoln, a president with great experience in the practice of law, died intestate, and his estate was divided, as it still would be in some states, into a third for his widow and a third for each of their two sons. In some instances this would work out well enough for all concerned. But in Lincoln's case one son was fully grown and the other was 12 years old, so the arrangement may not have been considered ideal by his widow.

The possibilities of inequities when there is no will are nearly endless. A hostile relative might be able to acquire a large share of your estate, for example, or a relative who is already well-fixed might be able to take legal precedence over needier kin.

So you need a will, a carefully drawn one. Oral, or nuncupative, wills are not legal in a number of states and cover only narrow circumstances where they are legal. Handwritten, or holographic, wills are legal in some states but can create complicated and expensive problems for the survivors.

That's why it makes sense to pay a competent lawyer a reasonable fee to write a document that delineates your wishes and will stand up later to scrutiny in probate court. Trying to save a few dollars, or even a few hundred if you have a complex estate, can cost far more in the long run.

Before you see a lawyer. A lawyer's time is money, so have some basics straight before you go to see one. Start with a list of your assets—real estate, bank accounts, stocks, bonds, cars, boats, life insurance, profit-sharing and pension funds, business holdings, money owed to you and the like. Note for the lawyer's benefit any trusts and jointly held property so he can determine whether they can pass under a will. You usually needn't list every piece of jewelry, every stick of furniture; making specific bequests of long lists of items in a will can needlessly complicate matters and lead to extra costs and delays. The executor of your estate can often carry out your separate instructions simply and directly. Ask your lawyer's advice on this.

Choose your executor carefully. Naturally, he should be someone you trust—a relative, a friend, your lawyer, anyone you feel is able to take on the responsible task of disposing of your estate. Remember, however, that the person should be willing, so check before you name someone who might later prove reluctant, forcing the court to appoint someone you perhaps would not have chosen.

A husband and wife should decide together whether to name each other or a mutually-agreed-upon person as executor in their wills.

If you have minor children, you'll also have to decide how you want them taken care of if you and your spouse both die. This involves setting up a guardianship, a task that has two principal functions. The first is to provide for the proper care of the children until they reach the age of majority. The second entails managing prudently the money and property you leave to the children and distributing it to them as you would wish.

You might pick one person for both tasks if you know someone who could handle them. Or you might name a warm-hearted relative to raise the children and a business-minded relative (perhaps the executor) to handle the financial end. Try to pick people who get along well together.

Next you'll have to decide how you want your estate distributed. This is obvious and straightforward in many instances, such as leaving everything to your spouse or to your children if both of you die.

What you want to do may be more complicated. Say you want an aged aunt to live in your house for the rest of her days and then you'd like the house to go to your two children in equal shares. Your lawyer can show you how to do that. Be concerned only with what you want to do and leave it to the lawyer to tell you how best to accomplish it. He might, for example, suggest one or more trusts of various sorts that would accomplish your aims and minimize taxes later.

Choosing a lawyer. If you don't already have a lawyer, ask an officer at your bank or a business acquaintance for recommendations. For simple wills a competent generalist should be able to do the job at a reasonable price. If your estate is substantial, it may be a good idea to consult an attorney who specializes in estate planning so you can minimize the effects of federal and state taxes. Don't conclude hastily that your estate is too small for you to worry about taxes. Insurance policies, company benefits, investments and rising real estate prices could make your estate larger than you think.

When you first talk to a lawyer, get a clear understanding of the fee. Depending on the lawyer, the size of the city or town, and the complexities of the document you need, the fee can range from as little as $35 for a simple will to $100 an hour or more for the time involved in planning a complex estate. There is no such thing as an average price, but a common one in a metropolitan area might be in the $150 to $300 range.

Using the lawyer. Once you get down to cases with your lawyer, state clearly and completely what you want to do. The lawyer will likely explain several ways of accomplishing your objective. If you specifically want to leave someone out of your will, especially a child, be sure to say so. Your lawyer will probably advise you to mention the person by name so that he can't later contest the will on the ground that you merely forgot.

You may want to specify in your will that the executor is to serve without bond. This can save your estate several hundred dollars in nonrefundable bonding fees that otherwise would be required.

The lawyer should recommend wording broad enough to cover a rise or drop in your fortunes and provisions for a common disaster that takes the lives of you, your spouse and your children.

Usually, your lawyer will supervise the signing and witnessing of the will to make sure it is done properly and can be probated with the fewest problems.

Don't worry about your situation changing in the future. You can always amend the will. But don't do it yourself. You could invalidate the entire document in the eyes of the court, thus undoing the good you've done so far. Go to the expense of having the lawyer make the changes.

Don't keep the will in a safe-deposit box because it may be sealed after your death, making the document unavailable for a period of time. Perhaps you can keep it in the lawyer's vault or with your other important papers. You may also want to give a copy to the executor or the principal beneficiary. Subject to your lawyer's advice, consider including a letter of last instructions that will help your executor gather your affairs together and carry out your wishes.

PLANNING YOUR ESTATE

Everything you own and property over which you exercise decisive control such as certain kinds of trusts are considered part of your estate when you die. In understanding the importance of planning for the distribution of your estate, consider all the things that can affect it.

Probate. This is the procedure by which state courts validate a will's authenticity, thereby clearing the way for the executor to collect and pay debts, pay taxes, sell property, distribute funds and carry out other necessary tasks involved with settling an estate.

Many states have simplified their probate rules in response to criticism over the past several years, but the process can still be slow and expensive. Probate fees average around 6% to 10% of assets, but they can run to much, much more.

Not all of your estate, though, will go through probate. Among the items exempted from probate—but not necessarily from taxes—are life insurance payable to a beneficiary other than your estate, property left in a trust, and such assets as bank accounts held in a joint tenancy form of ownership.

Trusts. Essentially, a trust is an arrangement whereby you give assets to a legal entity—the trust—created in a separate agreement to be administered by an individual or institutional trustee for a beneficiary, who may be yourself or some other person.

An *inter vivos,* or living, trust operates while you are alive. A *testamentary* trust goes into effect after your death. A *revocable* trust's provisions can be changed; an *irrevocable* trust can't be materially modified.

Trusts can reduce taxes. They also help in such situations as these:

- James is the sole support of his father. If James dies before his father, there is no assurance that the father will be able to care for himself. Therefore, instead of willing his money directly to his father, James sets up a testamentary trust with a bank as trustee. If James dies while his father is still living, the bank will invest the money and use the proceeds for the father's support. When the father dies, the remaining funds will be distributed to another beneficiary designated in the trust.

- Henry and Sally intend to leave a substantial sum to their son, now 21, but are concerned about his ability to handle that much money. Rather than give him the entire amount at once, they set up a trust that will pay him the income annually—half the capital when he reaches 25, the remaining half when he turns 30.

Banks and professionals such as attorneys charge fees for administering trusts. The cost might rule them out for small trusts. In any case, you might prefer to appoint a friend or relative who knows the trust's beneficiary and who might be willing to serve for a small fee or only expenses. Husbands and wives can sometimes act as trustees for each other's trusts. You may also want to appoint two or more trustees to guard against the possibility that one will be incapacitated and to name successor trustees who will take over and manage the assets if a trustee dies.

Joint tenancy. Property that is jointly owned with a right of survivorship—the form commonly used by married couples—automatically passes to the other owner when one owner dies.

The pluses and minuses of joint ownership are discussed in detail later on in the chapter. For now, suffice it to say that they are an important estate planning tool.

Estate and gift taxes. Unless you are quite well-to-do, the tax reduction bill passed in 1981 all but assures that your estate will have to pay little if any federal estate tax after you die. The liberalization of the law is substantial: In 1981, an estate had to amount to more than $175,625 before it began to incur any tax; by 1987, an estate of up to $600,000 will be able to pass to heirs tax-free. And with proper planning, married couples will be able to protect the entire estate of the first spouse to die.

Does this mean you needn't worry about estate taxes? Hardly. The phasing in of the new tax schedule will take six years, with the tax-free amount rising in stages rather than in one big leap. In the meantime, you need to plan for the possibility that you could wind up with an estate much larger than what you envision. You can use the net-worth worksheet in chapter 1 to see where you stand now.

(Actually, the increase in the estate-tax allowance is accomplished not by raising the allowance itself but by raising what's called the unified estate and gift tax credit. The credit stood at $47,000 in 1981, which was

up to $ 10,000		18%
over $ 10,000 to $ 20,000		$ 1,800 plus 20%
over $ 20,000 to $ 40,000		$ 3,800 plus 22%
over $ 40,000 to $ 60,000		$ 8,200 plus 24%
over $ 60,000 to $ 80,000		$ 13,000 plus 26%
over $ 80,000 to $ 100,000		$ 18,200 plus 28%
over $100,000 to $ 150,000		$ 23,800 plus 30%
over $150,000 to $ 250,000		$ 38,800 plus 32%
over $250,000 to $ 500,000		$ 70,800 plus 34%
over $500,000 to $ 750,000		$155,800 plus 37%
over $750,000 to $1,000,000		$248,300 plus 39%

enough to protect $175,625 in assets. It will rise in stages through 1987.)

You should also be aware that the federal government is not the only official authority wanting a piece of your estate when you die. Many state governments levy estate taxes that cut into much smaller estates than the federal tax. The most common state levy is an inheritance tax, which works a bit differently. An estate tax comes out of the estate before its proceeds can be divided up among the heirs. An inheritance tax, on the other hand, is paid by each of the heirs out of their inheritance unless the will directs that the estate cover it.

There is also the federal gift tax to take into consideration. Since 1942, the law has allowed you to give away up to $3,000 a year ($6,000 for couples) to as many people as you wished without incurring any gift tax at all. The new law raises the level of allowable tax-free gifts to $10,000 for individual givers and $20,000 for couples, starting in 1982. (To be strictly accurate, people rarely pay any gift tax. Rather, the tax incurred serves to reduce the estate tax credit available at death.)

If a tax on gifts seems unfair, think of the loophole its absence would create. People of means could give away much of their wealth to prospective heirs and thus escape the estate tax entirely.

At one time the government taxed gifts at a lower rate than estates, but for the past several years the gift and estate tax schedules have been the same. The table above shows the rates in 1981. (The percentages on the right apply to amounts falling between the two figures on the left on the same line.)

If you wanted to do the calculations, you would see that the $47,000 credit available in 1981 protects estates up to $175,625. That exclusion will be increased in stages through 1987: In 1982, a $62,800 credit will shield estates up to $225,000; in 1983, a $79,300 credit will cover up to $275,000 of assets; in 1984, a $96,300 credit will cover $325,000; in 1985, a $121,800 credit will cover $400,000; in 1986, a $155,800 credit will cover $500,000; and in 1987 and thereafter, a credit of $192,800 will cover estates of up to $600,000.

Despite the generosity of the new law, you still need to pay attention to estate planning. You should plan gifts in accordance with the higher annual limitations in effect for 1982 and after. You should familiarize yourself with state laws. And, if you are married, you should plan to use the marital deduction to the fullest.

Marital deduction. Gifts and estates are further protected from taxes by exemptions for gifts made by one spouse to another and for estates inherited by one spouse from another.

In 1981, you are entitled to a gift tax marital deduction for the first $100,000 of gifts to a spouse, plus 50% of the amount over $200,000. In addition, you are entitled to the standard $3,000 yearly exclusion for gifts to a spouse. Furthermore, half of your estate or $250,000, whichever is greater, can pass to a surviving spouse tax-free.

For gifts made and decedents dying in 1982 and after, the law is much more generous. There is no limit on gifts between spouses and there is no limit on the marital deduction. This means that, with proper estate planning, the marital deduction and the estate-tax exclusion can be used to pass estates of any size from one spouse to the other without incurring any federal estate tax. To make sure that you take full advantage of this opportunity, and to minimize estate taxes upon the death of the second spouse, consult with an experienced estate attorney familiar with the laws of your state.

INS AND OUTS OF JOINT OWNERSHIP

Joint ownership is a traditionally popular way for husbands and wives to hold property. It's a nice symbol of economic togetherness. As is customary, joint ownership is used here as shorthand for two ways of owning property: *joint tenancy with the right of survivorship* and *tenancy by the entirety*.

Although they differ in some respects and many states don't recognize the entirety variety, both forms provide a survivorship feature that's especially attractive to married couples. When one partner dies, the other joint owner automatically becomes sole owner of the property. Beyond the security offered by this assured continuity, joint ownership permits property to bypass probate, avoiding delays and usually trimming the costs of that final accounting process. In some states it can also ease the inheritance tax bite, and such property may be exempt from seizure by creditors of the deceased.

Possible problems. Those advantages, buttressed by some imagined benefits that don't actually exist, help explain the appeal of joint ownership.

Offsetting those advantages are several problems. For one thing, control of jointly held property is muddled. Depending on what's involved, one spouse may be able to dispose of it without the other's knowledge (as is generally the case with the entire balance of a joint checking or savings account). Or, each may be hamstrung, unable to sell the property without the other's consent (a situation that can apply to a home or to stocks and bonds not held in a joint brokerage account).

Joint ownership doesn't necessarily save taxes when you die, although the idea that it does is a sturdy misconception. Some people think none of the property would be taxed until the death of the survivor; others believe only half is taxed in the estate of the first to die. The truth is that joint ownership can result in such property being taxed twice: once when the first owner dies and again at the survivor's death.

Although jointly held property escapes probate, it's not immune from federal estate taxes. In 1981, the Internal Revenue Service generally presumes that property owned jointly belongs entirely to whichever owner dies first. Unless it can be proven that the survivor used his funds to help pay for the property—and evidence may be hard to come by if the property was acquired years ago—its entire value is included in the estate of the first to die. Any property still owned by the survivor at his death could be taxed again.

In 1982 and thereafter, this problem will be relieved by the new tax law. One half of the value of all property owned by a husband and wife as joint tenants will automatically be included in the estate of the first spouse to die. This change will eliminate the difficult task of determining how much each spouse contributed to the property in cases where responsibility for payments may not be clear.

For more information on joint ownership, including details on determining the value of gifts and the special rules applying to jointly owned farms and businesses, get a copy of IRS Publication 448, *A Guide to Federal Estate and Gift Taxation*. It's free from any IRS office.

Who should own what? Choosing the right kind of ownership can be tricky. It's clear that the more property you own, the more attention should be paid to the consequences of how you own it. Today's ownership decisions should be made with an eye to the future. There are clear advantages to joint ownership, and in many circumstances they easily outweigh the potential drawbacks. A lawyer well versed in federal estate and local property laws can help you make the right choice. You may decide that the best course for you and your spouse is a careful mix of joint and individual ownership, depending on the property involved.

• *House.* Joint ownership's survivorship feature may be especially appealing here. Talk with your lawyer about other options, though, and be sure to consider whether it would make sense to create a qualified joint interest.

• *Savings and checking accounts.* Joint accounts are convenient, but in some states part or all of the balance may be frozen at the death of either owner. Since that could strap the survivor at a difficult time, you may want to have individual accounts, too. Ask your banker about local rules.

• *Life insurance.* If you own a policy on your own life the proceeds will be included in your estate regardless of who receives them. It might be advisable for each mate to own the policies on the other's life. This keeps the proceeds out of the estate of the insured but also means that the insured must give up all "incidents of ownership," including the right to change the beneficiary and borrow against the cash value. Depending on your circumstances, creating a life insurance trust to own the policies may be beneficial. Check with your attorney or insurance agent for details.

• *Stocks and bonds*. Joint ownership could restrict flexibility in managing investments because both signatures are needed to buy or sell.

• *Car*. There's not much advantage to joint ownership and one drawback: The assets of both owners could be vulnerable to a suit for damages.

• *Safe-deposit box*. Pitfalls exist here, too. Check local laws. A jointly owned box may be sealed upon the death of either owner until authorities take inventory.

Community property states. Community property states add a special twist to the ownership puzzle. They are Arizona, California, Idaho, Louisiana, Nevada, New Mexico, Texas and Washington. (The rest are called common-law states.)

In those eight states salaries and assets acquired during marriage are generally considered community property, which means they are owned 50-50 by each spouse. Community property doesn't carry the right of survivorship, so when one spouse dies, the other does not automatically assume full ownership. The deceased partner's half is disposed of by will or the state's intestate rules and only that part is included in the estate for tax purposes.

Community property laws in these states usually permit couples to set up other types of ownership, either separate or joint. For details, check on local laws that apply to your circumstances. If you move from a common-law state to one with community property rules, or vice versa, be sure to review your family's ownership arrangements and estate plans.

INDEX